T0226222

Lecture Notes of the Institute for Computer Sciences, Social Informatics and Telecommunications Engineering 240

Editorial Board

Ozgur Akan
Middle East Technical University, Ankara, Turkey
Paolo Bellavista
University of Bologna, Bologna, Italy
Jiannong Cao
Hong Kong Polytechnic University, Hong Kong, Hong Kong
Geoffrey Coulson
Lancaster University, Lancaster, UK
Falko Dressler
University of Erlangen, Erlangen, Germany
Domenico Ferrari
Università Cattolica Piacenza, Piacenza, Italy
Mario Gerla
UCLA, Los Angeles, USA
Hisashi Kobayashi
Princeton University, Princeton, USA
Sergio Palazzo
University of Catania, Catania, Italy
Sartaj Sahni
University of Florida, Florida, USA
Xuemin Sherman Shen
University of Waterloo, Waterloo, Canada
Mircea Stan
University of Virginia, Charlottesville, USA
Jia Xiaohua
City University of Hong Kong, Kowloon, Hong Kong
Albert Y. Zomaya
University of Sydney, Sydney, Australia

More information about this series at http://www.springer.com/series/8197

Kazuya Murao · Ren Ohmura
Sozo Inoue · Yusuke Gotoh (Eds.)

Mobile Computing, Applications, and Services

9th International Conference, MobiCASE 2018
Osaka, Japan, February 28 – March 2, 2018
Proceedings

 Springer

Editors
Kazuya Murao
Ritsumeikan University
Kusatsu-shi, Shiga
Japan

Sozo Inoue
Kyushu Institute of Technology
Kitakyushu-shi, Fukuoka
Japan

Ren Ohmura
Toyohashi University of Technology
Toyohashi-shi, Aichi
Japan

Yusuke Gotoh
Okayama University
Okayama-shi, Okayama
Japan

ISSN 1867-8211　　　　　　ISSN 1867-822X　(electronic)
Lecture Notes of the Institute for Computer Sciences, Social Informatics
and Telecommunications Engineering
ISBN 978-3-319-90739-0　　　　ISBN 978-3-319-90740-6　(eBook)
https://doi.org/10.1007/978-3-319-90740-6

Library of Congress Control Number: 2018941547

© ICST Institute for Computer Sciences, Social Informatics and Telecommunications Engineering 2018
This work is subject to copyright. All rights are reserved by the Publisher, whether the whole or part of the material is concerned, specifically the rights of translation, reprinting, reuse of illustrations, recitation, broadcasting, reproduction on microfilms or in any other physical way, and transmission or information storage and retrieval, electronic adaptation, computer software, or by similar or dissimilar methodology now known or hereafter developed.
The use of general descriptive names, registered names, trademarks, service marks, etc. in this publication does not imply, even in the absence of a specific statement, that such names are exempt from the relevant protective laws and regulations and therefore free for general use.
The publisher, the authors and the editors are safe to assume that the advice and information in this book are believed to be true and accurate at the date of publication. Neither the publisher nor the authors or the editors give a warranty, express or implied, with respect to the material contained herein or for any errors or omissions that may have been made. The publisher remains neutral with regard to jurisdictional claims in published maps and institutional affiliations.

Printed on acid-free paper

This Springer imprint is published by the registered company Springer International Publishing AG
part of Springer Nature
The registered company address is: Gewerbestrasse 11, 6330 Cham, Switzerland

Preface

Welcome to the proceedings of the 9th EAI International Conference on Mobile Computing, Applications, and Services (MobiCASE 2018) held in Osaka, Japan. This was the first time that MobiCASE conference comes to Asia. The main objective of MobiCASE is to bring together scientists, engineers, and researchers from both network systems and information systems with the aim of encouraging the exchange of ideas, opinions, and experiences.

This year, MobiCASE received 35 papers for review. Each paper was carefully reviewed by at least three Technical Program Committee (TPC) members and reviewers. The TPC selected 11 full papers and 13 demo/poster papers to be presented during the conference. We would like to thank the 52 TPC members whose reviews and discussions formed the foundation of the MobiCASE 2018 program. MobiCASE 2018 hosted exciting keynote speakers, and the conference was accompanied by the Student Workshop.

The organization of an international conference requires the support and help of many people. A lot of people helped and worked hard for a successful MobiCASE 2018. First, we would like to thank all the authors for submitting their papers. We are indebted to TPC Chairs, Professor Ren Ohmura and Professor Sozo Inoue, who carried out the most difficult work of carefully evaluating the submitted papers and creating conference program. We would like to thank the Organizing Committee members including the Web chair, publicity and social media chair, workshop chair, sponsorship chair, demo and poster chair, and publication chair for their excellent work. We also would like to express our great appreciation to our keynote speakers, Dr. Takeshi Kurata and Dr. Tao Mei for accepting our invitation. We would like to give our special thanks to the Steering Committee chair, Steering Committee members, and the conference manager for giving us the opportunity to hold this conference and for their guidance in organizing the conference. We would like to thank the local chairs and local organization team at Ritsumeikan University, Japan, for making good local arrangements for the conference. We hope that you have an enjoyable and productive time during this conference and have a great time in Osaka, Japan.

April 2018   Kazuya Murao

Conference Organization

Steering Committee

Steering Committee Chair

Imrich Chlamtac — Create-Net, Italy

Steering Committee Members

Ulf Blanke — ETH Zurich, Switzerland
Martin Griss — Carnegie Mellon University, USA
Thomas Phan — Samsung R&D, USA
Petros Zerfos — IBM Research, USA

Organizing Committee

General Chair

Kazuya Murao — Ritsumeikan University, Japan

Technical Program Committee Chairs and Co-chairs

Ren Ohmura — Toyohashi University of Technology, Japan
Sozo Inoue — Kyushu Institute of Technology, Japan

Web Chair

Naoya Isoyama — Kobe University, Japan

Publicity and Social Media Chair

Hiroki Watanabe — Hokkaido University, Japan

Workshops Chair

Katsuhiko Kaji — Aichi Institute of Technology, Japan

Sponsorship and Exhibits Chair

Shoji Sano — Kanazawa Institute of Technology, Japan

Demos and Posters Chairs

Yu Enokibori — Nagoya University, Japan
Ismail Arai — Nara Institute of Science and Technology, Japan

Publications Chair

Yusuke Gotoh — Okayama University, Japan

Local Chairs

Kohei Matsumura	Ritsumeikan University, Japan
Ryosuke Yamanishi	Ritsumeikan University, Japan

Conference Manager

Dominika Belisova	EAI - European Alliance for Innovation

Technical Program Committee

Eve Schooler	Intel, USA
Jie Gao	Stony Brook University, USA
Petteri Nurmi	University of Helsinki, Finland
Polly Huang	National Taiwan University, Taiwan/Keio University, Japan
Rasit Eskicioglu	University of Manitoba, Canada
Rik Sarkar	University of Edinburgh, UK
Trevor Pering	Google, USA
Veljko Pejovic	University of Ljubljana, Slovenia
Tsutomu Terada	Kobe University, Japan
Kazushige Ouchi	Toshiba, Japan
Takuro Yonezawa	Keio University, Japan
Yasuyuki Sumi	Future University Hakodate, Japan
Katsuhiko Kaji	Aichi Institute of Technology, Japan
Yasue Kishino	NTT, Japan
Hiroshi Mineno	Shizuoka University, Japan
Hidekazu Suzuki	Meijo University, Japan
Christian Meurisch	TU Darmstadt, Germany
Susanna Pirttikangas	University of Oulu, Finland
Anja Exler	Karlsruhe Institute of Technology, Germany
Gerold Hlzl	University of Passau, Germany
Kaori Fujinami	Tokyo University of Agriculture and Technology, Japan
Kei Hiroi	Nagoya University, Japan
Masaki Shuzo	Kanagawa University, Japan
Shigeyuki Miyagi	The University of Shiga Prefecture, Japan
Yoshihiro Kawahara	The University of Tokyo, Japan
Md. Atiqur Rahman Ahad	University of Dhaka, Bangladesh
Yuuki Nishiyama	Keio University, Japan
Kota Tsubouchi	Yahoo! Japan
Yutaka Arakawa	NAIST, Japan
Samuli Hemminki	University of Helsinki, Finland
Yusheng Ji kei	NII, Japan
Shoji Kobashi	University of Hyogo, Japan
Shinichi Konomi	University of Tokyo, Japan

Takuya Maekawa	Osaka University, Japan
Kalika Suksomboon	KDDI R&D Labs, Japan
Till Riedel	Karlsruhe Institute of Technology, Germany
Philipp Scholl	Albert-Ludwigs University Freiburg, Germany
Moustafa Youssef	Egypt–Japan University of Science and Technology, Egypt/Google
Stephan Sigg	Aalto University, Finland
Moustafa Elhamshary	Tanta University, Egypt
Brahim Benaissa	Kyushu Institute of Technology, Japan
Paula Lago	Los Andes Univ., Columbia
Kanae Matsui	Tokyo Denki University, Japan
Naoki Ohshima	The University of Electro-Communications, Japan
Nararat Ruangchaijatupon	Khon Kaen University, Thailand
Ella Peltonen	University of Helsinki, Finland
Aaron Yi Ding	Technische Universität München, Germany
Martin Pielot	Telefonica Research Group in Barcelona, Spain
Abinav Mehrotra	University College London, UK
Simo Hosio	University of Oulu, Finland
Ekaterina Gilman	University of Oulu, Finland
Muneeba Raja	Aalto University, Finland

Contents

Keynote

Making Pier Data Broader and Deeper:

PDR Challenge and Virtual Mapping Party

Takeshi Kurata[1,2(✉)], Ryosuke Ichikari[1], Ryo Shimomura[1,2],
Katsuhiko Kaji[3], Takashi Okuma[1], and Masakatsu Kourogi[1,4]

[1] National Institute of Advanced Industrial Science and Technology,
Tokyo, Japan
{t.kurata, r.ichikari, takashiokuma,
m.kourogi}@aist.go.jp
[2] Tsukuba University, Tsukuba, Japan
[3] Aichi Institute of Technology, Toyota, Japan
kaji@aitech.ac.jp
[4] Sitesensing Co. Ltd., Tokyo, Japan

Abstract. Big data can be gathered on a daily basis, but it has issues on its quality and variety. On the other hand, deep data is obtained in some special conditions such as in a lab or in a field with edge-heavy devices. It compensates for the above issues of big data, and also it can be training data for machine learning. Just like a platform of pier supported by stakes, there is structure in which big data is supported by deep data. That is why we call the combination of big and deep data "pier data." By making pier data broader and deeper, it becomes much easier to understand what is happening in the real world and also to realize Kaizen and innovation. We introduce two examples of activities on making pier data broader and deeper. First, we outline "PDR Challenge in Warehouse Picking"; a PDR (Pedestrian Dead Reckoning) performance competition which is very useful for gathering big data on behavior. Next, we discuss methodologies of how to gather and utilize pier data in "Virtual Mapping Party" which realizes map-content creation at any time and from anywhere to support navigation services for visually impaired individuals.

Keywords: Lab-forming fields · Field-forming labs · Big data
Deep data · Pier data · PDR · IoT · IoH · VR · Service engineering

1 Introduction

To get a complete picture of an actual service field, the process involves measuring and modeling people, things, and environment with technologies such as geospatial internet of things (IoT) [1]. Then, based on the acquired situation, it "intervenes" in the field through augmented reality (AR)-based information support and robots, and promotes a behavioral change of customers and employees. This kind of methodology, involving the iteration of hypothesis and verification, could only be conducted in a laboratory. However, it is now becoming possible to transfer it to actual fields, a process that we call "lab-forming fields."

© ICST Institute for Computer Sciences, Social Informatics and Telecommunications Engineering 2018
K. Murao et al. (Eds.): MobiCASE 2018, LNICST 240, pp. 3–17, 2018.
https://doi.org/10.1007/978-3-319-90740-6_1

Figure 1 shows the optimum design loop of service (observation, analysis, design, and application) and the technologies involved in each phase. One of the methodologies that employ this optimum design loop to improve and innovate is lab-forming fields, but there is also the concept of "field-forming labs", which involves building or offering a virtual environment with high reproducibility to minimize the divergence with the actual field as much as possible, thereby bringing the knowledge obtained in a laboratory experiment (hypothesis and verification) closer to the knowledge that should be obtained in the real field.

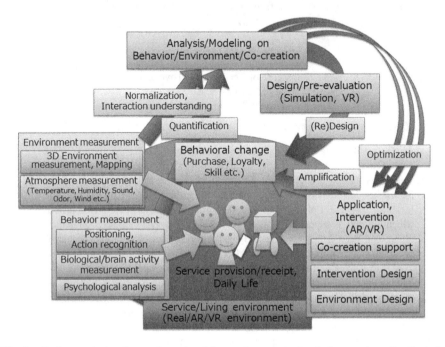

Fig. 1. Optimum design loop of service (observation, analysis, design, and application) for supporting human-centered co-creation.

2 Pier Data

Through lab-forming fields and field-forming labs, it is possible to acquire "big data" and "deep data". Big data can be collected on a daily basis without much effort, but it is difficult to maintain its quality, and it has limited types. At this point, there is no clear definition of deep data, but for this work, we consider that it has characteristics that supplement big data, such as high quality, heterogeneity (including correct image, motion, gaze, biometric information, and brain activity data), and that it includes subjective data (surveys and interviews). Deep data are used as training data for supervised machine learning that is applied to recognize something from big data, or as basic information to deepen the qualitative understanding of the field, but it can only be obtained in special circumstances, such as sensing in a laboratory or an edge heavy field, or by asking surveyees.

A pier has a structure in which the platform is supported by stakes. Figure 2 can be interpreted as a structure in which deep data support big data. It is also possible to assume that, typically, a so-called platformer is good at gathering big data, and a so-called stakeholder which has knowledge and know-how in each field is good at gathering deep data. For these reasons, we call this combination of big data and deep data "pier data" (in reference [1], we formerly called pier data "comb data" because of the appearance of its structure. We have now changed its name to "pier data," which we found more appropriate because it also contains the meaning of structure). By acquiring mainly big data with lab-forming fields and mainly deep data with field-forming labs, and by deepening and widening the pier data efficiently, we believe that it will be possible to comprehensively understand what is happening in the real world, especially in the service and manufacturing fields, which can then be more easily improved and innovated.

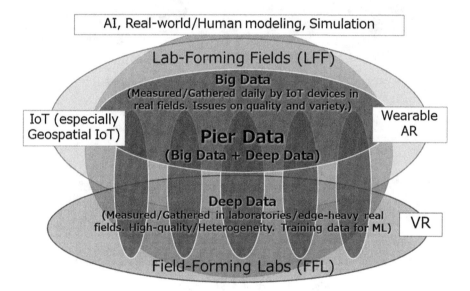

Fig. 2. Lab-forming fields and field-forming labs: Big Data + Deep Data = Pier Data

In this paper, we present two examples of activities that we are conducting to obtain wider and deeper pier data. The first is an outline of the PDR Challenge, a competition aimed at evaluating the performance of pedestrian dead reckoning (PDR, relative positioning for pedestrians), an efficient technology to collect big data by behavior measurement. Then, we discuss the methodology to collect and use pier data contained in a virtual mapping party that supports the map creation necessary for navigation for visually impaired people.

3 PDR

We have been engaged in R&D related to PDR [2, 3] since 2000 (Fig. 3). PDR is a technology that uses a group of sensors (commonly known as nine-axis sensors) that measure the physical quantity of three-axis components — acceleration, angular velocity, and magnetism — to estimate the posture of the sensors, as well as the travel speed and direction of the pedestrian carrying the sensors. With this, it is possible to learn the pedestrian's relative location.

Fig. 3. History of AIST's PDR study

In many cases where a positioning system is to be introduced into an indoor service or manufacturing site, the cost of developing the physical and information infrastructure becomes a barrier that raises questions about its cost-effectiveness. The introduction of indoor positioning is one of the fundamentals of lab-forming fields, and, although it is beginning to be understood better with the dissemination of IoT-oriented thinking, there are still cases in which the effect of its introduction needs to be represented by a monetary value (alone). As a reference to the Nobel prize in economics laureate R. Solow's productivity paradox theory, we call this situation an indoor positioning paradox/dilemma. This paradox or dilemma, which does not occur with the use of outdoor satellite positioning, can be eased with the use of a relative positioning method like PDR. The best example of it is the indoor navigation in "DoCoMo Map

Navi" [4]. With a nine- or ten-axis PDR, a map (pedestrian space network data) and interaction with the user, it enables indoor navigation in about 560 underground shopping centers and subway premises across Japan (as of November 2017) without installing a physical infrastructure.

PDR can be classified into the inertial navigation system (INS) type, which estimates three-dimensional positions, and the steps and heading system (SHS) type, which estimates two-dimensional positions [5]. The former method [6] can provide a highly accurate three-dimensional positioning without depending on how each person walks. It does, however, have some limitations: because it is a method based on double integration of acceleration, it requires an accelerometer with easy calibration and high sensitivity, and the nine-axis sensor must necessarily be attached to the toe or shoe, where zero-velocity update (ZUPT) is possible.

We have been conducting research mainly on the latter type of PDR, the SHS [2, 3, 7, 8]. It is mainly composed of (1) attitude estimation, (2) estimation of walking direction, and (3) walking motion detection and walking speed (pace) estimation. Compared to the INS-type method, it has fewer limitations related to the position of attachment of the nine-axis sensor and calibration of the accelerometer. However, although the SHS-type is less limited than the INS type in terms of attachment position, it did have some limitations of its own. For example, the measurement with the SHS-type must be done in a stable condition by fixing a nine-axis sensor on the waist or chest, or by walking while holding and looking at the screen of a smartphone with a built-in nine-axis sensor.

The popularization of smartphones in recent years, especially, is highly expected to ease the limitations related to attachment or holding conditions even further. The estimation of walking direction mentioned in [3] is an essential technology for this purpose, and the main methods that have been proposed are: (A) based on the PCA (Principal Component Analysis) of acceleration amplitude, (B) based on a FLAM (Forward and Lateral Acceleration Modeling), and (C) based on FIS (Frequency analysis of Inertial Signals). According to a research report that made a comparative evaluation between these [9], the method with FIS [3] has produced an overall better evaluation result than the others.

The measurement range of an SHS-type PDR is limited on the ground and floor that are included in the map and floor plan; in other words, the estimation in the height direction is limited on the map and floor plan. In many cases, however, this height information is sufficient to obtain the position information of the target public (residents, customers, employees, etc.); therefore, this limitation is hardly a problem. As pressure sensors become more accessible and accurate, a 10-axis sensor, which is a nine-axis sensor with a pressure sensor added, also begins to be more widely used. There are also attempts to measure the travel in the vertical direction using this 10-axis sensor [7, 8, 10].

While many other absolute positioning methods, in principle, provide a positioning result that is a set of independently obtained results, PDR generates a continuous trajectory. The shape and displacement (change of speed and angle) of this trajectory includes characteristics of the movement of the person being measured, and it also allows to measure the type and intensity of the movement [13, 14]. Therefore, in some cases, it is more appropriate to consider PDR a means to measure behavior rather than a positioning method.

4 PDR Challenge

Indoor positioning technologies such as PDR are becoming essential to service observation and lab-forming fields based on the same [1]. Also, the increasing number of related publications in international conferences and the popularity of the competitions [13–16] are the reflection of the rapidly growing number of domestic and international companies and universities engaged in R&D and implementation of PDR. Also, because PDR is a relative positioning method, it requires a different evaluation method than that used in absolute positioning methods such as Global Navigation Satellite System (GNSS) and Wi-Fi positioning. Also, the description of its efficiency in articles and specification sheets of products or services is unified.

In this context, we established the PDR Benchmark Standardization Committee [17] in 2014 (endorsed by 39 organizations as of November 2017) as a grassroots activity. In 2015, we collaborated with the "UbiComp/ISWC 2015 PDR Challenge" [13, 14], and, in 2017, we organized the "PDR Challenge in Warehouse Picking" [18], a PDR competition in a logistics picking scenario, at the International Conference on IPIN 2017. Table 1 summarizes the characteristics of these two PDR Challenges.

Table 1. Comparison of the characteristics of PDR Challenge

	Ubicomp/ISWC 2015 PDR Challenge	PDR Challenge in Warehouse Picking in IPIN 2017
Scenario	Indoor pedestrian navigation	Picking work inside a logistics warehouse
Walking/motion	Continuous walking while holding smartphone and looking at navigation screen	Includes many motions involved in picking work, not only walking
On-site or off-site	Data collection: on-site Evaluation: off-site	Off-site
Number of people and trial	90 people, 229 trials	8 people, 8 trials
Time per trial	A few minutes	About 3 hours
Remark	Collection of data of participants walking. The data are available at HASC (http://hub.hasc.jp/) as corpus data	Competition over integrated position using not only PDR, but also correction information such as BLE beacon signal, picking log (WMS), and maps

The PDR Challenge in Warehouse Picking was carried out as one of the four tracks of the IPIN 2017 indoor positioning competition. The competitors entered as teams, and a total of 20 teams (five from China, four from South Korea, three from Japan, two from Taiwan, and one each from Germany, France, Portugal, Chile, and Australia) participated in the four tracks. Five among these teams (two from Japan, and one each from South Korea, China, and Taiwan) participated in the PDR Challenge in Warehouse Picking, which was won by the KDDI R&D Labs team.

The preparation of the PDR Challenge in Warehouse Picking was carried out along with the preparation of the Frameworx Logistics Open Data Contest [19]. The data of eight picking workers carrying a smartphone was collected. It included 10-axis sensor data and BLE beacon reception data, warehouse management system (WMS) data related to barcode reading during the picking work, as well as map information. One part of the WMS data was kept undisclosed and used by the organizers as the correct value in the evaluation of positioning error (evaluation point). The remaining disclosed part was made available for the competitors to use for position correction. By changing the amount of this undisclosed part — that is, the length of the section and time where position correction with WMS did not work — trial data were created with two levels of difficulty and offered to the competitors. Data that had been obtained at a different warehouse for training for the competition were also offered as a sample. Each competitor calculated the trajectory of each trial using the positioning program that it developed and submitted the result to the organizers.

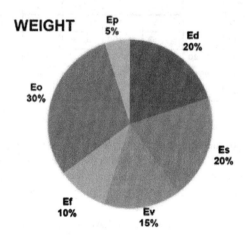

Indices related to accuracy
  E_d – Index related to integrated positioning error
  E_s – Index related to PDR error based on EAG
Indices related to the trajectory naturalness
  E_v – Index related to the naturalness of travel speed
  E_f – Index related to position measurement output frequency
Specific indices for warehouse picking scenario
  E_o – Index related to collision with obstacles
  E_p – Index related to motions during picking work

WEIGHT

Ep 5%
Ed 20%
Es 20%
Ev 15%
Ef 10%
Eo 30%

Fig. 4. Evaluation index (Top: individual indices; Bottom: weight of each individual index to total index Ec)

There were many discussions regarding the evaluation index and indicator at the PDR Benchmarking Standardization Committee and during the competition preparation, but we decided to use the individual indices shown in Fig. 4 and the total index, which is the weighted average of them. The detailed definition of each individual index can be confirmed on the website of The PDR Challenge in Warehouse Picking [18], but, in this paper, we discuss the "EAG (Error Accumulation Gradient)," the base of index Es, which is related to the error of PDR.

If the positioning result of PDR, which is a relative positioning method, is not corrected, the positioning error tends to accumulate. Reference [20] takes this into consideration and proposes using the positioning error per unit time (m/s) as an indicator. This proposed indicator, which we name EAG, is calculated based on the linear regression (intercept of 0) of the positioning error along with the elapsed time from measurement start time. Because PDR is often applied in real-time applications as in pedestrian navigation, the elapsed time from measurement start time is adopted to calculate the indicator.

Meanwhile, in cases where batch processing using all the data from measurement start to finish is possible, it is also possible to correct the position retroactively. Therefore, in the PDR Challenge in Warehouse Picking, we adopted the EAG obtained by linear regression (intercept of 0) of the positioning error along with the elapsed time to the past or future (the shorter one) from the time when position correction is possible as base of Es. In addition, after the competition, we also discussed the application of robust regression that takes the outliers into account (Fig. 5).

Table 2. Result summary of the PDR Challenge in Warehouse Picking

Team	Ec	Accuracy		Naturalness		Warehouse specific		Median error [m]	Error Accumulation Gradient (EAG) [m/sec]
		Ed	Es	Ep	Ev	Eo	Ef		
ETRI	5th 65.74	65.41	96.34	97.20	**100**	51.82	11.32	11.03	0.12
KDDI	1st 91.16	72.35	97.97	43.55	**100**	99.88	**100**	9.02	0.09
Nagoya	2nd 88.92	70.57	**99.20**	72.72	87.84	93.55	99.27	9.54	**0.06**
XMU	3rd 78.44	67.64	96.06	84.97	95.66	59.62	99.24	10.39	0.13
YZU	4th 77.95	**75.34**	97.74	**97.48**	99.09	45.53	**100**	**8.15**	0.09

The detailed results of the competition are posted on its website [18]. Although it is summarized in Table 2, here we discuss it further with the EAG as an example. This indicator can be used not only to evaluate the performance of PDR alone, but also to decide the design guidelines of the absolute positioning infrastructure to be included in integrated positioning.

For example, Nagoya University's team's EAG is 0.06 m/s, or 3.6 m/min. Supposing that there is a service or manufacturing site planning to introduce an integrated positioning system that includes this PDR system and that the specification for positioning error required for that field is within 4 m on average, it is possible to build a design guideline that states that it is necessary to incorporate an absolute positioning method capable of correcting the position with an error of 0.4 m or less about once per minute (3.6 + 0.4 = 4.0). In this case, ultrawideband positioning, BLE positioning with an AoA (angle of arrival) method, and positioning using installed cameras [21] are some absolute positioning methods that would apply.

Supposing that the required specification for positioning error is the same, less than 4 m on average, and that the absolute positioning methods had already been decided on multilateration or fingerprinting with BLE the average positioning error of which is around 3 m. In this case, even if the frequency of BLE positioning is once every 16 s, it is possible for PDR to update the positioning result in the interval between two positioning points with BLE and the result satisfies the required specifications (0.06 * 16 + 3.0 = 3.96).

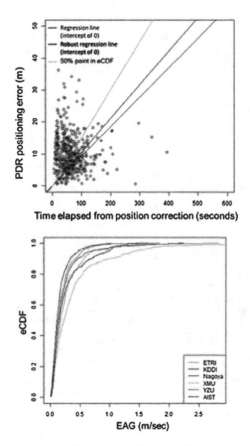

Fig. 5. Example of EAG (m/sec) (Top: Regression lines, Bottom: eCDF of EAG calculated from each evaluation point)

5 Virtual Mapping Party

In Sects. 3 and 4, we discussed the PDR, one of the essential positioning technologies to collect big data using lab-forming fields. This section and the next focus on the methodology to collect and use pier data based on field-forming labs and virtual mapping party, which supports the map making needed for walking navigation for visually impaired people [22].

Our research related to movement support for visually impaired people began with the development of a navigation system for visually impaired people that uses previously mentioned positioning technologies such as PDR and GNSS (satellite positioning) [23, 24]. "Point of Interest (POI)" information refers to general map content offered even in navigation for sighted people. This includes destination candidates, such as establishments and stores, as well as landmarks that can be recognized from distance. The navigation for visually impaired people, however, is expected to offer, in addition to POI, "Point of Reference (POR)" [25, 26] information. Examples of POR are braille blocks on the ground and floor, utility holes, car stoppers, stairs, environmental noise, smell, and other information that helps with the user's safety and current position grasp. Our navigation system was developed to provide both POI and POR, but because POR contents are not yet fully developed, collecting them was challenging.

Table 3. Different characteristics of mapping activities

Type of activities	Location	Time	Remarks
Conventional mapping party	On-site	Sync.	• Deep understanding of the local situation • Development of community through face-to-face liaison • Influenced by local weather and level of congestion • Difficult to participate from distance • Mandatory skill for organizing events
Mapping party using smartphones app.	On-site	Any time (Async.)	• Deep understanding of the local situation • Easy mapping during free time (e.g. while commuting) • The position accuracy of the registered information depends on the positioning method • Difficult to participate from distance
Mapping party using crowdsourcing image sharing service	Anywhere (Off-site)	Any time (Async.)	• Crowdsourcing • Possible to participate from any place, anytime • Require previous collection of pictures • Possibly difficult to understand the local situation
Virtual mapping party	Anywhere (Off-site)	Any time (Async.)	• Crowdsourcing • Possible to participate from any place, anytime • The system supports the positioning of registered information • Simulation of the local site through VR • Require previous collection of environmental information such as pictures • Cocreation type in which visually impaired people can participate using AR tactile map

There is an event called "Mapping Party", which is dedicated to making maps that include the collection of POI/POR. OpenStreetMap, the project that creates free map information that anybody can use, also frequently holds this mapping party event. Also, a mapping party aimed at creating maps for visually impaired people is specifically called a "Blind Mapping Party". This kind of time-and-space synchronous event has some problems, though. For example, the participants need to gather at the appointed location and time, the success of the event is dictated by the weather, and it involves geographical and time-related limitations. The use of ICT technology to increase the efficiency of local participation-type activities is becoming more common. One of the most common methods is the support and optimization of local activities through the use of smartphone applications [27].

There are also some attempts to lower the hurdles related to the need of physically visiting the site. For example, Hara et al. [28] are using Google Street View to research the accuracy of the registered bus stop information collected by crowdsourcing. It requires caution, however, because distributing map contents created from information provided from Google products, such as Google Maps, to services outside of Google, raises legal concerns. An effective way to tackle such concerns is to use more open shared platforms of street-level images such as Mapillary [29] and OpenStreetCam [30]. Voigt et al. [31] are engaged in a "lab-base" approach (which is close to field-forming labs), which uses Mapillary and OpenStreetMap to collect map information from places other than the site itself. Table 3 summarizes the characteristics of each kind of mapping activity.

Figure 6 is a conceptual drawing of a virtual mapping party. Below are some characteristics of the prototypes and preliminary demonstrations being developed to implement this concept [22, 26]:

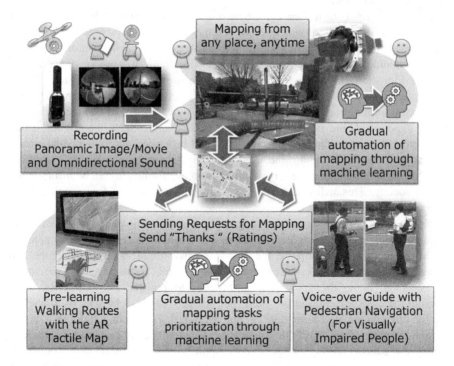

Fig. 6. Conceptual drawing of Virtual Mapping Party (includes items that have already been implemented and future challenges)

- Focused on supporting creation of map contents (especially POR) for visually impaired people
- Simulation of the field using a VR environment with omnidirectional movies and three-dimensional environmental sounds

- Uses information collected through the connection with other navigation and AR tactile map apps [26] and promotes the exchange of requests and evaluation between stakeholders
- The visually impaired users themselves can participate in the information collection activity
- Studying the feasibility of gradual automation of each task with machine learning

6   Virtual Mapping and Pier Data

The data collected with navigation applications and AR tactile maps (usage history, request to map a location, evaluation of map contents, etc.) is expected to be acquired while the service is used, and thus is considered typical big data. Because our virtual mapping applications can be linked with Mapillary, in case the environmental information used for mapping consists only of images, this environmental information may also be seen as big data.

However, images of the spaces where visually impaired people walk, such as sidewalks and indoor environments, are seldom registered in shared platforms of street-level images like Mapillary. Therefore, the environmental information for mapping should probably be considered close to deep data. If, however, the environmental information is composed of omnidirectional movies and three-dimensional environmental sounds, as well as their accurate position and orientation, then that environment information is naturally a deep data. When we are to conduct a demonstration experiment, the person handling the experiment collects the environmental information. We expect that, in the future, this will be carried out by the collaborators of users who require mapping, the users of navigation services, personal mobility, robots, drones, etc., and that the ecosystem to use this information will be incorporated into the society. This will enable the environmental information for mapping to be collected as big data.

We have developed a virtual mapping application that is intended to crowdsource the map-making process using environmental information. We are using this application in events like workshops at the National Museum of Emerging Science and Innovation (Miraikan) and preparing to distribute it so that it can be used in the way it was designed. Now, the application user needs to register the POI/PORs while browsing the environmental information, but this task can also be seen as a labeling task for environmental information — that is, a task of creating training data for machine learning. If the POI/POR candidates are automatically extracted by machine learning using these training data, so that the application user only needs to confirm it, the task efficiency should improve. If the learning process advances even further, automation will also become possible. This kind of gradual automation of the map-making process will be indispensable for a consistent development of map contents.

7   Conclusion

We outlined PDR, an effective technology to collect big data by behavior measurement, as well as its competition, the PDR Challenge. The definition of "pedestrians," according to the Road Traffic Act, includes wheelchair users, but since PDR is a relative positioning method based on the characteristics of biped walking behavior, it cannot be applied to wheelchair users. We previously proposed vibration-based vehicle dead reckoning as a method for relative positioning of wheeled vehicles [32]. These initiatives focused on implementing xDR (Dead Reckoning for x) or uDR (universal Dead Reckoning) and will certainly stimulate the collection of behavior-related big data and their use [33–35] even further.

The evaluation indicators related to benchmarking of vison-based spatial registration and tracking methods for mixed and augmented reality being discussed at the ISO [36] is divided into reliability indicators (error, completion rate), time indicators (frame rate, delay), and diversity indicators (number of trials, variety of trial content). This kind of discussion must be held at the PDR Standardization Committee and PDR Challenge as well, and it will probably be necessary to design indices and indicators related to efficiency (computational efficiency, energy consumption) and reproducibility (influence related to temperature hysteresis, local environment change, etc.).

We also discussed virtual mapping party, which supports the creation of the map contents necessary for navigation for visually impaired people. We mentioned our application cooperation with the open platform Mapillary to share street-level images, and our applications are also cooperating with the navigation application NavCog [37], which offers an open platform. We believe that this organic cooperation of the entire process, from map making to navigation and AR tactile map, will allow us to further widen and deepen the pier data to support the movement of visually impaired people.

Acknowledgment. The PDR Challenge in Warehouse Picking was carried out partially with the support of JST OPERA's "Elucidation of the Mechanism of Cooperation Between Humans and Intelligent Machines and the Creation of Fundamental Technology to Build a New Social System Based on Cooperative Value." The virtual mapping party was carried out with the support of JST RISTEX's "Development of a Movement Support System for Visually Impaired People by Multi-Generation Co-Creation."

References

1. Kurata, T., Ichikari, R., Chang, C.-T., Kourogi, M., Onishi, M., Okuma, T.: Lab-forming fields and field-forming labs. Serviceology for Services. LNCS, vol. 10371, pp. 144–149. Springer, Cham (2017). https://doi.org/10.1007/978-3-319-61240-9_14
2. Kourogi, M., Kurata, T.: Personal positioning based on walking locomotion analysis with self-contained sensors and a wearable camera. In: Proceedings of the ISMAR 2003, pp. 103–112 (2003)
3. Kourogi, M., Kurata, T.: A method of pedestrian dead reckoning for smartphones using frequency domain analysis on patterns of acceleration and angular velocity. In: Proceedings of the PLANS 2014, pp. 164–168 (2014)
4. DoCoMo Map Indoor Navigation Area. http://dmapnavi.jp/stc/enabled_device/

5. Harle, R.: A survey of indoor inertial positioning systems for pedestrians. IEEE Commun. Surv. Tutor. **15**(3), 1281–1293 (2013)
6. Foxlin, E.: Pedestrian tracking with shoe-mounted inertial sensors. IEEE Comput. Graph. Appl. **25**(6), 38–46 (2005)
7. Kaji, K., Kawaguchi, N.: 3D walking trajectory estimation method based on stable sensing section detection. Trans. Inf. Process. Soc. Jpn **57**(1), 12–24 (2016)
8. Kaji, K., Kawaguchi, N.: Estimating 3D pedestrian trajectories using stability of sensing signal. In: Proceedings of the Seventh International Conference on Indoor Positioning and Indoor Navigation (IPIN2016) (2016)
9. Combettes, C., Renaudin, V.: Comparison of misalignment estimation techniques between handheld device and walking directions. In: Proceedings of the IPIN 2015, 8 p. (2015)
10. Ichikari, R., Ruiz, L.C.M., Kourogi, M., Kitagawa, T., Yoshii, S., Kurata, T.: Indoor floor-level detection by collectively decomposing factors of atmospheric pressure. In: Proceedings of the IPIN 2015, 11 p. (2015)
11. Makita, K., Kourogi, M., Ishikawa, T., Okuma, T., Kurata, T.: PDR plus: human behaviour sensing method for service field analysis. In: Proceedings of the ICServ 2013, pp. 19–22 (2013)
12. Kanagu, K., Tsubouchi, K., Nishio, N.: Colorful PDR: Colorizing PDR with shopping context in walking. In: Proceedings of the IPIN 2017 (2017)
13. Kaji, K., Abe, M., Wang, W., Hiroi, K., Kawaguchi, N.: UbiComp/ISWC 2015 PDR challenge corpus. In Proceedings of the HASCA2016 (UbiComp2016 Proceedings: Adjunct), pp. 696–704 (2016)
14. Kaji, K., Kohei Kanagu, K., Murao, K., Nishio, N., Urano, K., Iida, H., Kawaguchi, N.: Multi-algorithm on-site evaluation system for PDR challenge. In: Proceedings of the Ninth International Conference on Mobile Computing and Ubiquitous Networking (ICMU2016), pp. 1–6 (2016)
15. Lymberopoulos, D., Liu, J.: The microsoft indoor localization competition: experiences and lessons learned. IEEE Signal Process. Mag. **34**(5), 125–140 (2017)
16. IPIN 2017 Competition. http://www.ipin2017.org/callforcompetition.html
17. PDR Benchmark Standardization Committee. https://www.facebook.com/pdr.bms/
18. PDR Challenge in Warehouse Picking. https://unit.aist.go.jp/hiri/pdr-warehouse2017/
19. Frameworx Logistics Open Data Contest. http://contest.frameworxopendata.jp/
20. Abe, M., Kaji, K., Hiroi, K., Kawaguchi, N.: PIEM: path independent evaluation metric for relative localization. In: Proceedings of the Seventh International Conference on Indoor Positioning and Indoor Navigation (IPIN2016) (2016)
21. Ishikawa, T., Kourogi, M., Kurata, T.: Economic and synergistic pedestrian tracking system with service cooperation for indoor environments. Int. J. Organ. Collective Intell. **2**(1), 1–20 (2011)
22. Ichikari, R., Kurata, T.: Virtual mapping party: co-creation of maps for visually impaired people. J. Technol. Persons with Disabil. **5**, 208–224 (2017)
23. Kurata, T., Kourogi, M., Ishikawa, T., Kameda, Y., Aoki, K., Ishikawa, J.: Indoor-outdoor navigation system for visually-impaired pedestrians: preliminary evaluation of position measurement and obstacle display. In: ISWC 2011, pp. 123–124 (2011)
24. Kurata, T., Seki, Y., Kourogi, M., Ishikawa, J.: Roles of navigation system in walking with long cane and guide dog. In: The 29th Annual International Technology and Persons with Disabilities Conference (CSUN 2014) (2014)
25. Denoncin, S.: AX'S: A New Indoor GPS Solution Designed for All, BLV-034, CSUN 2014 (2014)

26. Ichikari, R., Yanagimachi, T., Kurata, T.: Augmented reality tactile map with hand gesture recognition. In: Miesenberger, K., Bühler, C., Penaz, P. (eds.) ICCHP 2016. LNCS, vol. 9759, pp. 123–130. Springer, Cham (2016). https://doi.org/10.1007/978-3-319-41267-2_17

27. Miura, T., Yabu, K.-i., Noro, T., Segawa, T., Kataoka, K., Nishimuta, A., Sanmonji, M., Hiyama, A., Hirose, M., Ifukube, T.: Sharing Real-World Accessibility Conditions Using a Smartphone Application by a Volunteer Group. In: Miesenberger, K., Bühler, C., Penaz, P. (eds.) ICCHP 2016. LNCS, vol. 9759, pp. 265–272. Springer, Cham (2016). https://doi.org/10.1007/978-3-319-41267-2_36

28. Hara, K., Azenkot, S., Campbell, M., Bennett, C.L., Le, V., Pannella, S., Moore, R., Minckler, K., Ng, R.H., Froehlich, J.E.: Improving public transit accessibility for blind riders by crowdsourcing bus stop landmark locations with google street view: an extended analysis. ACM Trans. Access. Comput. (TACCESS) 6(2), 23 (2015). Article 5

29. Mapillary. https://www.mapillary.com/

30. OpenStreetCam. https://www.openstreetcam.org/

31. Voigt, C., Dobner, S., Ferri, M., Hahmann, S., Gareis, K.: Community engagement strategies for crowdsourcing accessibility information - Paper, Wheelmap-Tags and Mapillary-Walks. In: Proceedings of the ICCHP (2), pp. 257–264 (2016)

32. Kourogi, M., Kurata, T.: Vibration-based vehicle dead reckoning (VDR) for localization of wheeled vehicles. In: IEEE/ION PLANS 2018 Conference (2018, accepted)

33. Ichikari, R., Chang, C.-T., Michitsuji, K., Kitagawa, T., Yoshii, S., Kurata, T.: Complementary integration of PDR with absolute positioning methods based on time-series consistency. In: Proceedings of the IPIN 2016, 195_WIP (2016)

34. Fukuhara, T., Tenmoku, R., Ueoka, R., Okuma, T., Kurata, T.: Estimating skills of waiting staff of a restaurant based on behavior sensing and POS data analysis: a case study in a Japanese cuisine restaurant. In: Proceedings of the AH-FE2014, pp. 4287–4299 (2014)

35. Myokan, T., Matsumoto, M., Okuma, T., Ichikari, R., Kato, K., Ota, D., Kurata, T.: Pre-evaluation of Kaizen plan considering efficiency and employee satisfaction by simulation using data assimilation-Toward constructing Kaizen support framework.In: Proceedings of the ICServ 2016, 7 p. (2016)

36. Benchmarking of vison-based spatial registration and tracking methods for Mixed and Augmented Reality (MAR), ISO/IEC 18520

37. Ahmetovic, D., Gleason, C., Ruan, C., Kitani, K., Takagi, H., Asakawa, C.: NavCog: a navigational cognitive assistant for the blind. In: Proceedings of the MobileHCI 2016, pp. 90–99 (2016)

Conference Papers

DanceVibe: Assistive Dancing for the Hearing Impaired

Chi-Ju Chao[1], Chun-Wei Huang[2], Chuan-Jie Lin[3], Hao-Hua Chu[2],
and Polly Huang[1,2(✉)]

[1] GICE, National Taiwan University, Taipei, Taiwan
pollyhuang@ntu.edu.tw
[2] GINM, National Taiwan University, Taipei, Taiwan
[3] CSIE, National Taiwan Ocean University, Keelung, Taiwan

Abstract. Dancing to the rhythm in music comes natural for most of us. This however is a little far-fetched for the hearing impaired. Not being able to hear the music, the hearing impaired rely on visual aid and techniques such as mind counting to dance. To ease the learning process and alleviate the cognitive load in a dance performance, we propose DanceVibe, a wearable device that replays the beats in music via vibrations. In a 35-volunteer user study conducted over 3-month time, we find the system adds to the visual aid in the learning process and is effective enhancing dance performance. The system is particularly useful enabling on-stage performance without the need to memorize and mind count the beats. A word of caution before using DanceVibe and DanceVibe only on stage is that it does require practice and familiarity to the concept of rhythm.

Keywords: Assistive dancing · Wearable computing
Human computer interaction

1 Introduction and Background

For many of us, music is a daily necessity. The reason is simply that music works magic. Listening or moving along the rhythm in music is emotionally soothing and physically liberating [1, 2]. For those who are physically coordinated, performing dance on stage, adding to the music experience, creates a certain sense of self-fulfillment [3].

For the hearing impaired, these benefits of dancing or feeling along the emotions in the music could be far-fetched. The difficulty hearing music makes it hard to grasp the concept of rhythm which is crucial to performing dances. Getting the tones, particularly the volume, pitches, and flow of the sound requires sophisticated hearing aid. Until today, accessibility and affordability of the hearing aids remain an issue that requires continuous effort in well-developed countries [4], not to mention the level of effort required for the developing countries. Seeking alternatives that are potentially more affordable, efforts such as [5–7] investigate how assistive devices that communicate music through *vibrations* could enhance the experience of music appreciation for the hearing impaired.

© ICST Institute for Computer Sciences, Social Informatics and Telecommunications Engineering 2018
K. Murao et al. (Eds.): MobiCASE 2018, LNICST 240, pp. 21–39, 2018.
https://doi.org/10.1007/978-3-319-90740-6_2

There is little work done yet to assist dancing despite reports of hearing impaired performing dances publicly [8, 9]. For recreational performances, the dancers rely on visual aids such as video from displays or gestures from assisting staff nearby the stage. For professional performances, the dancers mind-count based on music tempos memorized by heart. The latter case is particularly challenging and the cognitive loads of these dancers are two-fold: the dance moves and the rhythm. Precise recollection of movement timings, just like precise execution of dance moves, might require a human being of exceptional talent to perform [10, 11].

Not only so, music and dance trainings in early childhood are known to benefit one's motor skill development and have long-lasting effect into the adulthood [12]. Dancing to the music, in particular, help perfect the arm and leg coordination [13]. More recent work finds music training has even broader influence to cognitive development, including memory, language, reading ability, and executive function [14].

Feeling the rhythm in the music can be made easy and affordable. Our premise in this work is that – DanceVibe, the proposed system, helps learning and performing dances for the hearing impaired, and therefore lowering the threshold for the hearing impaired to enjoy rhythm and dancing.

DanceVibe consists of two components. The Beat Extraction component pre-processes the music sound wave and captures the rhythm, i.e., timing of the beats, in the music. The rhythm file can be uploaded and later replayed on the DanceVibe gloves or belts. By feeling the vibrations generated by the wearable part of DanceVibe, the users receive continuous cues of the beats in the music. An analogy of the DanceVibe system is how we often convert the music into digital mp3 format today. We then can load the file to a mobile mp3 player and later listen to the music as we go. Unlike the usual mp3 experience, we extract only the beats in the music into a digital file, play the file back on a wearable module that vibrates at the time of the beats, and therefore communicating the rhythm to the listeners. The wearable part of DanceVibe is implemented in two wearable forms: glove and belt to accommodate different stage performance needs.

Thirty-five people of different degree of hearing impairment have volunteered to participate in the user study over 3-month time. In the experiment, each volunteer first learns the dance with the help of an instruction video and DanceVibe in the first phase and performs the dance in three different assistive dance performance settings: (1) DanceVibe and video, (2) video only, and (3) DanceVibe only. Professional dancers are invited to score the volunteers as they dance in the three different settings. The volunteers are also requested to fill out a pre-test questionnaire to inform us of their gender, age, level of hearing impairment, use of hearing aid, and prior experience with music and dancing. They are also asked to fill out a post-test questionnaire to express how they rate the DanceVibe experience subjectively.

The major findings are as follows. (1) DanceVibe adds to the conventional visual-aid-based method. In particular, DanceVibe works the best alongside the dance video. (2) DanceVibe does sustain for stage performances where placement of visual aids is restricted. (3) However, for recreational performances, visual aid is still more effective as we observe that DanceVibe works the best for volunteers who have prior music experience, whereas the visual aid approach does not require prior music experience and works well for all volunteers. This suggests that DanceVibe might not be for all the dancers to be. It does require practice and familiarity to the concept of rhythm. (4) Furthermore, according to the post-test questionnaire, feeling the rhythm via vibration is refreshing and interesting to the volunteers. This indicates the vibration-based user interface could help motivating the music and/or dance training for the hearing impaired. When this is done at the early age, the hearing impaired could potentially develop better motor, language, and execution skills.

To sum up, our contribution includes (1) the design and implementation of DanceVibe, (2) the user study on the effectiveness of DanceVibe, and (3) the analysis revealing the caution one should take before considering DanceVibe as a dance performance aid. In the sections to come, we first describe the design and implementation of DanceVibe. The evaluation is carried out progressively. First, we take on a small-scale trial study, which sets us on track for the formal, large-scale user study, which is described subsequently. Lastly, but not the least, we report the findings from both objective dance scores and subjective user feedback.

2 System Design and Prototype

The DanceVibe system consists of 2 components. The beat extraction component processes the music clip and generates the beat-only playback file. The file is transferred and store on a wearable module which vibrates at the beats and therefore communicates the rhythm to the user.

2.1 Beat Extraction

There are two phases of computation involved in identifying the beats in the music. In the first phase, the system estimates the peaks in the raw sound waves. Figure 1 shows

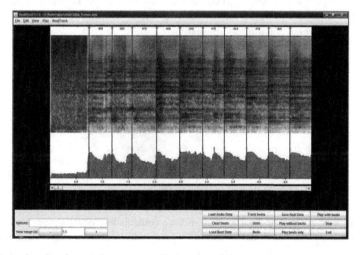

Fig. 1. Raw signals of a music segment. The peaks of the sound wave are the onsets of the beats. The time duration between the peaks are referred to as the inter-onset interval (IOI).

the raw signal of a music segment. The peaks in the plot indicate the onsets of the beats. Identifying timing of the peaks allows estimating of the inter-onset interval (IOI), which enables playback of the beats for the beat player component.

There are two approaches to identify peaks. One is to envelop a wave segment by tracing a pair of consecutive local maximums in the signal amplitude. The other is to exploit time-frequency processing such as the wavelet transform to identify the timing of the energy peaks at the frequency of interest. The challenge is however that both approaches could potentially be erroneous depending on the music, as well as the recording quality.

To mitigate the problem in peak estimation, more recent solutions [15–17] refine the peak estimations by aligning them to the tempo derived from multiple peak estimations in the music. We adopt BeatRoot [18], which is open source and shown outperforming prior works, for the beat extraction function.

2.2   Wearable Vibrator

The vibrator module consists of an 8-bit microcontroller, an IEEE 802.15.4 compliant radio transceiver, and a high-speed motor. Given the simplicity of the vibrating function, we choose the commonly used MSP430 and CC2420 chipsets for the control and communication functions on board. The only caution applied in the hardware design is the choice of the motor. Preliminary testing shows that low-power motors might not provide strong enough sensation when the users are more engaged in dance moves. On the other hand, high power motors can be too bulky to wear which does not serve the purpose of the system well either. The eventual choice, a 20000 RPM high-speed motor, is considerably small and sensible. See the small metal cylinder extending to the left of the main module in Fig. 2. The module is packaged into the glove form initially. After receiving feedback from the preliminary experiment, the belt form is developed. Both forms of DanceVibe are shown in Fig. 3. Note that the glove form can be implemented alternatively using a smart watch. Though, the prototype, using low-end microcontroller, is substantially lower in cost and for the waist belt form, there is no commercially available alternative.

Fig. 2. DanceVibe prototype: (1) The main module contains the MSP430 microcontroller and CC2420, a IEEE 802.15.4 compliant radio, (2) Vibrators are connected to the main module via GPIO.

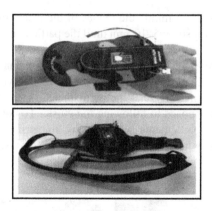

Fig. 3. DanceVibe in two wearing form: (1) Glove (top) and (2) Belt (bottom).

The vibrator is started by a remote controller. Currently, the remote control is implemented as a PC plugged in with the IEEE 802.15.4 radio transceiver. When the user initiates the play function on the PC, it transmits a packet to all Vibrator modules in the area and allows synchronized group dances.

3 Preliminary Study

To validate the design and to try out the prototype, we recruit three users with hearing impairment for a folksong dance lesson in the lab. The three participants, two male and one female, are in their 30s and live an active lifestyle. The dance is typical of folksong dances with 4 simple move sequences and each recurring twice till the end of the music.

The participants are first instructed to put on the DanceVibe glove (Fig. 4, Left). In the learning phase, the glove is on with vibrating beats as the instructor shows each of the move sequences with the music played synchronously. After observing a couple of

Fig. 4. Experimental procedure: (1) Trying out the DanceVibe Glove (Left). (2) Learning to dance by following the instructor's moves (Right).

times, the participants begin to mimic the moves of the instructor (Fig. 4, Right). The practice phase continues for some 5–10 min until the participants are confident dancing by themselves.

In the performing phase, the participants perform the full dance twice (Fig. 5, Left). Once with the music and beats in synchronization. The other with the music and beats off sync. We observe distinctively that the participants dance to the beats communicated from the glove, as opposed to following the music. To conclude the experiment, all of us, including the participants with hearing impairment and the experiment administrators with healthy hearing, dance to the beats and music respectively (Fig. 5, Right).

Fig. 5. Experimental procedure: (1) Dancing alone with the DanceVibe (Left) and (2) Group dancing by all with the DanceVibe (Right).

The three participants are interviewed following the experiment. The major findings are as follows. (1) All of them find the device odd but the experience interesting and fun. (2) The DanceVibe works intuitively and does not distract them visually while learning the dance moves. One participant, who has experience performing to the public, share openly that: (3) the device might be more of stage use where placement of visual aids on stage are often restricted. Dancers on stage rely on mind counts to keep in sync with the music. This can be difficult depending on the music the performers will be dancing to. (4) On the other hand, in the learning phase, visual aids are necessary anyway. It is not clear how much DanceVibe would help. (5) Although the DanceVibe is compact, it would provide more flexibility for costume design if more wear forms are available. The findings are encouraging and the feedback prompts us to implement the belt form DanceVibe.

4   User Study

The objective of the user study is to evaluate the effectiveness and usability of DanceVibe and compare it to the commonly used visual aid approach, i.e., showing of dance video. The test subjects are invited to the lab and instructed to follow an experimental procedure that is substantially extended from the preliminary trial. The sessions are recorded and each subject is asked to complete a pre-test questionnaire for basic information and a post-test questionnaire regarding the experience with DanceVibe.

4.1   User Selection

According to our observation and user feedback from the preliminary trial, it is likely that DanceVibe might be more of use for a certain population but not the others. To enable further analysis on a number of user-specific factors, we recruit volunteers of both gender, varying age, varying degree of hearing impairments, varying level of dance or music experience, and varying level of sports activities. 35 people of hearing impairment participate in the study.

Each volunteer is provided a pre-test questionnaire to complete before the experiment starts. See the questionnaire in Table 1. See also Table 2 for a detailed summary of the 35 volunteers and their attributes. There is a 43% to 57% gender balance in the population. There is also a significant age and hearing impairment severity span. As hearing aid is becoming economically affordable, a majority of the population wear hearing aid and live rather active lifestyles, with some degree of music, dance, and sports experience.

4.2   Procedure

The procedure is similar to the preliminary trial. Each volunteer is instructed to go through 4 stages of the experiment: (1) wear the DanceVibe, (2) learn the dance moves, (3) practice the dance, and (4) perform the dance.

To speed up the learning process, we record the instructor dancing to the music and edit the video so it runs in a karaoke-like style. In the video, captions indicating a sequence of moves are added. Figure 6 shows a user learning to dance by watching the dance karaoke video and feeling the vibrations from the DanceVibe (right wrist). At the bottom of the projection screen, the volunteer sees 8 moves. Translated, they mean move left, step, move right, step, move left, step, step, and stop. The moves are simple by design. This is to lower the learning curve and take the volunteer's cognitive load off from executing the moves, and therefore focusing on feeling the beats from DanceVibe. Note though the learning curve could still be steep for volunteers who has little experience with music or dance.

After learning the moves and the sequence, the volunteers are allowed to practice as many times as they want until they are comfortable for the final test dance. At the final stage, the volunteers are instructed to dances 3 times, first with the karaoke style dance video and DanceVibe, (2) with just the video, and (3) with just the DanceVibe. The test dance performances are video recorded for analysis later. When all 3 test dances are completed, the volunteers are asked to complete the post-test questionnaire (Table 3) and a short interview before receiving the compensation for their time and effort.

Table 1. Pre-test questionnaire.

1. Gender:	□ Male □ Female
2. Age:	□ ≤ 17 □ 18~35 □ 36~64 □ ≥ 65
3. Hearing Impairment:	□ Slight □ Moderate □ Severe
4. Are you wearing any hearing aid?	□ Yes □ No
5. Have you listened to music before?	□ Yes □ No (If no, jump to question 8)
6. Do you listen to music often?	□ Yes □ No
7. How do you listen to music?	□ Just listen □ Turn up the volume □ Sense the vibration □ Visual effect or dance move □ Body or sign language □ Headphone or earphone □ Others _____
8. Have you danced before?	□ Yes □ No (If no, jump to question 11)
9. Do you dance often?	□ Yes, for____year(s) □ No
10. How do you listen to the music while dancing: □ Just listen □ Turn up the volume □ Feel the vibration on the dance floor □ Mind count □ Visual aid from friends □ Others _____	
11. Do you do any sports regularly?	□ Yes □ No (If no, skip rest of the questions)
12. Frequency of sports activities:	□ < 1 □ once a week □ twice □ 3 times □ 4 or more
13. Duration of the sports sessions:	□ 30 mins □ 1 hr □ 2 hrs □ 3 hrs or more
14. Preferred sports activities :	□ swimming □ team sport such as baseball/basketball □ running □ yoga/aerobic □ others _____

4.3   Data Collection and Processing

User experience is multi-facet. Both subjective and objective measures are essential to a well-around understanding of the system. For the subjective user experience, we quantify the feedback provided by the volunteers in the post-test questionnaires. The 5 options, disagree, mildly disagree, neutral, somewhat agree, very much agree, are converted to numerical scores 1 to 5 respectively.

For objective user experience, we find the effectiveness of DanceVibe better captured by evaluating the dance performance. To quantify how well each volunteer dances in different settings, we invite 3 professional dancers to screen the video recordings and score each dance from 1 to 5. To be specific, the screeners are provided the scoring guideline (Table 4). Each video receives 3 scores.

The pre-test questionnaires are mainly to allow further analysis of how a user subgroup respond stronger or weaker to the use of DanceVibe.

Table 2. Summary of the test subjects.

Age	18–35	36–64	>65	Sum 35
	26(74.2%)	8(22.8%)	1(2.8%)	
Gender				
M	8	6	1	15(42.8%)
F	18	2	0	20(57.1%)
Hearing impairment				
Slight	6	0	0	6(17.1%)
Moderate	5	0	0	5(14.2%)
Severe	15	8	1	24(68.5%)
Wearing hearing aid				
Yes	25	1	0	26(74.2%)
No	1	7	1	9(25.7%)
Prior music experience				
Yes	25	3	1	29(82.8%)
No	1	5	0	6(17.1%)
Prior dance experience				
Yes	20	5	0	25(71.4%)
No	6	3	1	10(28.5%)
Regular sports activity				
Yes	21	6	1	28(80%)
No	5	2	0	7(20%)

Fig. 6. A volunteer dancing to the instruction video with the DanceVibe glove on his right wrist.

4.4   Hypotheses and Tests

The main hypotheses surround (1) whether different assistive settings, with or without DanceVibe, affects significantly the volunteers' dance performance, (2) whether any of the factors impact significantly the volunteers' dance performance, (3) whether any of

Table 3. Post-test questionnaire.

1. Dancing is fun.
□ Disagree   □ Mildly disagree   □ Neutral   □ Somewhat agree   □ Very much agree
2. The dance you just learned is not difficult.
□ Disagree   □ Mildly disagree   □ Neutral   □ Somewhat agree   □ Very much agree
3. It is interesting learning to dance via vibrations.
□ Disagree   □ Mildly disagree   □ Neutral   □ Somewhat agree   □ Very much agree
4. DanceVibe is helpful learning to dance.
□ Disagree   □ Mildly disagree   □ Neutral   □ Somewhat agree   □ Very much agree
5. DanceVibe is helpful learning to dance even without the video.
□ Disagree   □ Mildly disagree   □ Neutral   □ Somewhat agree   □ Very much agree

Table 4. Video scoring guideline.

1: Missing almost all beats
2: Missing more than half of the beats
3: Dancing to about half of the beats
4: Dancing to more than half of the beats
5: Dancing almost all move on beat

the factors impact significantly how the volunteers feel about dancing and using DanceVibe.

For the first main hypothesis (H1), 3 sub-hypotheses (H1-1 to H1-3) are tested to further analyze which pair of assistive settings are more different than the others.

- **H1**: The dance performance is significantly different among the assistive dance settings.
- **H1-1**: The dance performance is significantly different between the DanceVibe and Video vs. the Video only setting.
- **H1-2**: The dance performance is significantly different between the DanceVibe and Video vs. the DanceVibe only setting.
- **H1-3**: The dance performance is significantly different between the Video only vs. the DanceVibe only setting.

For the second main hypothesis (H2), 7 sub-hypotheses (H2-1 to H2-7) are tested to see if any of the volunteer-specific factors are more influential than the others.

- **H2**: The dance performance is significantly different depending on any of the factors.
- **H2-1**: The dance performance is significantly different between the 2 genders.

- **H2-2**: The dance performance is significantly different between the 2 age groups.
- **H2-3**: The dance performance is significantly different between the 3 hearing impairment level groups.
- **H2-4**: The dance performance is significantly different between the 2 groups wearing the hearing aid or not.
- **H2-5**: The dance performance is significantly different between the 2 groups having prior music experience or not.
- **H2-6**: The dance performance is significantly different between the 2 groups having prior dance experience or not.
- **H2-7**: The dance performance is significantly different between the 2 groups having prior sports experience or not.

For the third hypothesis (H3), we perform tests on each of the questions in the post-test questionnaires and check if any of the factors makes a difference. There are in total 5 by 7 sub-hypotheses. In the result, we present only the sub-hypothesis that at least one factor plays a statistically significant role in the subjective feedback.

- **H3**: Any of the questions in the post-test questionnaire is significantly different depending on any of the factors.

We apply commonly used statistical techniques to examine whether multiple data samples are significantly different. Specifically, the T test [19] is used to check if two data samples are from the same distribution and the ANOVA test [20] is used for the cases of 3 data samples or above.

The t-value and f-value represent how far apart the sample means are from each other for the T and ANOVA test respectively. From both tests, the generated p-value reflects the variation of the possible means. The smaller the variation, the more confident the test is about whether the sample means are from the same distribution or not. Typically, we seek a p-value smaller than 0.001 or 0.01. We mark a p-value smaller than 0.001 with *** indicating strong confidence and for p-value smaller than 0.01 with ** indicating moderate confidence.

In case we need to examine if certain factor pairs are correlated (so we can trace back to the root cause), the Chi Square test [21] is applied. When the p-value generated by the test is small, the correlation in the factor pair is statistically significant.

5   Result - Dance Performance

Each volunteer's dance is evaluated by 3 expert dancers. All 35 volunteers dance to the music in 3 different assistive dance settings: DanceVibe and video, video only, and DanceVibe only. Therefore, for each setting, we receive 105 scores for the statistical analysis. Below we present first the results of how well the volunteers dance in the 3 assistive settings (Hypothesis H1) and then analyze how the volunteer might react differently depending on factors such as hearing impairment severity and prior music experience (Hypothesis H2).

5.1   Comparison of 3 Assistive Settings

We pass the scores from each of the 3 settings through the ANOVA and T test. Table 5 shows the outcome of the ANOVA test. An f-value of 10.43 and a p-value of less than 0.001 suggests that some of the 3 settings are significantly different, confirming Hypothesis H1. Furthermore, applying the T test on each pair of settings (see Table 6) shows the 3 settings are significantly different from each other. Every pair shows a p-value of less than 0.001, which confirms Hypothesis H-1.1, H-1.2, and H-1.3.

Table 5. One-Way ANOVA test result.

Source	SS	df	MS	f-value	p-value
3 assistive dance settings	14.76	2	7.38	10.43	<.001
Error	72.13	102	0.70		
Total	86.90	104			

Table 6. Pairwise t-test result.

Test settings	# of Scores tested	t-value	p-value
DanceVibe and Video vs. Video only	105 vs. 105	4.51	<0.001
DanceVibe and Video vs. DanceVibe only	105 vs. 105	7.97	<0.001
Video only vs. DanceVibe only	105 vs. 105	5.87	<0.001

Now we examine quantitatively which of the 3 settings stands the best and which the worst. Table 7 enlists the average score and the standard deviation per assistive dance setting. One can observe that DanceVibe and video together work the best overall. An average score of close to 4 signifies that the volunteers are able to dance the majority of the moves on beat. The video only setting does not quite compare, which suggests that DanceVibe enhances the learning and performance process.

Table 7. Average and standard deviation of the dance scores.

Test settings	# of Scores collected	Average	Standard deviation
DanceVibe and video	105	3.94	0.81
Video only	105	3.56	0.77
DanceVibe only	105	3.02	0.92

The DanceVibe only setting however performs significantly worse than the video only setting. The message is that visual stimulus is more effective than vibrations as it communicates not just the beats but also the moves. Nonetheless, the average score of the DanceVibe only setting suggests that the volunteers on average catches half of the beats in a dance which would have been impossible for the severely hearing impaired. For circumstances that placement of visual aid might be restricted (e.g., stage performance), DanceVibe provides as a sensible alternative that is less intrusive to the environment.

5.2   Impact of Dancer-Specific Factors

To understand whether a certain population benefit more from DanceVibe than the others, we group the scores by a number of factors that we have surveyed in the pre-test questionnaire. For factors that are binary, we apply the t-test and examine the t-value and p-value to see if the difference between the 2 groups are significant. For factors that are trinary or higher, we apply the ANOVA test and examine the f-value and p-value to see if the difference among the groups are significant. Below, we present first the influence of the personal attributes such as gender, age, and hearing impairment level. Next, we discuss the influence of habit related factors such as wearing of hearing aid, experience with music, dancing, and sports activities.

5.2.1   Personal Attributes

Among the 3 personal attributes (Tables 8, 9 and 10), gender's influence to dance performance is minimum, and this is the case for all 3 settings. While the volunteers of varying degree of hearing impairment show some difference in the dance performance, the p-values suggest that the score variation is high and the difference in the average scores is not statistically significant.

Table 8. t-test result for the influence of gender in 3 test settings.

Test settings	Average score		t-value	p-value
	Male	Female		
DanceVibe and video	3.93	3.95	−0.059*	*<0.05
Video only	3.55	4.56	−0.04*	*<0.05
DanceVibe only	2.82	3.18	−1.14*	*<0.05

Table 9. t-test result for the influence of age in 3 test settings.

Test settings	Average score		t-value	p-value
	18–34	35–65+		
DanceVibe and video	4.16	3.29	3.11**	**<0.01
Video only	3.75	3.00	2.74**	**<0.01
DanceVibe only	3.28	2.29	3.07**	**<0.01

Table 10. t-test result for the influence of hearing impairment level in 3 test settings.

Test settings	Average score			f-value	p-value
	Slight	Moderate	Severe		
DanceVibe and video	4.39	3.87	3.85	1.10*	*<0.05
Video only	4.11	3.73	3.39	2.38*	*<0.05
DanceVibe only	3.78	3.2	2.81	3.07*	*<0.05

Age is a factor that incurs a significant difference. Younger volunteers dance better than the older ones. This could be partly that the younger volunteers are generally more agile and fond of physical activities. This could also be contributed by the fact that the hearing aids are growingly affordable and the support from the social welfare system has been strengthened. As a result, the younger generations of the hearing impaired are cared by specialists and wear hearing aids at an early age. We do observe commonly that the young volunteers cite their experience with sound and music in the pre-test questionnaire. To confirm the conjecture, we present how the three factors, age, hearing aid, and music experience, are correlated in Sect. 5.2.3.

Hearing impairment level does not influence the dance performance significantly. The chance is high that hearing aid has compensated the factor for most volunteers as we do observe a high percentage of volunteers participating in the study wearing a hearing aid.

In summary, Hypothesis H2-2 is validated while H2-1 and 2-3 are invalidated. Note that H2 is also validated as one of the H2-x is shown statistically true.

5.2.2   Habit-Related Factors

Influence of the remaining factors are discussed in this subsection. Firstly, we compare the dance scores of the groups with hearing aid vs. not are statistically different (Table 11). This is not entirely surprising, as being able to hear to some degree would have helped in addition to all the other aids. We are particularly interested in the result of the video only setting. Among the 3 settings, the video only setting shows less a difference. This is likely due to the visual nature of the setting. Being able to hear does not matter much. Though in the meantime, rhythm is indeed a non-negligible component in the learning and dancing process. The vibrations serve the purpose of adding to the visual aid and provide as a *richer* reminder to the volunteers.

Table 11. t-test result for the influence of wearing hearing aid in 3 test settings.

Test settings	Average score		t-value	p-value
	Hearing aid	No aid		
DanceVibe and video	4.17	3.25	3.34**	**<0.01
Video only	3.74	3.03	2.52*	*<0.05
DanceVibe only	3.28	2.29	3.07**	**<0.01

Prior music experience is a unique factor. It influences only one setting – the DanceVibe only setting (see Table 12). It appears that, in the 2 other settings, the volunteers are able to keep up with the moves provided the visual cues. This is understandable, as prior visual experience would matter more to the interpretation of the visual cues, rather than prior music expeirence. This suggests also, without the video in the DanceVibe only setting, vibrations are the only cues the volunteers are receiving and prior music experience is crucial interpreting the vibrations, i.e., the rhythm. Having a good sense of rhythm makes a difference when using DanceVibe, and such a sense is typically fostered by prior experience with periodic processes, e.g., listening to music.

Table 12. t-test result for the influence of music experience in 3 test settings.

Test settings	Average score		t-value	p-value
	Music exp	No exp		
DanceVibe and video	4.08	3.27	2.35*	*<0.05
Video only	3.68	2.94	2.25*	*<0.05
DanceVibe only	3.25	1.94	3.68***	***<0.001

Once the sense of rhythm is established, how frequent one practices the skill does not seem to matter much, as we see in Table 13 that the difference between the frequent and infrequent music appreciators is insignificant.

Table 13. t-test result for the influence of music appreciation frequency in 3 test settings.

Test settings	Average score		t-value	p-value
	Frequent	Not frequent		
DanceVibe and video	4.17	3.72	1.31*	*<0.05
Video only	3.82	3.16	1.54*	*<0.05
DanceVibe only	3.28	3.11	0.32*	*<0.05

In summary, Hypothesis H2-4 and H2-5 are validated.

The influence of the dance and sports activities is even less and not statistically significant. See Tables 14, 15 and 16. The reason is likely that the dance moves are simple by choice, so it does not require volunteers to be athletic to learn or perform. How often the volunteers dance and what sports they play are even less influential.

Table 14. t-test result for the influence of prior dance experience in 3 test settings.

Test settings	Average score		t-value	p-value
	Yes	No		
DanceVibe and video	3.93	3.96	−0.10*	*<0.05
Video only	3.64	3.36	0.93*	*<0.05
DanceVibe only	3.05	2.96	0.24*	*<0.05

Table 15. t-test result for the influence of dance frequency in 3 test settings.

Test settings	Average score		t-value	p-value
	Frequent	Not frequent		
DanceVibe and video	4.5	3.82	1.6*	*<0.05
Video only	4.33	3.50	2.12*	*<0.05
DanceVibe only	3.75	2.92	1.69*	*<0.05

In summary, Hypothesis H2-6 and H2-7 are invalidated.

Table 16. t-test result for the influence of prior sports experience in 3 test settings.

Test settings	Average score		t-value	p-value
	Yes	No		
DanceVibe and video	3.91	4.04	−0.37*	*<0.05
Video only	3.55	3.57	−0.03*	*<0.05
DanceVibe only	3.03	3.00	0.08*	*<0.05

5.2.3   Interaction Between Factors

To validate the conjecture that most young volunteers wear hearing aid and therefore more experienced with music, we show in Tables 17, 18 and 19 the percentage of volunteers at different age groups who wear hearing aid, volunteers at different age groups who have prior music experience, and volunteers wearing hearing aid who have prior music experience. The Chi Square test finds a p-value of less than 0.001 for all three factor pairs, indicating statistically significant correlation in all factor pairs.

Table 17. Correlation between age and hearing aid.

Age	18–34 N(%)	35–65+ N(%)	Sum N(%)
Wearing hearing aid			
Yes	25(71.43)	1(2.86)	26(74.29)
No	1(2.86)	8(22.86)	9(25.71)
Chi Square test output: $\chi^2 = 29.07$ p = 4.874E-07 (***<.001)			

Table 18. Correlation between age and prior music experience.

Age	18–34 N(%)	35–65+ N(%)	Sum N(%)
Prior music experience			
Yes	25(71.43)	4(11.43)	29(82.86)
No	1(2.86)	5(14.29)	6(17.14)
Chi Square test output: $\chi^2 = 15.71$ p = 0.0003887 (***<.001)			

Table 19. Correlation between prior music experience and wearing hearing aid.

Prior music exp	Yes N(%)	No N(%)	Sum N(%)
Wearing hearing aid			
Yes	25(71.43)	1(2.86)	26(74.29)
No	4(11.43)	5(14.29)	9(25.71)
Chi Square test output: $\chi^2 = 15.71$ p = 0.0003887 (***<.001)			

Table 20. Post-test questionnaire score average and standard deviation.

Question set	Average	Standard deviation
Q1: Dancing is fun	4.51	0.78
Q2: The dance I just learned is not difficult	4.37	0.59
Q3: It is interesting to feel the beats in music through vibrations	4.31	0.75
Q4: DanceVibe helps learning to dance	4.05	0.90
Q5: Without the video, DanceVibe helps performing dance	3.71	1.04

6   Result – Post-test Questionnaire

Summarized in Table 20 is the result of the post-test questionnaire. We can see that the volunteers in general find that (Q1) dancing is fun, (Q2) the dance they have learned in the experiment is not difficult, and (Q3) feeling the beats in the music via vibration is fun. We see in the standard variable of the scores that while the volunteers are more consistent about the difficulty level of the dance, the opinion on whether dancing or feeling the beats through vibration is interesting is more diverged. This indicates that there is some degree of variability in the volunteers' personal interest about dancing and music, which shows diversity in the volunteers participating in the user study.

More importantly, the users are positive that (Q4) DanceVibe helps in the learning process. This echoes the finding from the dance performance scores. The volunteers do learn better with not just the instruction video but also DanceVibe. Note that in the learning phase of the experiment, the instruction video is always in display. On the other hand, the volunteers agree only partially that (Q5) DanceVibe helps in dance performance. As we see in the testing phase, the volunteers perform the worst wearing only DanceVibe. The volunteers are self-conscious of their performance and their answers to Q4 and Q5 reflect so.

One particular result to present is the relative difference between volunteers who have prior dance performance experience and rely on mind counting to track the beats in the music while dancing. The average score to Q5 in this group of volunteers is 4.22, which is significantly higher than the overall average 3.71. This supports Hypothesis H3 and echoes what one of the volunteers in the preliminary trial has commented. DanceVibe would be helpful to stage performance that placement of visual aid is constrained.

7   Conclusion

In this study, DanceVibe is shown effective assisting dance learning and performing well aside the conventional video-based method. In particular, DanceVibe does sustain for stage performances that placement of visual aids is restricted. One word of caution though is that DanceVibe might not be for all the dancers to be. It does require practice and familiarity to the concept of rhythm.

A surprising finding is that the users do find the form of user interaction, i.e. feeling the rhythm via vibration, refreshing and interesting. This indicates the potential of DanceVibe as an aid in music or dance training for children. Children, relative to adults, are more prone to fun activities. With DanceVibe being fun, children of hearing impairment are more likely to accept music and dance training and therefore develop better motor, language, and execution skills in the long run.

Using vibration as an HCI has potential. To this point, the vibrations communicated are simply the beats extracted from the music. There is a good design space expressing the music through vibration patterns. For example, the power or sudden breakage of beats in the music can be cues for dramatic moves that are more expressive of the ambient emotion. Furthermore, there is an increasing number of performances embracing digital art forms. In these performances, synchronization among dancers and the on-stage projections can be critical. If the vibration feed takes into account how individual dancer reacts slower or faster to the vibrations, fine-grained synchronization might be possible and therefore creating a seamless flow. We are currently looking into these possibilities to enable richer dancing experience for the hearing impaired.

References

1. Salimpoor, V.N., Benovoy, M., Larcher, K., Dagher, A., Zatorre, R.J.: Anatomically distinct dopamine release during anticipation and experience of peak emotion to music. Nat. Neurosci. **14**, 257–262 (2011)
2. Sievers, B., Polansky, L., Casey, M., Wheatleya, T.: Music and movement share a dynamic structure that supports universal expressions of emotion. Psychol. Cogn. Sci. **110**(1), 70–75 (2013)
3. Michal Doron Harari: "To be on stage means to be alive" theatre work with education undergraduates as a promoter of students' mental resilience. Soc. Behav. Sci. **209**(3), 161–166 (2015)
4. Donahue, A., Dubno, J.R., Beck, L.: Accessible and affordable hearing health care for adults with mild to moderate hearing loss. Ear Hear. **31**(1), 2–6 (2010)
5. Goldstein, J.M.H., Proctor, A.: Tactile aids for profoundly deaf children. J. Acoust. Soc. Am. **77**, 258–265 (1985)
6. Darrow, A.A.: The effect of vibrotactile stimuli via the Somatron on the identification of rhythmic concepts by hearing impaired children. J. Music Ther. **26**(3), 115–124 (1992)
7. Nanayakkara, S., et al.: An enhanced musical experience for the deaf: design and evaluation of a music display and a haptic chair. In: Proceedings of the 27th International Conference on Human Factors in Computing Systems, Boston, MA, USA (2009)
8. Berselli, M., Lulkin, S.A.: Theatre and dance with deaf students: researching performance practices in a Brazilian school context. Res. Drama Educ. J. Appl. Theatre Perform. **22**(3), 413–419 (2017)
9. Hill, K.: Delightful! Deaf Dance Competitors Move to The Beat. The Gleaner, 15 May 2016
10. Peltier, C.: Inspirational Deaf Dancer Uses Vibrations to Coordinate His Moves And Proves Anyone Can Do Anything. A Plus. 31 Mar 2016
11. Traynor, R.: The Dance of a Thousand Hands. Hearing Health & Technology Matters, 4 April 2016
12. Costa-Giomi, E.: Does music instruction improve fine motor abilities? Ann. New York Acad. Sci. **1060**, 262–264 (2005)

13. Washburn, A., DeMarco, M., de Vries, S., Ariyabuddhiphongs, K., Schmidt, R.C., Richardson, M.J., Riley, M.A.: Dancers entrain more effectively than non-dancers to another actor's movements. Front. Hum. Neurosci. **8**, 800 (2014)

14. Miendlarzewska, E.A., Trost, W.J.: How musical training affects cognitive development: rhythm, reward and other modulating variables. Front. Neurosci. **7**, 279 (2013)

15. Duxbury, C., et al.: A hybrid approach to musical note onset detection. In: Proceedings Digital Audio Effects Workshop (DAFx) (2002)

16. Bello, J.P., et al.: A tutorial on onset detection in music signals. IEEE Trans. Speech Audio Process. **13**, 1035–1047 (2005)

17. Klapuri, A.: Sound onset detection by applying psychoacoustic knowledge. In: 1999 IEEE International Conference on Acoustics, Speech, and Signal Processing, ICASSP 1999, vol. 6, pp. 3089–3092 (1999)

18. Dixon, S.: Evaluation of the audio beat tracking system BeatRoot. J. New Music Res. **36**, 39–50 (2007)

19. Student: The probable error of a mean. Biometrika **6**(1), 1–25 (1908)

20. Fisher, R.A.: Statistical Methods for Research Workers. Oliver & Boyd, Edinburgh (1925)

21. Pearson, K.: On the criterion that a given system of deviations from the probable in the case of a correlated system of variables is such that it can be reasonably supposed to have arisen from random sampling. Philos. Mag. Ser. 5 **50**(5), 157–175 (1900)

Quick Browsing of Shared Experience Videos Based on Conversational Field Detection

Kai Toyama$^{(\boxtimes)}$ and Yasuyuki Sumi

Future University Hakodate, Hokkaido, Japan
k-toyama@sumilab.org, sumi@acm.org

Abstract. We propose a system to aid the browsing of shared experience data that includes multiple first-person view videos. Using this system, users can avoid the tedious task of searching through lengthy videos. Our system aids browsing by displaying situational information cues on the video seek-bar, and visualizing node graphs showing members participating in the scenes and their approximate location. Users of our system can search and browse events with the help of cues indicating participant names and their locations. We use auditory similarity to detect conversational fields in order to detect the dynamics of groups in crowded areas. We conduct an experiment to evaluate the ability of our system to decrease the time needed for finding specified scenes in lifelog videos. Our experimental results suggest that our system can aid the browsing of videos that include one's own experiences, but cannot be proven to aid the browsing of unfamiliar data.

Keywords: Smart video viewing · Information cues
First-person view videos · Conversational fields

1 Introduction

We propose a system that helps users to quickly browse videos capturing social events by providing cues showing the chronological history of conversation groups generated during the events. We use a method to detect conversational fields as cues based on the similarity of auditory situations among the participants.

We define conversational fields as a topological area in which multiple persons join the same conversation. As participants in the conversational fields, we consider not only people speaking but also people listening to them. Recognizing group activities such as group conversations is an important technique to enable context-aware applications for enriching social activities, e.g., groupware. For example, at conferences, there are activities of different spatial sizes; these include oral presentations, poster presentations, and social gatherings. We must recognize differences in spatial sizes and perform the appropriate service. The purpose of this paper is to realize an efficient browser for searching a user's lifelog data as a context-aware application based on recognized conversation fields.

© ICST Institute for Computer Sciences, Social Informatics and Telecommunications Engineering 2018
K. Murao et al. (Eds.): MobiCASE 2018, LNICST 240, pp. 40–55, 2018.
https://doi.org/10.1007/978-3-319-90740-6_3

Because advancing camera technology enables us to record videos for long periods of time, we can record our experiences and share them with others. However, it is difficult to find a specific event from a lengthy video. We consider conversation partners and their approximate location to be important information for recalling memories. Therefore, we use conversational fields as a cue for browsing video.

The remainder of the paper is organized as follows. Section 2 provides an overview of the problem addressed in our research by presenting related work. Section 3 presents our system for quick browsing of shared experience videos as an application that uses detected conversational fields based on situated sound similarity. Section 4 presents an experimental evaluation showing that our system can provide the ability to quickly find any scene from lengthy lifelog videos. We describe limitations of our study and future work in Sect. 5. We conclude the paper in Sect. 6.

2 Related Work

2.1 Detecting Conversation Groups as a Social Context

Hall [1] introduced a concept called proxemics, i.e., measurable distances between people as they interact. Many studies in the domain of ubiquitous computing have attempted to detect social contexts by estimating users' positions and mutual orientations based on proximity detection via infrared tags [2,3], location detection according to signal intensity of Wi-Fi access points [4], the use of Bluetooth Low Energy (BLE) [5], visual tracking of groups of people [6,7], and various other techniques. In addition, Kendon [8] proposed F-formation as a measure of social interaction. F-formation detection [9–12] involves analyzing physical clusters of people as well as proximity detection.

Physical clusters of people could be candidates for conversational fields. However, it is difficult to determine conversational fields according to cluster size because the physical size of conversational fields can easily vary depending on the size and shape of the space, the crowdedness of people, and the particular social situation.

Previous works have aimed to estimate ad-hoc groups based on ambient sound similarity. Techniques that use sound to detect groups and their locations can be roughly divided into two categories: those that are analogous to fingerprinting [13–15] and those that analyze the similarity of each sound [16–18]. To utilize techniques analogous to fingerprinting, the environmental sound of each place must be recorded in advance. For example, Aoki et al. [19] proposed a method to detect conversation groups from collocated multiple simultaneous conversations. Their method needs prior training with users' speech data. In contrast, Wirz et al. [20], whose aim and approach are similar to ours, reported a detailed performance evaluation of their proximity estimation method. Their method records ambient sound on each microphone synchronously, and calculates similarities. We are more interested in application development with simple and light implementation, and this paper aims to provide practical findings from our trials in various fields.

Nakakura et al. [21] proposed a system called Neary, which detects conversational fields containing people in a conversation by comparing sound similarity among them. The similarity in auditory situations between each pair of users is measured according to the similarity in the frequency properties of sound captured by the users' head-worn microphones.

Intuitively, users whose microphones receive similar sounds (voice of a certain person, ambient sound, etc.) are regarded as the members of a conversation. In this method, people situated in the same sound environment are naturally grouped in the same conversational field, independent of its physical size. The conversational fields detected by this method match the granularity of social activities such as meetings, lectures, and group tours. The method is also adjustable to various conversational field sizes, from ad-hoc chatting to a lecture in a large hall (Fig. 1).

The state of conversational fields in a crowded area

The physical size of conversational fields depending on social activities

Fig. 1. Distance between participants and the physical size of conversational fields depending on social activity and situation.

Neary is implemented using a simple algorithm and runs on portable PCs. Preliminary experimental results show that Neary can successfully distinguish groups of conversations and track dynamic changes in them. This study aims to deploy Neary to track users' participation in conversational fields during daily activities, and provide a browser that can quickly search the users' lifelog videos.

2.2 Smart Video Viewing

There are two categories of techniques that enable users to browse videos quickly: fast-forwarding techniques [22,23] and video summarization techniques [24–27]. Fast-forwarding techniques reduce camera shaking and fast-forward the video by resampling frames. However, fast-forwarding does not consider the events in the video. On the other hand, video summarization techniques extract scenes in the video based on cue detection achieved by hand activity recognition [28–30], face recognition [31], and activity segmentation [32]. However, users cannot know the context of an extracted scene. Additionally, if the detection result is wrong, it is possible that an important scene has been missed.

Higuchi et al. [33] proposed EgoScanning, which facilitates rapid browsing of egocentric videos. Hand activity, face recognition, and the movement of the person who recorded the video are used as cues; these are shown on the video timeline to indicate regions of detection. The aims of their study are similar to ours. We facilitate browsing using conversational fields as cues, and show them on the seek bar.

3   Detection of Conversational Fields and Its Application

3.1   Detecting Conversational Fields

System Overview. Figure 2 shows our vision of context-aware applications using conversational field detection, which is described in this section. Neary, our previously proposed system, used a small computer and detected conversation groups by using a peer-to-peer approach. We implemented a Neary server in this study in order to increase the flexibility of access to conversational field information by client applications.

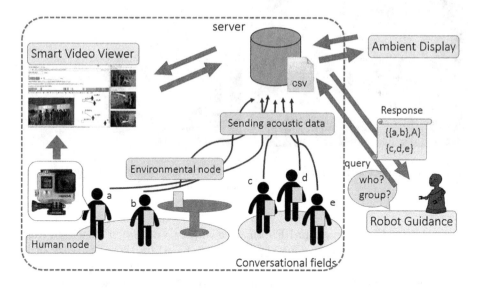

Fig. 2. Overview of our applications based on conversational field detection.

Additionally, we aim to detect approximate locations of conversation groups by installing the same device with ones worn by the participants. The device, which is installed on an object or some part of the environment, is called an environmental node, and it enables us to recognize the position and physical size of conversational fields. Meanwhile, the device-wearing participants are called human nodes.

Our goal is to propose applications based on conversational field recognition systems, such as ambient displays or robot guidance. Hence, we use smartphones for detecting conversational fields. For this study, we built a smart video viewer system that depends on conversational fields based on auditory similarity.

Sound Sensing by Mobile Devices. In this subsection, we outline our method of sensing by mobile device, which enables us to run our client software. We used the Nexus 5 as a mobile device, after considering the frequency response of the microphone; in order not to worry about the differences in the sound frequency characteristics between devices, we made all devices Nexus 5.

Figures 3 and 4 respectively show people wearing the device as human nodes and the device installed as an environmental node on a poster. Installing the device in the environment enables recognition of the positions of conversation groups and the sizes of conversational fields, because if human nodes and a group being recorded by the environmental node on the poster are judged by our method to be the same group based on auditory similarity, we can deduce that people are near the poster.

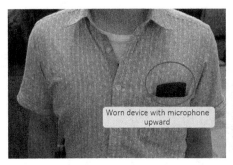

Fig. 3. Worn device (Human node).

Fig. 4. Environmentally installed device (Environmental node).

Detection of Conversational Fields. We employ a detection algorithm that analyzes auditory similarity. Our algorithms are based on those of Neary [21], because Neary has a sufficiently high precision ratio and is lightweight. We optimized the parameters of the algorithm in accordance with the devices used for conversational field detection in this study.

The Neary algorithm obtains the similarity between each pair of devices and judges whether or not there are conversation groups, based on a threshold. The algorithm is as follows:

1. Record audio by microphone-equipped smartphone.
2. Process the sound data using a fast Fourier transform (FFT) every six seconds.

3. Extract frequency characteristics ranging from 50 Hz to 1600 Hz in 1 Hz increments.
4. Compare feature amounts obtained via cosine similarity to that of other devices, using the following formula:

$$Cos(u, v) = \frac{\sum_{i=0}^{1550} (u_i) \times (v_i)}{\sqrt{\sum_{i=0}^{1550} (u_i)^2} \times \sqrt{\sum_{i=0}^{1550} (v_i)^2}} \tag{1}$$

u and v are device identifiers
5. Every 80 s, count the number of instances in which the threshold of 0.75 is exceeded.
6. If number of instances in which the threshold is exceeded is increasing, judge these devices as belonging to the same conversational fields.

We made a few modifications to the Neary algorithm. In Neary, one second of non-silent content is extracted from a six-second buffer (feature amount extraction step 2); however, its performance suffers owing to the time lag on each device. Therefore, in this study we use the entire six seconds of sound data for calculation. Moreover, the threshold was defined as 0.775 in Neary, but we adjusted it to 0.75 (step 5), because we use different microphone-equipped smartphones.

Next, our system performs the smoothing of sequentially obtained results using the above algorithm. Conversational field information is obtained once every second. If the degree of similarity exceeds the threshold more times than it does not until 36 s before the end of the time period, these devices are considered co-located. In addition, smoothing is performed on conversational fields using two values. However, these parameters were determined based on the data, and this algorithm generates time-lag between judgement results and videos; thus, we synchronized the video to the result.

Scene of Detecting Conversational Fields. We show a scene in which conversational fields are detected and comprehended.

Figure 5 shows movement among three conversation fields. The left side of the figure shows actual video images used as ground truth data. The right side of the figure shows a graphical representation of corresponding scenes based on detection results produced by our system. Human nodes are expressed as human pictograms, and environmental nodes are expressed as rectangles. There were three conversation groups in this scene. In addition, some participants were wearing the devices. Devices were installed on all tables as environmental nodes. The man surrounded by red circles was moving among the conversation groups, and he wore a device identified as 3d6db. His activity is tracked as shown in the node graph.

Figure 6 shows the combining of two conversational fields into one. At the beginning the participants were talking in two different groups, but later they began conversing between the two conversational fields. Therefore, the physical

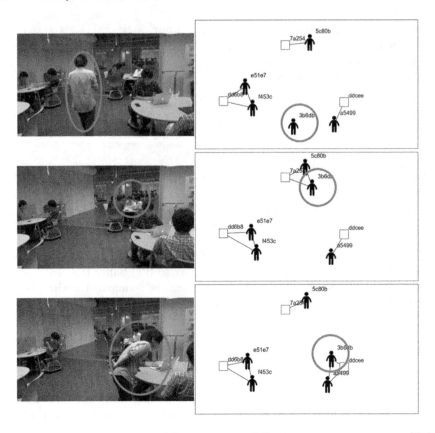

Fig. 5. Tracking a participant who moves across different conversation groups. (Color figure online)

size and dynamics of conversational fields can be detected by our method, as shown in the node graph.

In contrast, Fig. 7 shows a state of separation. The man surrounded by red circles was a moderator, and he was calling participants. However, there were two participants who were talking at presentation booth 1, and ignoring the moderator. In this case, these two participants are close to the moderator, but we believe they should be regarded as another group. However, the classical approach based on physical clusters of people cannot distinguish them. In contrast, our proposed system can distinguish between participants in such situations.

We can recognize approximate physical size and dynamics of conversational fields, and distinguish conversational fields. Using these comprehensions, our proposed system can facilitate video browsing.

3.2 Indexing Shared Experience Videos by Detected Conversation Groups

Figure 8 shows our proposed system that aids the browsing of shared experience videos. The system displays a cue on the seek-bar and visualizes conversational

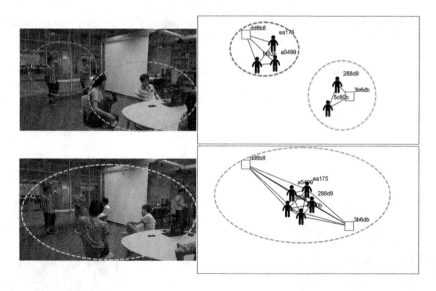

Fig. 6. Two conversational fields merged into one.

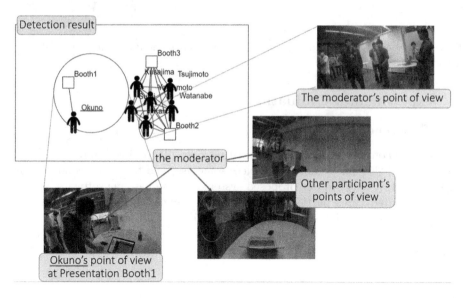

Fig. 7. Two participants are talking while the moderator is speaking. (Color figure online)

fields as node graphs. Users can browse multiple videos using cues based on members, conversation groups, or their positions.

A cue is expressed in n-colors (where n is the number of conversational fields in the data) depending on conversational fields that contain information on conversation group members and their positions. Accordingly, if there are no groups, the cue is colorless. Moreover, we assign similar colors for similar conversational fields. We explore scenes in multiple first-person videos using cues based on conversational fields.

In addition, if the user searches for a certain conversation group member, the system only shows cues that include the chosen member. Thus, if the member being searched for does not belong to any conversation groups, the cue is expressed as colorless.

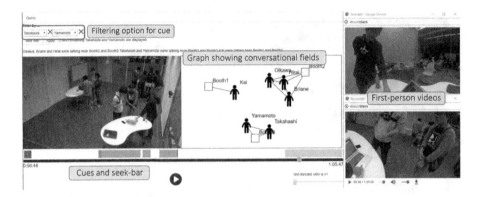

Fig. 8. Proposed system: Showing cues and node graphs based on conversational field detection.

4 Experimental Evaluation

4.1 Experiment

We compared our proposed system to existing video playback software (baseline). We measured the time taken to complete some assigned tasks and conducted a significance test between our proposed system and the baseline software.

We recruited three participants (subjects 1, 2, and 3), and assigned them eight tasks from two datasets (datasets A and B). We observed the subjects to gauge their reaction to our proposed system, in order to confirm whether conversational field information is useful. Finally, we conducted a semi-structured interview.

Datasets Used for Experiment. We prepared two datasets (datasets A and B), and recruited some participants who belong to the same laboratory as the evaluation experiment participants. These data were recorded in a poster presentation session, because we are confident that our proposed method can detect conversational fields in crowded areas and easily detect the dynamics of conversational fields as participants move to listen to a presentation.

Figure 9 depicts poster presentation situations from datasets A and B. These datasets are markedly different in terms of scale. Further details on datasets are listed in Table 1.

Fig. 9. Circumstances of poster presentation in datasets.

Table 1. Dataset details (video was recorded using cameras worn by participants.

	Dataset A	Dataset B
Participants	about 30	about 600
Presentation booth	9	61
Human node	6	6
Environmental node	3	2
Videos	3	5
Video length	01:12:00	00:57:31
Time elapsed after recording	6 months	2 months

We assigned four tasks for each dataset. The four tasks for dataset A were referred to as A-1, A-2, A-3, and A-4 (likewise for dataset B).

Dataset A included a video that was recorded by subject 1. However, subjects 2 and 3 did not participate in the presentation in dataset A. In other words, dataset A was not familiar to them. Meanwhile, dataset B included a video that was recorded by subjects 2 and 3. Accordingly, subject 1 was unfamiliar with the videos in dataset B.

Finding Task for Specified Scene. We prepared tasks such as determining "When did participant A converse with B by poster X ?" Figure 10 shows an example of solving a task.

When given the task question "When did participant A converse with participant B," one should watch multiple videos recorded by participants A and B, then make a judgement based on their video images and voices. If it is uncertain whether they conversed, it is necessary to watch other videos recorded by other subjects from a third-person viewpoint.

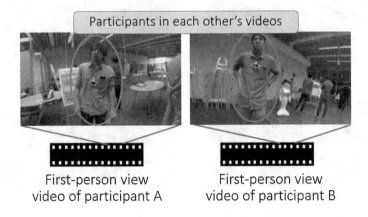

Fig. 10. Example of task for finding specified scenes.

4.2   Results of Time Taken to Complete Tasks

Task completion times for each task and subject is presented in Table 2 and Fig. 11. The cells shaded green in Table 2 indicate the amounts of time taken to complete the task with the help of our proposed system. The figures in red indicate the amount of time the subjects needed to complete tasks that involved watching their own data.

Figure 11 shows a comparison between the proposed system and the baseline software. The blue bar in the graph represents the completion time achieved by

Table 2. Amounts of time needed to complete tasks (in seconds): Red figures represent times measured when subjects watched their own data. Black figures represent times measured when subjects watched the data of others.

	A-1	A-2	A-3	A-4
Subject 1	68	83	18	31
Subject 2	261	128	13	90
Subject 3	58	352	59	71

	B-1	B-2	B-3	B-4
Subject 1	147	42	80	67
Subject 2	43	179	162	216
Subject 3	52	276	30	54

Amounts of the time
needed to complete tasks (in seconds).

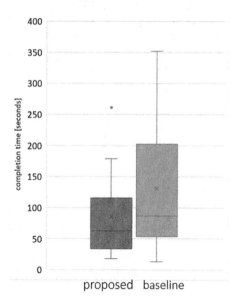

Fig. 11. Task completion times (overall): These graphs show a comparison between our proposed system and the baseline software.

using our proposed system, and the green bar represents the completion time achieved by using the baseline software. Conducting a statistical significance test ($p < 0.05$) revealed that, in the case of browsing video data of other people, there was little difference between the proposed system and the baseline software, because the measured time did not vary widely.

In contrast, we observed a significant difference in the case of subjects browsing videos that included their own data (see left side graphs in Fig. 12). As a result, it was confirmed that our proposed system can aid the watching of videos that include the user's own data.

4.3   Observation and Interview

We observed the subjects to confirm their reactions while using our system. We noted that it appeared difficult for subjects to determine who someone was conversing with, because it is difficult to confirm conversation groups from videos. Moreover, our cue information is nonfigurative, and we defined conversational fields as groups hearing the same voices or environmental sounds. In other words, we regard hearing and conversation as the same; thus, the subjects were confused by the task.

After the tasks were completed, we conducted a semi-structured interview with the subjects. First, we asked them about the cue, and received the comment that "The cue is almost correct." Next, we asked them why they had difficulty completing the task, and were told "It is difficult to judge instantly, because these videos occasionally lose conversation partners," and "I was confused by the expression of the task."

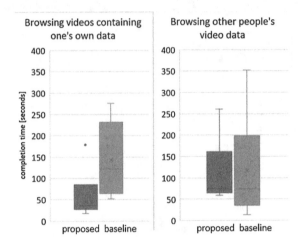

Fig. 12. Task completion times (separated): Graphs on left show a comparison between the proposed system and the baseline software when watching familiar videos; graphs on right represent watching unfamiliar videos.

5   Limitations and Future Work

Our experimental results suggest that our system can help users browse videos that include one's own experience. However, our evaluation and analysis were inadequate. Three participants did not allow adequate assessment of the proposed system. Moreover, the analysis method was insufficient, because we only conducted interviews and measured task completion times in our evaluation. Therefore, our observations and results were not fully supported.

We would like to perform an evaluation with more participants. We will provide data that support observations based on eye-tracking analyses and log data analyses. Moreover, we aim to design a questionnaire that supports the effectiveness of the proposed system.

6   Conclusion

We proposed a system to aid the browsing of shared experience data that includes multiple first-person view videos. With this system, users can avoid the tedious task of searching through lengthy videos. Our system aids browsing by using the video seek-bar to display indices based on conversational field information, including that related to participants and approximate location of group conversations.

We conducted an experiment to evaluate the ability of the indices to decrease the time needed for finding specified scenes in lifelog videos. Our experimental results suggest that our system can aid the browsing of multiple videos that include one's own experiences. On the other hand, the system has not been proven to aid the browsing of unknown data.

References

1. Hall, E.T.: The Hidden Dimension. Doubleday, New York (1966)
2. Borovoy, R., Martin, F., Vemuri, S., Resnick, M., Silverman, B., Hancock, C.: Meme tags and community mirrors: moving from conferences to collaboration. In: Proceedings of the 1998 ACM Conference on Computer Supported Cooperative Work (CSCW 1998), pp. 159–168. ACM, New York (1998)
3. Wyatt, D., Bilmes, J., Choudhury, T., Kitts, J.A.: Towards the automated social analysis of situated speech data. In: Proceedings of the 10th International Conference on Ubiquitous Computing (UbiComp 2008), pp. 168–171. ACM, New York (2008)
4. Yoshida, H., Ito, S., Kawaguchi, N.: Evaluation of pre-acquisition methods for position estimation system using wireless LAN. In: Proceedings of the Third International Conference on Mobile Computing and Ubiquitous Networking (ICMU 2006), pp. 148–155 (2006)
5. Do, T.-M.-T., Gatica-Perez, D.: Contextual grouping: discovering real-life interaction types from longitudinal bluetooth data. In: IEEE 12th International Conference on Mobile Data Management (MDM 2011), vol. 1, pp. 256–265, June 2011
6. Intille, S.S., Davis, J.W., Bobick, A.F.: Real-time closed-world tracking. In: Proceedings of IEEE Computer Society Conference on Computer Vision and Pattern Recognition (CVPR 1997), pp. 697–703, June 1997
7. McKenna, S.J., Jabri, S., Duric, Z., Rosenfeld, A., Wechsler, H.: Tracking groups of people. Comput. Vis. Image Underst. **80**(1), 42–56 (2000)
8. Kendon, A.: Conducting Interaction: Patterns of Behavior in Focused Encounters. Cambridge University Press, Cambridge (1990)
9. Vascon, S., Mequanint, E.Z., Cristani, M., Hung, H., Pelillo, M., Murino, V.: A game-theoretic probabilistic approach for detecting conversational groups. In: Cremers, D., Reid, I., Saito, H., Yang, M.-H. (eds.) ACCV 2014. LNCS, vol. 9007, pp. 658–675. Springer, Cham (2015). https://doi.org/10.1007/978-3-319-16814-2_43
10. Vascon, S., Mequanint, E.Z., Cristani, M., Hung, H., Pelillo, M., Murino, V.: Detecting conversational groups in images and sequences: a robust game-theoretic approach. Comput. Vis. Image Underst. **143**, 11–24 (2016). Inference and Learning of Graphical Models: Theory and Applications in Computer Vision and Image Analysis
11. Alameda-Pineda, X., Yan, Y., Ricci, E., Lanz, O., Sebe, N.: Analyzing free-standing conversational groups: a multimodal approach. In: Proceedings of the 23rd ACM International Conference on Multimedia (MM 2015), pp. 5–14. ACM, New York (2015)
12. Vázquez, M., Steinfeld, A., Hudson, S.E.: Parallel detection of conversational groups of free-standing people and tracking of their lower-body orientation. In: IEEE/RSJ International Conference on Intelligent Robots and Systems (IROS 2015), pp. 3010–3017, September 2015
13. Lane, N.D., Georgiev, P., Qendro, L.: DeepEar: robust smartphone audio sensing in unconstrained acoustic environments using deep learning. In: Proceedings of the 2015 ACM International Joint Conference on Pervasive and Ubiquitous Computing (UbiComp 2015), pp. 283–294. ACM, New York (2015)
14. Kannan, P.G., Venkatagiri, S.P., Chan, M.C., Ananda, A.L., Peh, L.-S.: Low cost crowd counting using audio tones. In: Proceedings of the 10th ACM Conference on Embedded Network Sensor Systems (SenSys 2012), pp. 155–168. ACM, New York (2012)

15. Azizyan, M., Constandache, I., Choudhury, R.R.: SurroundSense: mobile phone localization via ambience fingerprinting. In: Proceedings of the 15th Annual International Conference on Mobile Computing and Networking (MobiCom 2009), pp. 261–272. ACM, New York (2009)

16. Zhang, B., Trott, M.D.: Reference-free audio matching for rendezvous. In: IEEE International Conference on Acoustics, Speech and Signal Processing (ICASSP 2010), pp. 3570–3573, March 2010

17. Nirjon, S., Dickerson, R., Stankovic, J., Shen, G., Jiang, X.: sMFCC: exploiting sparseness in speech for fast acoustic feature extraction on mobile devices - a feasibility study. In: Proceedings of the 14th Workshop on Mobile Computing Systems and Applications (HotMobile 2013), pp. 8:1–8:6. ACM, New York (2013)

18. Tan, W.-T., Baker, M., Lee, B., Samadani, R.: The sound of silence. In: Proceedings of the 11th ACM Conference on Embedded Networked Sensor Systems (SenSys 2013), pp. 19:1–19:14. ACM, New York (2013)

19. Aoki, P.M., Romaine, M., Szymanski, M.H., Thornton, J.D., Wilson, D., Woodruff, A.: The Mad Hatter's cocktail party: a social mobile audio space supporting multiple simultaneous conversations. In: Proceedings of the SIGCHI Conference on Human Factors in Computing Systems (CHI 2003), pp. 425–432. ACM, New York (2003)

20. Wirz, M., Roggen, D., Tröster, G.: A wearable, ambient sound-based approach for infrastructureless fuzzy proximity estimation. In: International Symposium on Wearable Computers (ISWC 2010), pp. 1–4, October 2010

21. Nakakura, T., Sumi, Y., Nishida, T.: Neary: conversational field detection based on situated sound similarity. IEICE Trans. Inf. Syst. **E94–D**(6), 1164–1172 (2011)

22. Kopf, J., Cohen, M.F., Szeliski, R.: First-person hyper-lapse videos. ACM Trans. Graph. **33**(4), 78:1–78:10 (2014)

23. Poleg, Y., Halperin, T., Arora, C., Peleg, S.: EgoSampling: fast-forward and stereo for egocentric videos. In: IEEE Conference on Computer Vision and Pattern Recognition (CVPR 2015), pp. 4768–4776 (2015)

24. Lee, Y.J., Ghosh, J., Grauman, K.: Discovering important people and objects for egocentric video summarization. In: IEEE Conference on Computer Vision and Pattern Recognition (CVPR 2012), pp. 1346–1353, June 2012

25. Arev, I., Park, H.S., Sheikh, Y., Hodgins, J., Shamir, A.: Automatic editing of footage from multiple social cameras. ACM Trans. Graph. **33**(4), 81:1–81:11 (2014)

26. Lee, Y.J., Grauman, K.: Predicting important objects for egocentric video summarization. Int. J. Comput. Vis. **114**(1), 38–55 (2015)

27. Lu, Z., Grauman, K.: Story-driven summarization for egocentric video. In: IEEE Conference on Computer Vision and Pattern Recognition (CVPR 2013), pp. 2714–2721, June 2013

28. Fathi, A., Farhadi, A., Rehg, J.M.: Understanding egocentric activities. In: Proceedings of the 2011 International Conference on Computer Vision (ICCV 2011), pp. 407–414. IEEE Computer Society, Washington, DC (2011)

29. Li, C., Kitani, K.M.: Pixel-level hand detection in ego-centric videos. In: IEEE Conference on Computer Vision and Pattern Recognition (CVPR 2013), pp. 3570–3577, June 2013

30. Cai, M., Kitani, K.M., Sato, Y.: A scalable approach for understanding the visual structures of hand grasps. In: IEEE International Conference on Robotics and Automation (ICRA 2015), pp. 1360–1366, May 2015

31. Yonetani, R., Kitani, K.M., Sato, Y.: Ego-surfing first person videos. In: IEEE Conference on Computer Vision and Pattern Recognition (CVPR 2015), pp. 5445–5454, June 2015

32. Poleg, Y., Ephrat, A., Peleg, S., Arora, C.: Compact CNN for indexing egocentric videos. In: IEEE Winter Conference on Applications of Computer Vision (WACV 2016), pp. 1–9 (2016)
33. Higuchi, K., Yonetani, R., Sato, Y.: EgoScanning: quickly scanning first-person videos with egocentric elastic timelines. In: Proceedings of the 2017 CHI Conference on Human Factors in Computing Systems (CHI 2017), pp. 6536–6546. ACM, New York (2017)

Evaluating Mobile Music Experiences: Radio On-the-Go

Anupriya Ankolekar, Thomas Sandholm, and Louis Lei Yu[✉]

Gustavus Adolphus College, St. Peter, MN 56082, USA
lyu@gac.edu
http://homepages.gac.edu/~lyu/

Abstract. Music has become an accompaniment to everyday activities, such as shopping and navigating. Although people listen to music in a context-driven manner, music recommendation services typically ignore where a user is listening to the music. They also typically select music based on a single seed song, rather than ordering a user's created playlists for the best user experience. The contributions of this paper are three-fold: (1) We present a survey of 15 DJs of college radio stations to identify their heuristics in creating playlists for radio shows. (2) We present an experimental study design to evaluate various scheduling (track ordering) strategies for mobile music consumption *in situ*, which is used to (3) conduct a field experiment that compares the user experience of three scheduling strategies (tempo, genre and location) against the gold standard of a playlist created by an experienced DJ (This work was completed when Anupriya Ankolekar and Thomas Sandholm were both researchers, and Louis Lei Yu was a postdoctoral research fellow at Hewlett Packard Labs. The majority of the experiments were conducted during the summer of 2011. The authors are listed here in alphabetical order).

Keywords: User experience · Mobile music consumption
Music scheduling · Experiment design

1 Introduction

Listening to music on-the-go has been a fundamental part of our culture ever since the introduction of the transistor radio in 1954. With the popularity of portable digital players, people began to use music as an accompaniment to everyday activities, such as shopping and navigating [6,7]. DeNora [11] has described the way music has begun to serve a personal function for people: encouraging concentration during important tasks, reducing stress, providing mental preparation and even as a way of organizing people's memories of key events. Personally chosen collections of music are organized by people into playlists as a way of accessing these personal functions as and when needed.

© ICST Institute for Computer Sciences, Social Informatics and Telecommunications Engineering 2018
K. Murao et al. (Eds.): MobiCASE 2018, LNICST 240, pp. 56–73, 2018.
https://doi.org/10.1007/978-3-319-90740-6_4

Over the last decade, automatically generated playlists [5, 23, 26] through digital music recommendation services, such as Pandora[1], Last.fm[2], and Spotify[3], and music player services such as the iTunes Genius Mix and Google Play's instant mixes, have become popular. The Echo Nest[4] is a platform that offers personalized music selection as a service to music and radio providers.

Although automatic music selection on music streaming services has proven popular, there is relatively little literature on music scheduling[5] strategies. In current music selection approaches, the scheduling of tracks emerges from individual track recommendations, rather than being designed for a smooth listening experience the way radio show producers or DJs do. Furthermore, although people's music listening is often driven by their physical context, playlist generation methods rarely take this into account (with the notable exception of [24]).

In this paper, we address this research gap through three contributions: (1) We present the results of an informal survey of 15 DJs of college radio stations, to compile and examine the heuristics they use in creating radio shows. (2) We present an experimental study design to evaluate various scheduling strategies for mobile music consumption *in situ*. Using this experimental design, we present the results of a small-scale field experiment that compares the user experience of three music-feature based scheduling strategies against the gold standard of a playlist or *schedule* created by an experienced DJ.

The experiment has been designed to measure user experience without disrupting the users' experience of the flow of music, while mitigating the effect of users' musical preferences. We present the requirements for our music scheduling field experiment and develop an experiment design that fulfills these requirements. Using this experiment design and based on the heuristics used by DJs, we compared 3 scheduling strategies: *genre-based scheduling, tempo-based scheduling*, and *location-based scheduling* against an expert schedule in terms of user experience for people listening to music on-the-go.

The organization of the paper is as follows: We begin with describing the related literature on music consumption and on automatically generated playlists. We then present the results of our informal survey with DJs in Sect. 2.3 and derive scheduling strategies to be used in the experiment. In the following section, we describe the requirements of an experiment design for scheduling music for mobile consumption, and the actual field experiment design and analysis. In the Experiment section, we describe the schedulers used in the experiment and the experiment procedure. The results of the experiment are reported next, in terms of perceived user experience based on explicit user ratings as well as users' self-reported emotional response to the various scheduling conditions. The paper ends with a discussion of the results and the generality of the experiment design.

---

[1] pandora.com.

[2] last.fm.

[3] spotify.com.

[4] echonest.com.

[5] In this context, meaning the order in which we choose to play songs.

2   Related Work

2.1   Music Consumption: Mobile and Location-Aware

DeNora [11] has conducted seminal research on how people consciously use music in their everyday life to perform various functions, such as encouraging concentration during important tasks, reducing stress, providing mental preparation and even as a way of organizing people's memories of key events. The ubiquitous culture of listening to music on mobile devices has been described by Bull [6,7], who has documented how people listen to music while carrying out outdoor activities, such as shopping or navigating. Several studies have examined mobile music consumption in urban areas [22] and by youth [18], and how culture has a significant impact on how music is consumed. Nettamo et al. [22], in particular, describe how playlists are used to filter and organize vast and diverse collections of music to suit certain moods or contexts of use.

Recently, researchers began to examine the use of audio, and in particular music, for navigation outdoors. Nemirovsky and Davenport [21] developed a system called GuideShoes that utilizes a custom mobile music player built into shoes with GPS to deliver musical cues for street navigation. Warren et al. [28] present the Ontrack system to adapt audio continuously to help users navigate to a destination. Finally Gaye et al. [13] provides a good survey of mobile music research and early attempts to use location-based features with music.

In the last couple of years, location-aware music recommendation has flourished, with services like Soundtracker[6] and Soundtracking[7], and apps like RjDj[8], to name a few. Musicians have created location-aware albums, such as Bluebrain's the National Mall and Central Park, which are musical albums meant to be heard within a particular location, where the music heard is affected by the user's path. Music has also been shown to be an effective way to guide people to certain points of interest [3].

Although people commonly create personal playlists for different contexts, such as listening to music on-the-go, no existing system examines how to enhance the user's experience of music and their location by better scheduling the existing tracks in a user's playlist.

2.2   Automatic Playlist Creation

There is a parallel body of literature on automatic playlist creation within the music information retrieval community. The methods developed typically rely on various kinds of features of the audio, e.g. the metadata (such as artist, genre etc.) and content features (such as amplitude, beats etc.) to define similarity between audio. Ragno et al. [26] describe a way of automatically infer similarities between songs based on derived measures such as artists, genre, pitch, and

---

[6] soundtracker.fm.

[7] soundtracking.com.

[8] rjdj.me.

tempo. Several playlist creation methods use such similarity metrics to automatically generate playlists of similar songs [5,23]. In addition, automatic playlist generation methods typically rely on some form of explicit user preferences, such as a search query [25], a seed song [2,19], or user skipping behaviour [5,23].

PATS [24] generates playlists that suit a particular context-of-use, i.e. the real world environment in which the music is heard (such as music for work). To create playlists, it uses a dynamic clustering method in which songs are grouped based on a weighted similarity of attributes. An alternative approach to playlist generation treats the problem of selecting relevant music for a user as a collaborative filtering problem [17] and attempts to help the user find new music that matches their taste profile. Flycast [16] is another system that uses collaborative filtering techniques to generate a playlist based on the request histories of the current listening audience. Although not a collaborative filtering system, CoCoA Radio [4] allows users to collaborate on creating playlists for certain themes.

Unlike these approaches, our focus is not on selection of music, rather on scheduling a given set of songs into coherent and pleasant-sounding segments. Although these problems are related, the scheduling problem is more challenging, because the set of music to order is significantly smaller. Furthermore, as we shall see in the next section, DJs create engaging playlists by creating a sense of progression or movement within a schedule, which goes beyond methods that simply choose the 'best next song'. Finally, besides [24], none of the systems evaluate the performance of these techniques in a mobile context.

2.3 DJ Techniques

In order to better understand how DJs select and sequence songs for their shows, we conducted an informal survey of 15 DJs from college radio stations in the U.S. and Canada[9]. In addition, we examined the on-air training manuals for several college radio stations to understand how radio DJs develop radio programs[10]. In the following, we summarize our findings on the techniques DJs use when creating their shows.

College radio DJs typically select and sequence music from a large collection of vinyls, CDs, cassettes and digital downloads to produce a show. Most radio slots are 1–2 h long and consist of more than 15 songs. A rule of thumb that many DJs use to keep listeners engaged for this long is to break the show up into segments of 3–4 songs [8], keeping each segment to be "a maximum of three

---

[9] The radio stations are (1) CFRC 101.9 FM, Queens University Radio (http://cfrc. ca), (2) CFUV 101.9 FM, University of Victoria Radio (http://cfuv.uvic.ca), (3) KUSF 90.3 FM, University of San Francisco Radio (http://savekusf.org), (4) CFYT 106.9 FM, Dawson City Community Radio (http://cfyt.ca) and (5) WRHU 88.7 FM, Hofstra University Radio (http://www.hofstra.edu/Academics/Colleges/SOC/ WRHU).

[10] Unlike commercial radio stations whose playlists have been automatically generated [27] to get the best possible ratings [12], college radio stations still tend to have DJs who choose and schedule the music for their own shows.

songs or 15 min, which ever comes first." [9]. In between these segments, DJs might talk on air or play promos, announcements or commercials. These breaks provide some change to the listeners and provide natural points at which the DJs can change the pace of the program, in some sense, clearing the slate of one segment to start afresh in the next.

When selecting music, DJs often try to find a coherent theme to tie songs together. E.g. a DJ may dedicate an entire show to "songs of summer", or "songs by San Francisco bands", or "songs about food" etc. [8] Instead of focussing on a whole show, another common technique is to "put music together in sets connected by style, genres, or content, to promote continuity and help with transitions" [8]. It is jarring for the audience to listen to, e.g. a classical piece followed by a metal/hardcore song, followed by a traditional Irish jig followed by a jazz tune. Thus, many DJs group music of the same genre together in one segment, or group pieces that otherwise flow together. In our survey, many DJs also reported using the lyrics of each song to create sequences of related songs [8], e.g. if one segment is around "songs about food", then the next might be "songs about drinks". The tie between the lyrics and segments keeps listeners engaged [10].

Within each segment or even the show as a whole, the DJs we surveyed tended to order songs by pitch, tempo or loudness to manipulate the mood of the show. E.g. the DJ may start with a slow song followed by a slightly louder and faster song followed by an even louder and faster song. This will build up the energy of the show to a kind of climax at the end. Alternatively, a DJ may start with a set of fast and loud rock songs and gradually slow down towards the end of the segment or show. Of course, DJs may both increase and decrease the energy of the music within the same segment or show.

Finally, DJs are encouraged to "watch their transitions" [10]: good transitions are seamless, blending the song fading out with the following song while avoiding silent gaps between songs. E.g. a song with a metal tune that ends with a cello solo could be mixed with a classical music piece that starts with a violin, followed by a folk song that starts with a fiddle. Even though these three songs are not of the same genre, the beginning and the end of each song makes for a smooth transition, and the natural difference in pitch, loudness and tempo between each genre can allow the DJ to play with the mood of the segment. Good transitions are difficult to define; typically DJs will rely on their intuition about music to finds songs which fit best together.

While most of these practices rely on the musical knowledge and experience of DJs, some of the techniques outlined above can be formalized and used to automatically create pleasant and coherent playlists within an online or mobile music service. To our knowledge, bundling songs into coherent themes and varying the 'energy' of music within each segment have not been examined by the automatic playlist generation research.

3   Experiment Design

In order to effectively compare music scheduling strategies for music on-the-go, the following requirements must be fulfilled:

R1. Compare Schedules, Not Music Choice

The goal of the experiment is to evaluate the scheduling of music, hence the experiment design must not be biased by the choice of songs in a given playlist schedule. To ensure this, we fix the selection of music tracks used in the experiment. Each condition plays exactly the same set of songs; the sole difference is the order in which the tracks are played. The set of experiment songs must be designed to support reasonable, yet highly diverse playlists for all the strategies being compared.

R2. Evaluate Music Consumption *in situ*

To realistically examine the user experience of various kinds of schedules, a field experiment is necessary. The advantages of field experiments for mobile guides have been extensively discussed in Goodman et al. [15]. While the levels of potential confounding variables, such as noise levels, traffic and weather conditions cannot be kept consistent, their variation manifests itself randomly across conditions. Like [14], we consider this to be acceptable because variation in such variables is an integral part of real-world usage. By using actual locations and authentic environmental conditions, we obtain vital data on the experience of music on-the-go in practice.

R3. Be Independent of Users' Musical Tastes

To mitigate the song bias caused by users' personal preferences for certain songs or genres, users' musical preferences are measured via a Web-based survey a couple of days before the actual experiment. Users were asked to listen to and rate a superset of the songs used in the experiment on a 5-point Likert scale. The songs were presented in random order without any identifying information and include songs the users would hear eventually as part of the experiment. This rating is done on a per-song basis, but this allows us to compute an expected score for each user and schedule, depending on how much the user liked the songs in that schedule. Each user's schedule rating in the experiment is discounted by this expected score, thus removing any bias in rating caused by whether the user liked the songs in that particular playlist.

R4. Obtain Clear Signals of User Experience

Based on prior experience, we know that people tend to rate music more positively during an experiment, which can obscure the differences among scheduling methods. That is, schedules might be rated more positively simply because users enjoyed walking on a street and listening to music. To mitigate this bias, the data analysis will focus on negative ratings, which are a clearer signal of user preferences, rather than the raw user ratings of schedules.

R5. Use Experience Sampling to Evaluate Transitions
The user experience of song transitions are a critical reflection of the quality of scheduling. To better capture the users' experience of these and reduce reliance on recall, we use the experience sampling method (ESM), asking users to rate the songs and transitions between 'bundles' of songs, i.e. segments of 5 songs each.

4   Experiment

We now present an experiment that examines the effect of four basic music scheduling strategies on user experience. These scheduling strategies are inspired by the practices of DJs described in Sect. 2.3.

4.1   Scheduling Methods

We now define the 4 kinds of scheduling methods or *schedulers* that we will evaluate in the field study. We assume that a *candidate set* of songs is already available. Given this candidate set, the task of the scheduler or scheduling method is to order these songs into a playlist such that each song is played exactly once. As an organizing strategy, each scheduler will segment the candidate set into equal-sized *bundles* (i.e. fixed subsets of songs) that all share (or differ minimally in) some feature, thus creating a smoother, less jarring listening experience.

The automatic scheduling methods we define essentially only differ in terms of which feature is used to create the bundles. Some of the methods maintain a coherent order across bundles, whereas others just order songs within bundles and then randomize the order of the bundles.

Expert Scheduling. The *Expert* scheduling method is a baseline, just used for our experiments, that was created manually by an experienced DJ using the principles described in the previous section. Thus, in addition to scheduling music by pitch, tempo and genre, the schedule also takes into account song transitions and attempts to cluster songs with lyrics referring to similar entities (e.g. a food cluster may include songs with lyrics referring to sushi and pizza). This schedule can therefore be considered to be ordered both within and across bundles.

Genre Scheduling. The *Genre* scheduler relies on the genre meta-data of the songs to cluster songs such that each bundle contains songs of the same genre. There is no ordering across bundles, and there is no natural order within the bundle. Genres for songs are derived from the genre meta-data specified on Wikipedia or All Music[11]. This method is an representation or instantiation of a meta-data-based scheduler. In our experiment, the genre clusters used were Jazz, Rock, Electronic, and World.

---

[11] http://allmusic.com.

Tempo Scheduling. The *Tempo* scheduler uses the amplitude or loudness of the song[12] combined with the beat of the song[13]. These features were extracted from the part of the song that was scheduled to play[14]. Given

$$S_a \equiv sort(S, amplitude), S_b \equiv sort(S, beat)$$

where $sort(S, x)$ is the playlist S ordered by feature x, and

$$idx_a \equiv idx(s_a, S_a), idx_b \equiv idx(s_b, S_b)$$

where $idx(s_x, S)$ is the rank order of feature x of song s in the ordered playlist S. For example, the song with the lowest amplitude has rank order 1 and the one with the highest amplitude has rank n, where n is the size of the candidate set to be scheduled. The tempo based order of songs $S_{a,b}$ is then defined as:

$$S_{a,b} \equiv sort(S, idx_a + idx_b).$$

In other words, the candidate set is first rank-ordered in terms of amplitude and beat separately; then re-ranked based on the sum of the two rankings. Next, the ordered list of songs, $S_{a,b}$, is split into bundles, maintaining the tempo rank order within each bundle. The resulting bundles are then ordered randomly to maintain the perception of bundles. This method is an instantiation of a content or audio-feature based scheduler.

Location Scheduling. The *Location* scheduler is a novel scheduler that assumes a set of songs with associated physical locations (e.g. assigned by a DJ) and orders the songs based on the expected path taken by the listener. Thus, it always plays the song whose 'location' is closest in distance to the user. There is hence a natural order in this schedule for both within and between bundles. In the following section, we describe the song selection process for the experiment, in particular our method to pick songs for a location.

Song Selection. The set of experiment songs was chosen by the same experienced DJ who also then ordered them in the *Expert* schedule. The candidate set was chosen by first identifying songs for points of interest (POIs) in the experiment location, then filtering these songs to a set of 20 that would provide reasonable schedules when ordered by all the schedulers.

To choose songs for a given POI, we identified key distinguishing features of the POI and then chose audio to convey those features[15], e.g. through the

---

[12] RMS amplitude extracted using the sox tool (sox *audiofile.wav* stats | grep "RMS amplitude" | awk {'print $3'}). We got the same ordering results when extracting loudness using the RMS lev dB feature. We also found that pitch extraction did not produce any useful schedules so we dropped it.

[13] Number of beats detected by the aubiocut tool (aubiocut -b -i *audiofile.wav* | wc -l).

[14] In our system we normalize this to 1 min for all songs.

[15] All the audio used in the experiment can be heard at http://www.crowdee.com/dj.

melody, tempo, rhythm or lyrics of the songs. E.g., the key feature of a Thai restaurant could be "restaurant", or "Thailand", but since there were many restaurants in the vicinity, we chose to convey the feature "Thailand" with a traditional Thai folk song. For concrete features, e.g. "coffee" (for a coffee shop) or "pizza" (for a pizza restaurant), we relied on lyrics to communicate the features, e.g., choosing "The Coffee Song" by Frank Sinatra where the lyric "they've got an awful lot of coffee in Brazil" is mentioned prominently and repeatedly in the song. For abstract features that are more difficult to convey explicitly, e.g. "India" or "France", we relied on instrumental music to remind listeners of those cultures.

The process used to filter this larger set of songs was somewhat ad hoc with trial and error to identify a candidate subset of 20 songs that yielded reasonable schedules when ordered by all four schedulers. In practice, the two main restrictions were location distribution (for the *Location* scheduler) as described in the previous section and genre coverage (for the *Genre* scheduler), i.e. we needed 5 songs in each of 4 genres. The other two schedulers (*Expert, Tempo*) did not impose any substantial restrictions on the chosen song set.

4.2   Experiment Design

Participants were asked to take a guided walk along a few blocks of a busy downtown street in Palo Alto while listening to a playlist of songs (see Fig. 1). The experiment compared the user experience of four conditions, corresponding to the scheduling methods used to generate the playlist, namely: *Expert, Location, Genre* and *Tempo*. Each participant experienced 2 conditions, but the conditions are fully counterbalanced. Thus, for each condition, half of the par-

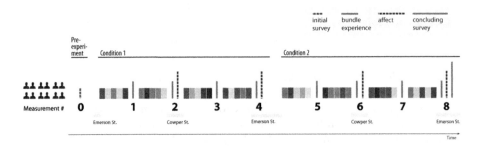

Fig. 1. Experiment design: In the pre-experiment stage, each participant rated a superset of the songs that would be used in the experiment (Measurement #0). During the field experiment, each participant participated in a guided walk during which they were exposed to 2 conditions. Each condition consisted of 4 bundles of 5 songs each, depicted by the 4 sets of 5 colored boxes. After hearing each bundle, participants were asked to report on their experience of that bundle and the transitions within that bundle. In addition, we measured their emotional response (i.e. affect of the condition) after every two bundles. At the end of the experiment (Measurement #8), participants filled out a concluding survey. (Color figure online)

ticipants experienced it as the first condition, and the other half as the second condition.

We tested the following hypotheses. We define μ as the (average) user experience for a particular condition:

Hypothesis 1:
μ is greater for the Location condition than for Expert

Hypothesis 2:
μ is greater for the Tempo condition than for Genre

The first hypothesis compares the 2 conditions that used contextual information for scheduling music. The Location schedule used knowledge of the location to order music. The Expert schedule used many different sources of information, including location and previous songs in the schedule, to order future songs. The second hypothesis examines the 2 conditions that used features of the songs themselves to order music.

4.3   Participants

We recruited 12 participants (over 90% of age 25–34 years, 4 female) from the Palo Alto area for the 45-min experiment. The participants were only moderately familiar with the experiment location, visiting it relatively infrequently (once every month or less). Most of the participants accessed the mobile Internet daily (7/12) and about half used location-based services on a weekly or daily basis (6/12). All of them had used smartphones before, with Android and iOS tied as the most common platforms (9/12 altogether). With 12 participants, our study comprised 48 trials all together, with 6 participants per condition. We randomized the order of each pair of conditions, so that for each condition, 3 participants experienced it as the first condition and another 3 as the second condition.

Location. The experiment location had to be chosen such that it could support a location-based music schedule and would be pleasant enough to walk while listening to the other schedules. We chose a busy shopping street that provided a high density of POIs and was nevertheless very 'walkable'. The POIs chosen to be represented within the location schedule constituted a balanced mix of large and small places, as well as prominent and obscure places. They were generally equally spaced within each stretch. For the *Location* condition, the schedule was restricted to only play songs about POIs that were on the side of the street the participant was instructed to walk on. Furthermore, the songs in the *Location* schedule were ordered sequentially based on the direction of the participants' walk to mimic a natural stroll on the street. However, the stretches corresponding to a bundle were short enough that participants could potentially walk back and forth in case they walked past a relevant POI.

4.4 Experiment Procedure

Participants were randomly assigned to two of the four conditions, which they heard while walking two loops of 4 street blocks (corresponding to the 4 bundles created for each condition). After an initial briefing on experiment procedure, the experiment device was introduced to the participants. The experiment device was an Android smartphone with a custom-built Android experiment app that presented a playlist of songs to the participant depending on the condition they were in. For the *Location* condition, the experiment app simulated the behavior of an LBS without using GPS or mobile Internet connectivity. Since the goal of the experiment was to compare the relative performance of different kinds of scheduling methods rather than evaluate the performance of a prototype, this allowed us to eliminate a potential source of confounds that might be caused by technical issues. Participants were given the prepared Android phone and a pair of earphones, and were instructed to walk at a leisurely pace.

The schedule for each condition consisted of 4 bundles of 5 songs, i.e. 20 songs played for one minute each. In line with the radio station techniques, songs were faded in and out for all the methods. The schedules were also chosen such that they were as different as possible from each other.

On the routes, the experimenter walked at a distance away from the participant to avoid disturbing and impacting the experiment, while still being able to observe and detect problems. To minimize experimenter demand effects and erroneous samples, the experimenter was available only at the end of each stretch to answer questions, while the participant filled out a mood questionnaire rating the emotional experience of that stretch. The experimenter would then also start the experiment app for the next stretch. At the end of the experiment, participants filled out a concluding survey with some open-ended questions about the experiment and their background.

As depicted in Fig. 1, we took measurements four times during the experiment, i.e. after every bundle. Participants were asked to rate the bundle they just heard (on a 3-point Likert scale) in terms of basic enjoyment and smoothness of song transition (see Fig. 2). We obtained user ratings for both measures so that users would pay attention to both the choice and order of songs in each bundle. These two ratings are however highly correlated, so in the ensuing analysis, we treat them as an aggregate rating.

Experience Sampling. After every two bundles, participants noted their emotional state, using a modified PAD (Pleasure, Arousal, Dominance) Semantic Differential Scale (PAD scale) [1,20]. The PAD scale consists of a set of bipolar adjective pairs that are rated along a five-point scale, which corresponds to 3 dimensions of emotional response: pleasure, arousal and autonomy. To make it amenable to frequent experience sampling, we modified and condensed the scale to only include word pairs that were appropriate and easy to interpret for our experiment. This resulted in a modified scale, consisting of six pairs of words in random order.

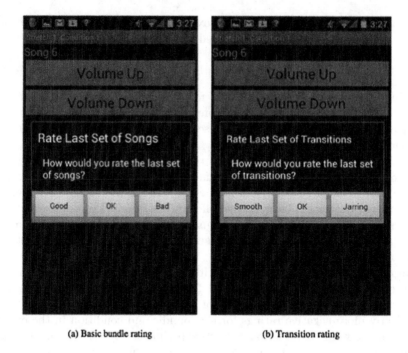

(a) Basic bundle rating   (b) Transition rating

Fig. 2. Mobile experiment app

5   Experimental Results

5.1   Analysis

A general issue facing the analysis of measurements is making sure that the samples are independent to avoid a bias in the results, i.e. we want to extract only the true signals of user preferences. The pre-experiment survey was used to remove user bias of specific song preferences, whereas various aggregation and filter operations were used to make sure that the observations could be reasonably assumed to be independent and identically distributed (i.i.d.), a necessary condition for statistical tests. Only negative ratings were counted and the samples that were filtered out were highly correlated with the ones included, therefore the true signals they represented were already present within the data retained. If the correlations in the data set are not properly accounted for, they can have a substantial effect on the statistical conclusions.

In the following, we describe how we aggregate and filter the measured user experience for each condition. The measured experience, m, of the user for a condition is obtained for each bundle as follows:

$$m = E[m] - n_b - n_t \tag{1}$$

where $n_b \in \{0, 1\}$ denotes the number of negative basic ratings (see Fig. 2) for a bundle during the walk, $n_t \in \{0, 1\}$ denotes the number of negative transition ratings, and $E[m]$ denotes the a priori expected experience based on the pre-experiment ratings. This value is obtained as follows:

$$E[m] = \lfloor n_o/2 \rfloor \tag{2}$$

where n_o corresponds to the number of negative ratings across the 5 songs in the bundle in the pre-experiment. The pre-experiment rating of both *Don't like it* and *Really dislike it* (the bottom two scores of the 5-point Likert scale) were considered negative.

In analyzing the data, we discovered that it was difficult to detect whether a user really liked a bundle or just tolerated them. Participants tended to give positive ratings as long as they did not actively dislike the bundle. This tended to obscure the differences between the different conditions. However, when users gave a negative score, it was a clear signal that the bundle resulted in a bad user experience. When we relied on the negative scores, the differences between conditions became much clearer.

We note that both the measured rating $(n_b + n_t)$ and this expected rating fall on the discrete increasing scale $\{0, 1, 2\}$. Thus $m \in \{-2, -1, 0, 1, 2\}$ is also on an increasing scale. A value of -2 for m, for instance, indicates that there were clearly more negative ratings for this bundle and condition in the experiment than one would expect from the pre-experiment ratings. We can therefore conclude that the condition had a negative impact on the experience for that user. Conversely an m-value of 2 indicates that there were clearly fewer negative ratings than one would expect from the pre-experiment ratings and thus the condition had a positive effect on the experience of that user.

5.2   User Experience

We now examine the impact of various scheduling methods on the user ratings of bundles. We take both pre-experiment and *in situ* (during the experiment walk) ratings into account. Examining the data, we found that the *in situ* ratings were generally higher than the pre-experiment ones across all the conditions, as expected. However, this does not affect the data, since we are comparing various conditions *in situ*.

The values of m are shown by bundle in Fig. 3. There were 8 samples of m for each user (see Fig. 1), however certain sample points were highly correlated for all users. These were samples 2, 3, 6 and 7 (corresponding to the measurement number in Fig. 1), and represent the 2nd and 3rd bundles for each user in each condition. By using only the samples for the 1st and 4th bundle in each condition to compare the user experience across conditions, these large correlations disappear, and we can treat the resulting set of samples as i.i.d. The largest correlation left after this second filter is .22, which is acceptable for our purposes. With this setup we have a total of 24 independent samples of m in the experiment: 4 samples per user and 6 samples per condition. The user experience μ for a condition is then the average value of m across all 6 samples, i.e:

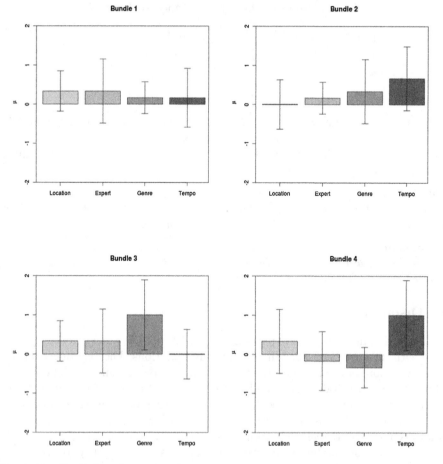

Fig. 3. Bundle-by-bundle results of user experience μ across conditions. The height of the bar represents the mean, and the error bars mark one standard deviation from the mean.

$$\mu_c = \frac{1}{6} \sum_{i=1}^{6} m_{i,c} \qquad (3)$$

where c is the condition. We then conducted one-sided, two-sample, unpaired t-tests to determine whether the differences in means of the 6 samples per condition were significantly greater than 0.

Now we can evaluate our two hypotheses:

Hypothesis 1:
μ is greater for the Location condition than for Expert

Hypothesis 2:
μ is greater for the Tempo condition than for Genre

The values of μ_c and the p-values (Bonferroni-compensated) of the corresponding t-tests are shown in Table 1.

Table 1. Results of Bonferroni-compensated t-tests

Hypothesis			p-value
1	μ_{Loc} .33	μ_{Exp} .08	$H_0 : \mu_{Loc} \leq \mu_{Exp}$ .40
2	μ_{Tem} .58	μ_{Gen} $-.08$	$H_0 : \mu_{Tem} \leq \mu_{Gen}$ .04

We recall that a higher mean of m signifies a better experience of that condition. We note that the *Location* condition appears better than the *Expert* condition but not at a significant level. However, the *Tempo* condition is significantly better than the *Genre* condition.

Conclusion 1:
We do not find significant support for Hypothesis 1, that the Location condition yields a better user experience than the Expert condition

Conclusion 2:
We find significant support for Hypothesis 2, that the Tempo condition results in a better experience than the Genre condition.

6   Discussion

In the concluding survey, most participants (8/12) reported being generally satisfied with the quality of scheduling within the conditions. The experience on the street was more enjoyable than that of the online pre-experiment. The different scheduling strategies do seem to affect the user experience, indicating that our experimental manipulation worked. Our study participants preferred the *Tempo* and *Location* conditions and were less favorable to the *Expert* and *Genre* conditions. One possible reason why the *Expert* condition did not perform as well might be that the candidate set was too small and restricted (by location and genre distribution) in our experiment to allow for the more sophisticated human techniques to fully play out.

The strongest result from our study is that *Tempo* (a linear combination of amplitude and beat rankings) yields a better user experience than *Genre* bundling. This could be because a meta-data based approach like genre scheduling requires more cultural knowledge and music expertise to appreciate whereas the *Tempo* condition is more neutral and can work well across all subjects. The genre scheduling performed particularly poorly in the last bundle that played World music. World music is itself a very heterogeneous category, but its poor performance highlights the problem of relying on, to some level, subjective categorizations. Another possible reason that *Tempo* performed well compared to *Genre* could be that it made people aware of the pace of the walk and matched it within certain bundles. A couple of people reported in the concluding survey that this was very enjoyable and suggested that the system should automatically match the tempo of the songs to the pace at which the user was walking[16].

---

[16] In fact, there are several applications that do this already, e.g. SynchStep (synchstep.com) and TrailMix (trailmixapp.com).

Our experiment design enabled us to study the various scheduling strategies in a field experiment and extracting statistically significant results. We used the smallest possible number of subjects to be able to derive basic statistical test results on our key conditions. The scheduling strategies we used were relatively simple. More complex strategies, using for example, features from music intelligence platforms like the Echo Nest, could be successfully evaluated for mobile consumption using our experiment design. Although this is not common practice, using purely negative ratings to obtain clearer user signals is likely to benefit the analysis of other user experience studies. Our filtering strategy to remove highly correlated samples and clean user signals could be fruitfully used by other small user experience studies to obtain stronger results.

7   Conclusions

In this work, we evaluated different scheduling methods on the user experience of music consumed on the go. We show that different schedules do affect the user experience and that techniques developed by radio station DJs to produce cohesive and smooth radio shows can be applied successfully for scheduling mobile music. Bundling, in particular, seems to be a useful technique that can help organize disparate content into coherent, aurally pleasant clusters. However, simply replicating rules as used by radio station DJs may not always yield the best experience, given that location relevance appeared to be an important determinant of the mobile music user experience. We found that ranking the songs within the set of candidate songs with respect to the amplitude and beats and then ordering the songs using a linear combination of these two rankings yielded the best user experience.

We presented the results of a survey of DJs for college radio stations, with the heuristics and techniques they use to create playlists for radio shows and how they ensure smooth and engaging user experiences. We also presented a field experiment design to evaluate scheduling strategies in terms of user experience. Our work has implications for music recommendation systems in improving the user experience of music consumed on the go. We consider this to be a promising research approach and encourage future work in this area.

Acknowledgments. This work was completed during the authors' time at Hewlett Packard Labs. The authors would like to thank Bernardo Huberman, senior HP fellow, for his guidance.

References

1. Agarwal, A., Meyer, A.: Beyond usability: evaluating emotional response as an integral part of the user experience. In: Proceedings of CHI 2009, pp. 2919–2930. ACM (2009)
2. Alghoniemy, M., Tewfik, A.H.: User-defined music sequence retrieval. In: Proceedings of the Eighth ACM International Conference on Multimedia, Multimedia 2000, pp. 356–358. ACM, New York (2000)

3. Ankolekar, A., Sandholm, T., Yu, L.: Play it by ear: a case for serendipitous discovery of places with musicons. In: Proceedings of CHI 2013, pp. 2959–2968 (2013)
4. Avesani, P., Massa, P., Nori, M., Susi, A.: Collaborative radio community. In: De Bra, P., Brusilovsky, P., Conejo, R. (eds.) AH 2002. LNCS, vol. 2347, pp. 462–465. Springer, Heidelberg (2002). https://doi.org/10.1007/3-540-47952-X_61
5. Bosteels, K., Pampalk, E., Kerre, E.E.: Evaluating and analysing dynamic playlist generation heuristics using radio logs and fuzzy set theory. In: Proceedings of ISMIR (2009)
6. Bull, M.: Sounding Out the City: Personal Stereos and the Management of Everyday Life. Berg, Oxford (2000)
7. Bull, M.: Sound Moves: iPod Culture and Urban Experience. Routledge, Abingdon (2008)
8. CFRC 101.9 FM: CFRC Volunteer Manual, December 2010. http://cfrc.ca/blog/wp-content/uploads/2009/03/volunteer-manual-32.pdf
9. CFUV 101.9 FM: CFUV Orientation Guide, November 2009. http://cfuv.uvic.ca/cms/wp-content/uploads/2012/03/Orientation-Manual-09-10-6th-edition-1.pdf
10. CJSR 88.5 FM: Music Show Basics, December 2001. http://www.firststage.ca/csirp/training/articles/musicshowbasics.html
11. Denora, T.: Music in Everyday Life. Cambridge University Press, Cambridge (2000)
12. Eastman, S., Ferguson, D.: Media Programming: Strategies and Practices. Thomson/Wadsworth, Belmont (2008)
13. Gaye, L., Holmquist, L.E., Behrendt, F., Tanaka, A.: Mobile music technology: report on an emerging community. In: Proceedings of the 2006 Conference on New Interfaces for Musical Expression, NIME 2006, pp. 22–25 (2006)
14. Goodman, J., Brewster, S.A., Gray, P.: How can we best use landmarks to support older people in navigation? J. Behav. Inf. Technol. **24**, 3–20 (2005)
15. Goodman, J., Brewster, S., Gray, P.: Using field experiments to evaluate mobile guides. In: Proceedings of HCI in Mobile Guides, Workshop at Mobile HCI 2004 (2004)
16. Hauver, D., French, J.: Flycasting: using collaborative filtering to generate a playlist for online radio. In: 2001 Proceedings of First International Conference on Web Delivering of Music, pp. 123–130, 23–24 November 2001
17. Hayes, C., Cunningham, P.: Smart radio: building music radio on the fly. In: Expert Systems, vol. 2000, pp. 2–6. ACM Press (2000)
18. Komulainen, S., Karukka, M., Häkkilä, J.: Social music services in teenage life: a case study. In: Proceedings of the 22nd Conference of the Computer-Human Interaction Special Interest Group of Australia on Computer-Human Interaction, OZCHI 2010, pp. 364–367 (2010)
19. Logan, B.: Content-based playlist generation: exploratory experiments. In: Proceedings of 3rd International Conference on Music Information Retrieval, Paris, France (2002)
20. Mehrabian, A., Russell, J.A.: An Approach to Environmental Psychology. M.I.T. Press, Cambridge (1974)
21. Nemirovsky, P., Davenport, G.: Guideshoes: navigation based on musical patterns. In: CHI 1999 Extended Abstracts on Human Factors in Computing Systems, CHI EA 1999, pp. 266–267 (1999)
22. Nettamo, E., Nirhamo, M., Häkkilä, J.: A cross-cultural study of mobile music - retrieval, management and consumptiom. In: OZCHI 2006, pp. 87–94. ACM (2006)
23. Pampalk, E., Pohle, T., Widmer, G.: Dynamic playlist generation based on skipping behavior. In: Proceedings of ISMIR (2005)

24. Pauws, S., Eggen, B.: PATS: realization and user evaluation of an automatic playlist generator. In: ISMIR, pp. 222–230 (2002)
25. Pauws, S., Verhaegh, W., Vossen, M.: Music playlist generation by adapted simulated annealing. Inf. Sci. **178**(3), 647–662 (2008)
26. Ragno, R., Burges, C.J.C., Herley, C.: Inferring similarity between music objects with application to playlist generation. In: Proceedings of the 7th ACM SIGMM International Workshop on Multimedia Information Retrieval, MIR 2005, pp. 73–80. ACM, New York (2005)
27. Surhone, L., Tennoe, M., Henssonow, S.: Radio Computing Services
28. Warren, N., Jones, M., Jones, S., Bainbridge, D.: Navigation via continuously adapted music. In: CHI EA 2005, pp. 1849–1852 (2005)

Smartphone-Based Estimation of a User Being in Company or Alone Based on Place, Time, and Activity

Anja Exler[✉], Marcel Braith, Kristina Mincheva, Andrea Schankin, and Michael Beigl

Karlsruhe Institute of Technology (KIT), TECO, 76131 Karlsruhe, Germany
exler@teco.edu

Abstract. Whether a person is *in company* is an important indicator for several research fields such as monitoring a patient's mental health states in clinical psychology or interruptibility detection in experience sampling. Traditionally, social activity is assessed using self-report questionnaires. However, this approach is obtrusive. The best solution would be an automatic assessment. Smartphones are suitable sensing systems for this task. In this paper, we investigate relations between being *in company* and place types. First, we present results of an online survey taken by 68 persons. Within the survey, we assessed how likely users are to be *in company* at specific place types provided by the Google Places API. We identified that places such as night club, bar, movie theatre, and restaurant are primarily visited *in company*. Places such as post office, gym, bank, or library are visited rather *alone*. Some place types are undecidable and require additional context information. As a next step, we ran an in-field user study to gather enriched real-world data. We logged temporal features, user activity, place type, and self-reported company indicators as ground truth. We gathered data of 24 participants over a period of three weeks. Using information gain and χ^2, we identified that *place type* and *hour of day* correlate with being *in company* with statistical significance shown by Cramér's *V*. Using machine learning, we trained different classifiers to predict being *in company*. We achieved an accuracy of up to 91.1%. Our approach is a first step towards an automatic assessment of being *in company* as it is more accurate than pure guessing. We propose to enrich it with further context information such as transportation mode or a more accurate activity classifier.

Keywords: Context recognition · Place type · Social activity

1 Introduction

Context-aware systems, which adapt their functionalities to the current context without explicit actions of the user, are supposed to have a better usability and user experience. This is, in particular, the case for mobile devices which

© ICST Institute for Computer Sciences, Social Informatics and Telecommunications Engineering 2018
K. Murao et al. (Eds.): MobiCASE 2018, LNICST 240, pp. 74–89, 2018.
https://doi.org/10.1007/978-3-319-90740-6_5

may adapt their functionalities with regard to the user's location, time or other properties of the environment.

The current social context, i.e. if a user is *in company* or *alone* might be another interesting contextual factor. For example, our social context influences our interruptibility and how we respond to smartphone notifications [14,17]. Also, the social context or a change in social context might be useful to support the detection of states and state changes in bi-polar personality disorder or depression to perform an appropriate treatment [10,18,19].

Commonly, the social context is provided by the users themselves via self-reports at discrete and sparse points in time. However, automatic context-aware systems require continuously gathered information. In this paper, we explore if it is possible to detect whether a user is *in company* or *alone* based on (a) different place types, (b) temporal features, and (c) the user activity. First, we propose a relationship between different place types and the probability of being *in company* or *alone*. We test this hypothesis within an online survey. Second, we enrich location features with temporal features and activity, because activities change during the day according to our biorhythm and habits [2,11]. This approach has been evaluated within a field study. Analyses include identification of feature importance and evaluating predictive models based on their accuracy.

2   Related Work

Many of these approaches rely on Bluetooth-based recognition of nearby devices [7,12]. However, due to raising privacy-awareness and security reasons, the visibility of devices using Bluetooth was restricted by the mobile OS during the last years. Smartphones with active Bluetooth are only visible if the user is currently in the Bluetooth settings. Hence, this approach is no longer an option. Alternative approaches for social sensing collected location data and transfered it to a server [7]. Every phone who installed this app provides data and allows a comparison of the data so check if devices are nearby. In this paper, we focus on a group activity recognition approach that relies on data from one single device only and that does not share the data with any server but instead runs all processes on the device itself.

The usefulness of activity, location, or temporal features for group activity detection was already proved by related work. A common method is to extract information from videos and analyse it with the objective to differentiate activities which can later on be labeled as group or single activities [1,4,16]. Some of these approaches focused on the spatio-temporal evolution of crowd behavior, so-called crowd context [4] while others relied on temporal and spatial information [1,16] – proving that spatio-temporal data is well-fitted for recognizing group activities. However, these approaches have the drawback that they use intrusive, non-privacy-aware, and high energy-consuming video techniques. It would be less energy-consuming and more privacy-aware to predict being *in company* based on automatically available and more abstract smartphone data and process this data directly on the phone itself – which is what we will do in this paper.

A connection between self-reported place types with social activity was already shown, e.g. to infer interruptibility [14]. Though, we focus on automatically detected location and place types as they are generalizable and do not require user involvement. In addition, place types are more abstract and hence more privacy-aware than raw GPS values. Our idea is to combine location data with temporal features and activity information. While related work focused on detecting groups and group activity we choose a more abstract approach and focus merely on recognizing being *in company*.

3   Exploring the Relation Between Place Types and Being in Company

We conducted an online survey to assess if users tend to visit a place rather *in company* or *alone*. We highlighted that being *in company* applies even if the user is only accompanied by one other person.

As mentioned before, locations were based on the place types that are offered by the Google Places API[1]. To reduce the number of questions within the survey the high number of over 120 place types[2] was reduced to 20 places as explained in [9].

In addition, we defined place categories to allow further abstraction of our results. Related work mostly focused on place categories for private [20] or business issues [12,13,15]. We intend to include both. We adapted the five categories proposed by Zheng et al. [20], namely: *Food & Drinks, Sports & Exercises, Movies & Shows, Shopping,* and *Recreation & Amusement.* We added the category *Work and Education* to cover both business matters and education.

For each place type we asked:

1. "In which category would you assign the currently displayed place type?" and offered the defined categories in form of *select many* checkboxes
2. "Do you visit the displayed place type rather alone or in company?" and offered a rating in form of a 5 point Likert scale ranging from "always alone" (1) to "always in company" (5)

The categories were assessed to be able to abstract the social activity to more abstract places. This might proof useful in the future as it allows to include new place types for which only the category but no probability for social activity is known. The answers to the Likert scale can be interpreted numerically as a likelihood of being *in company*, i.e. 1 being "always alone/never in company" and 5 being "never alone/always in company".

---

[1] https://developers.google.com/places/.
[2] https://developers.google.com/places/supported_types.

3.1   Participants

The survey was created with Google Forms and performed online. To recruit participants we spread the link to the survey via social media. 68 people answered the survey, 50% male and 50% female. The average age was 33 years (±12). Almost all participants had a school degree that qualified them for higher education. 63% even had a university degree which is a strong bias. The largest occupational category was information- and communication technology.

3.2   Results

The results of the survey are summarized in Tables 1 and 2. Analyzing the place types (see Table 1), it is visible that users are usually *in company* when visiting night clubs, bars, movie theatres, restaurants, and cafés. In contrast, users tend to visit post offices and gyms preferably *alone*. In addition, there are some places which are visited *alone* as well as *in company*. Prominent examples for these are shopping malls, universities and meal takeaways. For these places more

Table 1. Average answer per place type stating if a user visits a place rather *in company*(5) or *alone*(1).

Place type	Average	Standard deviation
Night Club	4.74	0.56
Bar	4.65	0.54
Movie Theatre	4.49	0.73
Restaurant	4.37	0.69
Café	4.08	0.71
Park	3.39	0.85
University	3.11	1.10
Shopping Mall	3.03	0.68
Meal Takeaway	2.87	0.75
Clothing Store	2.76	0.82
Parking	2.77	0.76
Store	2.69	0.62
Bus or Subway Station	2.60	0.65
Grocery Store	2.37	0.75
Bakery	2.29	0.55
Gas Station	2.28	0.76
Library	2.11	0.97
Bank	2.04	0.86
Gym	1.89	1.12
Post Office	1.77	0.64

Table 2. Likelihood of being *in company* per defined place category.

Place type	Likelihood
Movie & Shows	84.8%
Recreation & Amusement	67.2%
Food & Drink	61.7%
Work & Education	40.2%
Shopping	39.0%
Sports & Exercise	33.3%

information about the users and their activities are required to decide whether they are *in company* or *alone*.

Considering categories (cf. Table 2) we computed a likelihood for being *in company* while being in such places. Attending *Movies & Shows* is usually done *in company*. According to the place categories, *Recreation & Amusement* and *Food & Drinks* locations are visited *in company* in 2 out of 3 cases. *Sports & Exercises* are performed *in company* only in 1 out of 3 cases, probably depending on the kind of sport. *Work & Education* and *Shopping* are not decidable. The decision probably depends on the purpose of the business (e.g. having a meeting vs. writing a paper) or the shopping purpose (e.g. doing the weekly shopping vs. buying new clothes).

Overall, it becomes clear that location alone is not a distinct feature to differentiate between being *in company* and *alone*. It is necessary to investigate its combination with further contextual data such as activity or time. Thus, we conduct a user study to collect and analyze data.

4   In-Field User Study

4.1   Study Design

The purpose of the study was to gain insight about the context in which people are *in company* or *alone*. The time frame for the study was set to take place in February 2017 and to last three weeks.

There was an initial meeting with the participants in which we described the purpose of the study. Participants were free to ask questions about the study. We informed them that they were free to drop out of the study if they feel uncomfortable at any time. Afterwards, we asked them to sign a consent form to confirm their participation and to allow us using their personal data anonymously and for scientific purposes only. Next, we installed our app on their smartphone. We asked the participants to keep the location service enabled and only switch it off if they need to, for example to save battery, if they do not want a place to be recorded, or when they are outside the country and needed to prevent network access. We explained to them how to respond to notifications and how to add data later on using the retrospective log functionality of our app. After three weeks, we met again to export the recorded data and to ask the participants for feedback, such as problems or difficulties.

4.2   Participants

We recruited 30 participants, of which 24 started the study. The others had exclusion criteria, such as not having a cellular connection for large parts of the study or finally decided not to participate in the study because of privacy concerns. The participants were between 19 and 31 years old with an average of 24 years. 10 participants were female and 14 male. There was an equal distribution of students and working population.

4.3   Data Assessment App

Sensor Measurements. We developed an Android app to assess the desired features: place types (via Google Places API), user activity (Google Activity Recognition API), and temporal features (via system time).

To assess the location, we send longitude and latitude to the Places API which returns a collection of *PlaceLikelihood* objects, one for each probable place the user could currently be at. For simplicity, we visualized the structure of such a result returned by the API in JSON notation (see Fig. 1). We decided to always consider the most likely place and the first (i.e. most suitable) place type.

The Activity Recognition API relies on data from physical sensors such as accelerometer and gyroscope, but also GPS. It returns the most probable activity and the confidence of the classifier.

For temporal features, the app stores the internal system time as a unix timestamp. From the timestamp, we can derive features such as hour of day, day of week, or workday.

Subjective User Feedback (Ground Truth). Whenever a location change happens, i.e. the app detected a new place type, the user is prompted for feedback by a smartphone notification. The user has the choice to respond now or add the information later using the retrospective log functionality. Whenever reacting to the response, promptly or later on, the user is confronted with questions similar to the following example:

1. Are you currently at this place? *University*
2. *If yes:*
    (a) Are you *in company* at this place?
        → push either *in company* button or *alone* button
3. *If no:*
    (a) At which place are you currently?
        → select place type out of a drop down list
    (b) Are you *in company* at this place?
        → push either *in company* button or *alone* button

```
{
    "likelyPlaces": [
        {
            "likelihood": 0.4,
            "place": {
                "name": "ZKM Karlsruhe",
                . . .
                "placeTypes": [66, 5, 1013]
            }
        },
        {
            "likelihood": 0.12,
            "place": {
                "name": "Filmpalast",
                . . .
                "placeTypes": [64, 34]
            }
        },
        . . .
    ]
}
```

Fig. 1. Simplyfied representation of objects returned by the Google Places API in JSON notation.

The retrospective log function of the app presented a list of all places that a user visited that day. Each row showed the time of arrival and departure as well as the detected place type. Only visits of the same day were shown. A longer period would require to show dates as well and would eventually bloat the list with a lot of entries. In addition, retrospective bias or memory gaps might have occurred. A click on a list entry started the same interface that was used in case a user responds to a feedback prompt. This ensured that the user did not have to learn a new design but was already used to the same feedback interface.

5　Descriptive Data Analysis

The final dataset consisted of 1745 instances from 24 different participants. There were more instances in the dataset of class *in company* (993) than *alone* (752). A common comment was that the participants sometimes felt it was difficult to decide whether to declare a situation as being *in company* or *alone*, because there were other people present but the degree of social interaction was low.

Place types were also imbalanced and distributed very unevenly. As Table 3 shows, only 13 places had more than 10 occurrences. Some places, on the other hand, were strongly represented, e.g., "at home" with almost 700 instances.

Table 3. Number of recorded visits for each place type ordered by decreasing occurrence.

Place type	Occurances	% in Company
Movie Theatre	1	100.00
Bar	22	95.45
Fast Food Store	12	91.67
Work	72	90.28
Restaurant	41	87.80
Café	27	85.19
Clothing Store	12	83.33
Gym	11	81.82
Other	48	77.08
Shopping Mall	18	61.11
Department Store	12	58.33
Grocery Store	39	51.28
At Home	697	50.65
Bakery	6	50.00
Bank	3	33.33
Bus/Train Straion	77	29.87
Gast Station	7	28.57
Park	8	12.50
Parking Lot	8	12.50
Post Office	1	0.00

A frequent observation was that places were often detected incorrectly and required correction by the user. Also, some place types were detected multiple times although no change of place had happened. Both errors are probably caused by GPS drifts or inaccuracies of the Places API.

Precision of the Google Places API. To evaluate how well the place recognition itself worked, we compared the place types detected by the Google Places API with the place types provided by the participants (ground truth). It is calculated how often the users rejected the suggested place and picked a different one.

If the user labeled the place as "at home", "on the way", "work", or "other" the datum was not counted, because those places were not detectable by the Google Places API. Based on the ground truth, the service achieves a precision of 73%. This result is significantly better than guessing. Results might be enhanced by considering more place types than only the most probable one that is returned by the Google Places API. We only considered the place type that had the highest probability. However, the Google Places API returns a list of suitable place types with probabilities. Elhamshary and Youssef already showed that considering the top 5 venues is advisable: their approach yielded a 99% precision for the actual venue to be in the top 5 candidate list [8]. For future studies, a weighted approach considering the five most probables places should be considered.

Analysis of Place Type, Time, and Activity. Figure 2 presents the distribution of being *in company* or *alone* plotted against all considered place types and the hour of day. "Bars" and "restaurants" were frequently visited *in company*. In contrast, "bus or train stations" were mostly visited *alone*. The distribution of being *in company* or *alone* was rather balanced for places such as "at home", "on the way", "other", and "university".

Focusing on the hours of the arrival times (y axis) it can be seen that firstly, place and arrival time were dependent and secondly, that at night many places were visited *in company*. Though, there was not very much data with this pattern.

It is visible that there were more records of activities performed *alone* than *in company*. This phenomenon might be biased by the labeling process. If a participant labeled data only in case of being *alone* and never while being *in company* – for example, because it would be impolite to use the smartphone while being with others – such an imbalance could occur. In addition, the definition of being *in company* was strongly dependent on the participant's interpretation. According to the user feedback it was also hard to judge where being *in company* began and where it ended. One example for this it "at home" where it was not easy to tell if the fact of living in a shared apartment or with a partner always counted as being *in company* or only when performing joint activities. For "at home" and "university", it happened that participants were *in company* but not actually involved in a common activity. This is obvious for such place types as there might be individual activities performed in the presence of other people. In these cases the place seems to be no useful indicator for social activity.

User activities per se were also not very separating as shown in Fig. 3. There were almost no patterns between the activities and being *in company* or *alone*. The closest explanation would be that the shares of activities were not sufficient to discriminate between the classes, and time sequences play a large role there.

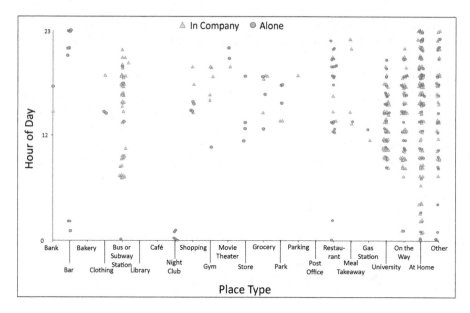

Fig. 2. Distribution of being *in company* (blue triangles) or *alone* (red circles) while being at a specific place typ (x axis) at a specific hour of day (y axis). (Color figure online)

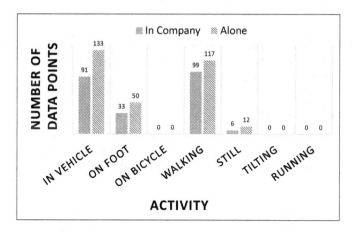

Fig. 3. Distribution of being *in company* (blue) or *alone* (red) per physical user activity. (Color figure online)

6   Feature Analysis

To assess the quality of our features we calculated the information gain and χ^2 with Cramér's V. Those numbers reveal how the features perform and how they compare to each other. However, they do not reveal how combinations of the features might be correlated to being *in company*, but give a tendency. The combination of features is measured with the performance of the classification.

6.1 Information Gain

Information gain is a measure of how much the entropy of the class distribution is reduced when only considering the different values of a feature. A reduction of entropy is desirable. For example if the data is separated by place type, it would be beneficial if within each place the class value would either be mainly *in company* or *alone*. The stronger the social activity indicator leans to one side, the lower the entropy. Information gain cannot be calculated on numeric attributes. Therefore, we binarized numeric attributes, i.e. transformed the attribute into the values zero and non-zero.

Table 4. Overview of the information gain for each feature of the mixed dataset for predicting being *in company* or *alone*.

Feature	Information gain
Place	0.11481
Weekday	0.02976
HourofDay	0.02678
Activity	0.00113

Table 4 shows the information gain for each feature. Place is by far the best feature according to this metric. Temporal features perform not as good but still have some gain. User activity however provides marginal information gain.

6.2 χ^2 and Cramér's V

χ^2 is a metric to test distributions of variables for independence. It is calculated by the sum of squared differences between observations. If the corresponding p-value, which indicates the likelihood that the difference in the observations is caused by statistical error, is smaller than the significance level α of usually 0.05 then the variables are dependent. The purpose of the test in the present case is to see if the selected features are actually dependent on being *in company* and, most importantly, if the results are significant despite the low amount of data.

Cramér's V is a measure of association between two variables and is based on χ^2. It shows the strength of the correlation between the variables. Equation (1) shows a bias-corrected version of Cramér's V which is used to ensure comparability between features that differ in the number of values [3]. The measure is used to judge which features are worth investigating further and which are neglectable.

$$\tilde{V} = \sqrt{\frac{max(0, \dfrac{\chi^2}{n} - \dfrac{(k-1)(r-1)}{n-1})}{min(k-1, r-1)}} \qquad (1)$$

Table 5. Overview of χ^2 values for each feature and its significance in form of p-values and Cramér's V.

Feature	χ^2	p-value	Significant	$\widetilde{V}$
Place type	104.42	<0.00001	Yes	0.2446
Hour of day	38.777	0.02099	Yes	0.1491
Weekday	5.708	0.04567	Yes	0.05719

Table 5 shows χ^2 values for all features compared with the class attribute, i.e. being *in company*. It also displays if there is a significant correlation between the feature and the class attribute, determined by the p-value. If true, Cramér's V is presented to indicate the strength of the correlation. The place type seems certain to be an indicator for being *in company* with a clear correlation expressed by a V of about 24%. Hour of day is also significantly correlated with a V of about 15%. According to Cohen [5] both qualify as a weak effect size. The weekday has no apparent significance which might be caused by the inhomogenity of the sample as students and working population have different schedules for each day.

Since place type and all temporal features are not only significant but also qualify for a small effect size, they are considered useful in classification.

7 Prediction of Being in Company

7.1 Preliminary Considerations

To evaluate the features that have been picked and to measure the potential of the approach for real world applications, a predictive model is built using machine learning. The result of our classification model is binary: a participant is either *in company* (1) or *alone* (0). Pure guessing would result in 50% accuracy on average. However, there are more instances in the dataset of class *alone* than *in company*. Always choosing *in company* would result in 57% accuracy on average. This value represents the baseline for the recognition accuracy of our predictive model. One question is which accuracy would be optimal. However, this heavily depends on the use case. For an ambulatory assessment with a socio-psychological component information about social activities, i.e. being *in company* or *alone*, are highly relevant and high recognition accuracies are required; misclassification might lead to misdiagnoses and wrong treatment. For context-dependent notifications lower accuracies might be more acceptable as missing a notification or being notified one time more might not have that severe consequences.

7.2 Classification

Based on the identified features, we evaluated different classification algorithms from the Weka[3] toolkit and compared them in terms of recognition accuracy, i.e.

---
[3] http://www.cs.waikato.ac.nz/ml/weka/.

the ratio of correctly classified instances and total number of instances. Accuracy is a good measure if the detection of both classes is equally important. It is used due to its neutrality as no specific use case is evaluated at this point. It is also already appropriate for a scenario such as counting the number of moments per month a participants was *in company*. In addition, we calculated precision, recall, and F1 measure.

For each classifier a 10-fold cross-validation was performed. That means the dataset is randomly split into 10 parts of equal size and the tested 10 times, each time with 9 parts being trained and one used for testing. The results are then averaged to give a final accuracy. All classification algorithms have reasonable default parameters. We did not perform any parameter tuning during this evaluation.

The selected classifiers are popular representatives from different types of classification methods. We considered J48 (C4.5) and Random Forest as tree-based methods, IB1 (1-Nearest-Neighbor) as a lazy learning method, SMO (Support Vector Machine) with polynomial kernel, Multilayer Perceptron as an Artificial Neural Network, Naive Bayes and Bayes Net as probabilistic methods, Logit Boost with Decision Stump to include a method with logistic regression, and VFI (Voting Feature Intervals) [6] as an alternative.

Table 6. Overview of the classification results.

Classifier	Accuracy	Precision	Recall	F1 measure
J48	91.90%	92.00%	91.90%	91.90%
Random Forest	91.90%	92.00%	92.00%	92.00%
IB1	91.50%	91.70%	91.50%	91.60%
SMO	77.60%	76.80%	77.60%	76.70%
Multilayer Percertron	86.20%	86.20%	86.30%	86.20%
Naive Bayes	76.10%	75.50%	76.10%	75.70%
Bayes Net	76.80%	76.60%	76.90%	76.70%
Logit Boost	77.70%	77.10%	77.70%	76.00%
Vote	68.60%	47.10%	68.70%	55.90%
Average	82.03%	79.44%	82.08%	80.30%

Table 6 shows the results. Tree-based methods, Nearest Neighbor classification, and Multilayer Perceptron perform best on our dataset. All others yield mediocre results. All classifiers perform significantly better than guessing and also much better than picking the majority class.

We considered the cardinalization of the place type feature in form of an a priori probability calculated from the results of the survey. However, it was found to be harmful for classification results except for Naive Bayes, a probabilistic approach. Hence, we neglected the a priori probabilities as a feature.

8   Conclusions

Automatically assessed indicators for being *in company* or *alone* are a desired feature in many areas of social sciences and computer science. Smartphones, as personal wearables and ubiquitous sensor system, are a suitable platform for an automatic assessment of this feature. Several researches investigated how to infer group activity based on sensor measurements such as audio data, video, detected bluetooth devices or GPS locations. However, none is known that relied on the place types provided by the Google Places API in a data protective and opportunistic manner.

8.1   Online Survey – Conclusion

As a first step towards a location-aware detection system we ran an online survey to assess a basic separability of being *in company* or *alone* based on the place type. We identified that place types with a high frequency of being *in company* usually belong to the *Recreation & amusement* category, e.g. "night clubs", "bars", or "movie theatres", or belong to the *Food & Drink* category, e.g. "restaurants" or "cafés".

In contrast, users tend to visit place types on their own if they are assigned to the place category *Sports & Exercise*, e.g. visiting the "gym". For some place types and categories a differentiation is not possible without further information. Example place types are "universities", "parks" or "shopping malls". We assume that temporal features such as time of day, weekday or information about the physical activity might improve the differentiation between being *alone* or *in company* at a specific place type.

8.2   User Study – Conclusion

These results encouraged us to run a user study to gather real world location data in combination with activity and time. The study lasted three weeks and was taken by 24 participants.

The gathered data consisted of place, temporal features such as day of week and hour of day, and the user activity. We calculated information gain and χ^2 in combination with Cramér's V to rate the feature importance. Both showed a significance for place, with a medium effect V value of 0.37, and temporal features, with a small effect V value between 0.21 and 0.23.

Based on these features, we built and evaluated different classifiers using the Weka toolkit. Results of up to 91.9% recognition accuracy are above the baseline of 50% (guessing) or 57% (predicting the most frequent class), respectively. Still, this recognition accuracy is pretty high, but still has room for improvement which is required for the classifier to be applicable for example in social sciences where accurate predictions of social activity is important. Though, it is also considerable to have a classifier that works automatically and only asks for user feedback in case its confidence is below a threshold.

Some place types showed to be reliably separable, such as "restaurants" and "bus or subway stations". For other place types the distribution seems random, e.g. "universities". For those places, further information is required.

The imbalance in the dataset and specifically the sparse data for some places impacted the results negatively. Some places might be very well distinguishable in terms of being *in company* or *alone*, but correlations, for example with hour of day, were indicated but without confirmable statistically significance.

8.3 Summary and Future Work

In summary, our research showed that smartphone-based features possess the power to support automatic distinction between being *in company* and *alone*. We identified significant relevance of spatio-temporal features. Classification models trained on study data achieved a higher recognition accuracy than the baseline. However, the models need further improvement to be suitable for real-world application.

Within this paper, we investigated generalized models due to two reasons: First, because the online survey was performed on a wider range of participants. Second, because the location sample from the user study was fairly sparse and we would not have had sufficient samples per place type per person. However, in future work, personalized models should be investigated stronger. The online survey already suggested that there are either interpersonal differences or external factors that influence the decision of being *in company* or *alone* at a specific place. Hence, further context and sensor sources, e.g. enhanced activity classifiers, calendar information, or device usage statistics, should be considered.

Presuming that smartwatches become more widespread, more complex activities could be detected without specialized hardware or laboratory setups. Furthermore, there is potential in recognizing long-term patterns and routines of individual persons, such as regular sport events or working hours.

References

1. Amer, M.R., Xie, D., Zhao, M., Todorovic, S., Zhu, S.-C.: Cost-sensitive top-down/bottom-up inference for multiscale activity recognition. In: Fitzgibbon, A., Lazebnik, S., Perona, P., Sato, Y., Schmid, C. (eds.) ECCV 2012. LNCS, vol. 7575, pp. 187–200. Springer, Heidelberg (2012). https://doi.org/10.1007/978-3-642-33765-9_14
2. Bachmann, A., Klebsattel, C., Budde, M., Riedel, T., Beigl, M., Reichert, M., Santangelo, P., Ebner-Priemer, U.: How to use smartphones for less obtrusive ambulatory mood assessment and mood recognition. In: Adjunct Proceedings of Ubicomp 2015, pp. 693–702. ACM (2015)
3. Bergsma, W.: A bias-correction for Cramér's and Tschuprow's. J. Korean Stat. Soc. **42**(3), 323–328 (2013)
4. Choi, W., Shahid, K., Savarese, S.: Learning context for collective activity recognition. In: 2011 IEEE Conference on Computer Vision and Pattern Recognition (CVPR), pp. 3273–3280. IEEE (2011)

5. Cohen, J.: Statistical Power Analysis for the Behavioral Sciences, 2nd edn. Hillsdale, New Jersey (1988)
6. Demiröz, G., Güvenir, H.A.: Classification by voting feature intervals. In: van Someren, M., Widmer, G. (eds.) ECML 1997. LNCS, vol. 1224, pp. 85–92. Springer, Heidelberg (1997). https://doi.org/10.1007/3-540-62858-4_74
7. Eagle, N., Pentland, A.S.: Reality mining: sensing complex social systems. Pers. Ubiquit. Comput. **10**(4), 255–268 (2006)
8. Elhamshary, M., Youssef, M.: Checkinside: a fine-grained indoor location-based social network. In: Proceedings of the 2014 ACM International Joint Conference on Pervasive and Ubiquitous Computing, pp. 607–618. ACM (2014)
9. Exler, A., Braith, M., Schankin, A., Beigl, M.: Preliminary investigations about interruptibility of smartphone users at specific place types. In: Adjunct Proceedings of Ubicomp 2016. ACM (2016, to appear)
10. Faurholt-Jepsen, M., Frost, M., Vinberg, M., Christensen, E.M., Bardram, J.E., Kessing, L.V.: Smartphone data as objective measures of bipolar disorder symptoms. Psychiatry Res. **217**, 124–127 (2014)
11. Halberg, F., Tong, Y.L., Johnson, E.A.: Circadian system phase - an aspect of temporal morphology; procedures and illustrative examples. In: von Mayersbach, H. (ed.) The Cellular Aspects of Biorhythms, pp. 20–48. Springer, Heidelberg (1967). https://doi.org/10.1007/978-3-642-88394-1_2
12. Liang, G., Cao, J., Zhu, W.: CircleSense: a pervasive computing system for recognizing social activities. In: 2013 IEEE International Conference on Pervasive Computing and Communications (PerCom) (2013)
13. Liao, L., Fox, D., Kautz, H.A.: Hierarchical conditional random fields for GPS-based activity recognition. In: Thrun, S., Brooks, R., Durrant-Whyte, H. (eds.) Robotics Research. Springer Tracts in Advanced Robotics, vol. 28, pp. 487–506. Springer, Heidelberg (2005). https://doi.org/10.1007/978-3-540-48113-3_41
14. Pejovic, V., Musolesi, M.: InterruptMe: Designing Intelligent Prompting Mechanisms for Pervasive Applications (2014)
15. Riboni, D., Bettini, C.: OWL 2 modeling and reasoning with complex human activities. Pervasive Mob. Comput. **7**(3), 379–395 (2011)
16. Ryoo, M., Aggarwal, J.: Stochastic representation and recognition of high-level group activities. Int. J. Comput. Vis. **93**(2), 183–200 (2011)
17. Ter Hofte, G.H.: Xensible interruptions from your mobile phone. In: MobileHCI 2007 (2007)
18. Trull, T.J., Ebner-Priemer, U.: Ambulatory assessment. Ann. Rev. Clin. Psychol. **9**, 151 (2013)
19. Trull, T.J., Ebner-Priemer, U.W.: Using experience sampling methods/ecological momentary assessment (ESM/EMA) in clinical assessment and clinical research: introduction to the special section (2009)
20. Zheng, V.W., Zheng, Y., Xie, X., Yang, Q.: Collaborative location and activity recommendations with GPS history data. In: International World Wide Web Conference 2010, New York, USA (2010)

GERMIC: Application of Gesture Recognition Model with Interactive Correction to Manual Grading Tasks

Kohei Yamamoto[1]([envelope]), Fumiya Kan[1], Kazuya Murao[1], Masahiro Mochizuki[2], and Nobuhiko Nishio[1]

[1] College of Information Science and Engineering, Ritsumeikan University,
1-1-1 Noji-higashi, Kusatsu, Shiga 525-8577, Japan
{moi,fumiya}@ubi.cs.ritsumei.ac.jp, {murao,nishio}@cs.ritsumei.ac.jp
[2] Research Organization of Science and Technology, Ritsumeikan University,
1-1-1 Noji-higashi, Kusatsu, Shiga 525-8577, Japan
moma@ubi.cs.ritsumei.ac.jp

Abstract. Gesture-based recognition is one of the most intuitive methods for inputting information and is not subject to cumbersome operations. Recognition is performed on human's consecutive motion without reference to retrial or alternation by user. We propose a gesture recognition model with a mechanism for correcting recognition errors that operates interactively and is practical. We applied the model to a setting involving a manual grading task in order to verify its effectiveness. Our system, named GERMIC, consists of two major modules, namely, handwritten recognition and interactive correction. Recognition is materialized with image feature extraction and convolutional neural network. A mechanism for interactive correction is called on-demand by a user-based trigger. GERMIC monitors, track, and stores information on the user's grading task and generates output based on the recognition information collected. In contrast to conventional grading done manually, GERMIC significantly shortens the total time for completing the task by 24.7% and demonstrates the effectiveness of the model with interactive correction in two real world user environments.

Keywords: Handwriting recognition · Recognition error correction

1   Introduction

Human activity recognition has received much attention because it is considered one of the most natural methods for improving quality of life by monitoring and supporting human life and work [1–4]. Some famous systems include a system that monitors a nurse provider and automatically outputs the nurse's notes [5] and a system that monitors an assembly worker and displays procedures [6,7]. These systems recognize human motions based on sensor values, store them as data memory in the virtual world, and then output the information in the

© ICST Institute for Computer Sciences, Social Informatics and Telecommunications Engineering 2018
K. Murao et al. (Eds.): MobiCASE 2018, LNICST 240, pp. 90–105, 2018.
https://doi.org/10.1007/978-3-319-90740-6_6

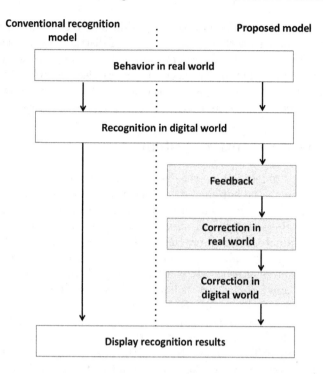

Fig. 1. Different process flows between the conventional recognition model and the proposed recognition model.

real world. However, recognition is performed on a user's consecutive motion without regard to retrial or alternation by the user even though that is likely to occur. Thus, a mechanism that allows the user to interactively correct recognition errors is needed to better fit an existing human activity model by allowing repeat motion, alternation, and suchlike unanticipated behavior.

Hence, we propose a gesture-based recognition model with a mechanism for correcting recognition errors by the user without affecting the real world. The different process flows between the conventional recognition model and the proposed recognition model are described in Fig. 1. We developed a recognition system based on the proposed model to support manual grading tasks, and verified its effectiveness. Our system, named GERMIC, consists of two major modules: handwritten recognition and interactive correction. The handwritten module recognizes diagrams such as "○", "△", and "/" drawn by a user with a pen-shaped mouse; moreover, the module recognizes numbers drawn by user too. Diagrams are recognized by image feature extraction and numbers are recognized using convolution neural network (CNN) on a PC. The interactive correction module is called on-demand by a user-based trigger, i.e., clicking a button embedded in the pen-shaped mouse. The interactive correction mechanism is then activated over voice feedback and the user can correct any occurrence of recognition errors or any recognition of unintended action. In addition, voice feedback enables the user to make corrections without slowing down or distracting the user by having to look at the PC screen. Each recognition result is stored in the system to be used to generate an output spreadsheet. Hence, we designed GERMIC to assist with grading tasks without impacting the user's conventional way of grading manually while reducing the user's mental and physical workload.

2 Existing Recognition Systems

There is a number of research on the systems and services that support graders. For instance, paper-based automated grading systems like "Glyph" [8] by Xerox[1] using a formatted sheet or systems using Optical Mark Recognition (OMR)[2] [9–11] help score papers, tests, and surveys automatically, reducing the burden on graders or evaluators. However, these systems require a rich infrastructure: formatted sheets, software, hardware, optical recognition capabilities, and so on. The sheets themselves are severely constraining as these systems do not accept responses in just any format, such as handwritten characters or diagrams, which take away flexibility and convenience for users.

There are also tablet, cloud, and web-based learning and grading technologies to assist graders. A project called CLP [12–14], conducted by MIT (Massachusetts Institute of Technology), is one of the most famous tablet-based learning and grading systems, which focuses on student-teacher interaction using a pen and tablet with the capability of accepting various answer formats. However, utilizing the tablet requires a lengthy and cumbersome setup including inputting all the types of questions and answers that will appear on each tablet. The system is thus focused on recognizing and collecting various type of answers efficiently without regard for errors in recognition so that it is hardly used in the real environment. In addition, the infrastructure and costs for supporting the use of tablets are considered prohibitive. With respect to cloud and web-based learning and grading, there is a lot of research and development on expanding Web-CAT (Web-based Center for Automated Testing) [15,16], which is the most widely known open source automated grading system for programming. These types of systems can accept richly expressive codes but are limited to programming assessments. Some other systems [17–19] that focus on more generic uses, such as automated scoring of students' writing, appears to be highly flexible with the ability to evaluate complex natural language but requires installation of a huge infrastructure, requires every user to own a PC, and does not recognize handwritten formats.

There has been a lot of research and development on recognition systems of handwritten characters [21–24]. Amma et al. [21] proposed an interactive handwriting input method using motion sensors such as accelerometer and gyroscope. They focus on the modality and intuitivity of their 3D recognition system but the system has very limited practical application. On recognition algorithms,

---

[1] Xerox: https://www.xerox.com/.

[2] Remark: http://remarksoftware.com/products/office-omr/.

Ahmad et al. [22] proposed using a support vector machine to recognize hand-written characters, while others following a main current in handwriting recognition systems are utilizing deep neural network architectures such as recurrent neural network [23]. To investigate recognition accuracy, Suen and Tan [24] introduced eight different classifiers for identifying handwritten digit errors. Despite these developments, none of the handwriting recognition systems have yet to be applied to the task of grading student work.

Research which assists graders investigated thus far has been forcing the user to drastically change their attitudes to grading tasks, even if the research is based on mobile assisting system, this point must be burdensome for the user. Furthermore, although it is a major way for graders and teachers to perform grading manually, a system to assist such scenes have not been investigated thus far and consequently it requires them to score each paper and to tally the final results with burdens. Therefore, a practical system that supports manual graders without affecting their conventional attitudes to grading is needed.

3 Proposed System

This section describes system requirements and we developed the system which meets the requirements named GERMIC (GEsture Recognition Model with Interactive Correction).

3.1 User Application Requirements

Currently, grading is done manually because students are still required put their answers down on paper. There is a huge demand for a system that supports manual grading, that is able to store and query the results for output and analysis, and that provides a mechanism for users to interactively correct recognition errors by the system. We propose a system that supports manual grading tasks in a class environment defined by paper-based assignments and exams.

For instance, the user will be able to grade a student paper using a pen-shaped mouse to manually draw a diagram such as a "◯" for a correct answer, "△" for a partially correct answer, and "/" for an incorrect answer. The user can also draw a number as partial point after recognition of "△". The results are collected and stored in a database and to be used for output and analysis (e.g., automatic calculation of an individual student's scores to obtain a total score for that student). The system is set up to provide information to the user on the recognition results to enable the user to easily correct any recognition errors. The system physically consists of a PC for storing recognition results to a database and the pen-shaped mouse for reading the trail of hand gesture while their grading papers.

3.2 System Overview

A system flowchart of GERMIC is shown in Fig. 2. To begin, GERMIC reads essential information from a csv file set (e.g., number of answers, number of questions, and allotment of scores). GERMIC then classifies diagrams drawn by the

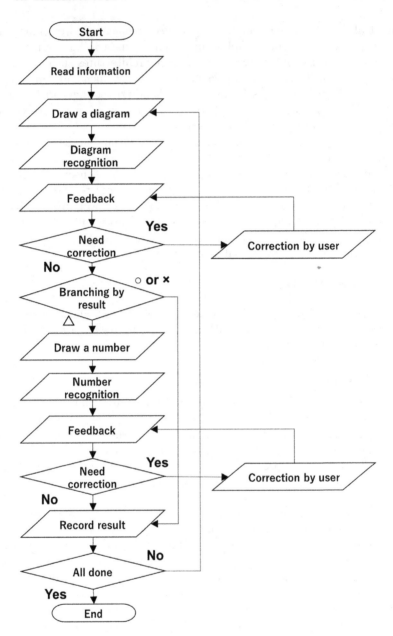

Fig. 2. Flowchart of GERMIC.

user into three groups: "○" (correct answer), "△" (partially correct answer), and "/" (incorrect answer) by image feature extraction. GERMIC provides results of the recognition to the user over voice feedback. Whenever the user catches a recognition error, the user can correct it by pressing the button embedded

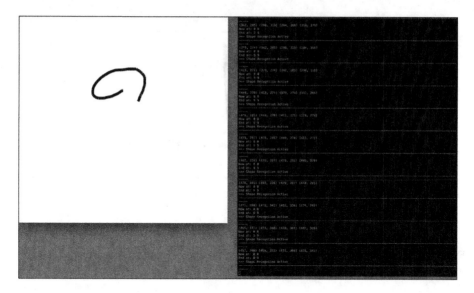

Fig. 3. Screen shot of the application window opened on the desktop.

in the pen-shaped mouse. The user is notified of the correction through voice feedback too. If the system recognizes a "◯" or "/" the score is stored in a database according to how the information was initially set up in the csv file for GERMIC. If the system reads a "△" the user is enjoined to write a number as a grade for a partially correct answer, which is recognized by the CNN trained system. The user can also correct faulty recognition of numbers by pressing the button on the pen. When the recognition conditions are satisfied, the user is instructed to proceed to the next grading task.

Once the user is done with grading, the system automatically calculates the score and output the results in a spreadsheet. The following provides details on how GERMIC recognizes the user's handwritten notation, how recognition is achieved through image extraction, and how voice feedback works with the mechanism for interactive correction.

3.3   Acquisition of the User's Drawing

GERMIC, which is implemented in Python (ver. 3.6.1) comprising libraries related to automated computation, is as an application that run on macOS Sierra (ver. 10.12.4). After the start-up of GERMIC, a window appears on the desktop of the computer and the cursor is automatically positioned at the center of the window on the left side as shown in Fig. 3. As the user draws a form with the cursor, the trailing coordinates of the form are recorded by GERMIC from beginning to end. The entire window is stored as image data once the drawing is done. GERMIC then performs image recognition of the trailing coordinates and the form is classified within the diagram or number category. When the user draws something, the user does not have to push or hold the button.

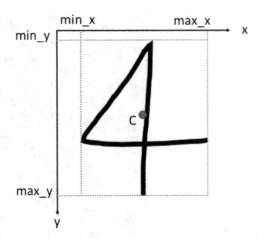

Fig. 4. The algorithm to cutout a number from the entire window at the time of number recognition.

3.4 Image Recognition

GERMIC performs image recognition on diagrams and numbers drawn by the user once the entire window is converted to image data. How image recognition is materialized is described below.

Cutout a Drawing Trail. When image recognition is performed on diagrams, the system processes the entire window since diagram recognition involves classifying the diagram based on the number of feature points contained in the window. For number recognition, the input must match the scale ratio of the image data (square image of a number) used in CNN training (to be discussed later). Thus, number recognition involves the process of cutting out the square image of the hand-drawn number on the window frame.

Figure 4 shows the algorithm for a number cutout. First, the entire window is converted to gray scale and each pixel is scanned as the top left is zero. Then the maximum x coordinate max_x, the minimum x coordinate min_x, the maximum y coordinate max_y, the minimum y coordinate min_y, and the center coordinate C of the hand-drawn number are calculated. If the drawn number is longer on the x-axis than the y-axis, then the number is squared by the size $max\_x - min\_x$ centered on C. If the drawn number is longer on the y-axis than the x-axis, the drawn number is squared by the size $max\_y - min\_y$.

Diagram Recognition. Diagram recognition classifies drawn diagrams into one of three diagram types: "◯", "△", and "/". Thus, the expected output of a diagram recognition is any one of the three diagram types. There are several ways to classify diagrams but most do not execute fast enough to provide real-time feedback. Therefore, we adopted the FAST algorithm [20] for performing diagram

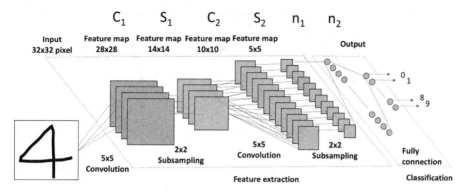

Fig. 5. Diagram of convolution neural network used in number recognition.

recognition. FAST algorithm detects feature points based on the condition as to whether a certain pixel p is continuously lighter or darker than the circumference of the surrounding pixels. If the condition can be satisfied, pixel p is registered as a feature point. Details of the algorithm is not provided herein.

GERMIC uses the number of feature points for classifying diagrams. Image feature extraction using FAST algorithm is implemented with OpenCV3.0 (ver. 3.2.0) library[3]. From our preliminary experiment, a diagram is recognized as "/" if the number of feature points is less than nine, as "$\triangle$" if greater than or equal to nine but less than 23, and as "$\bigcirc$" if greater than or equal to 23. In addition, if the number of feature points is less than three, the diagram is read as an unintended motion error and thus ignored.

Number Recognition. When GERMIC instructs the user to draw a number, the user is required to draw a one-digit number from one to nine as credit for a partially correct answer. The number zero is not recognized by GERMIC because "/" is consider its equivalent. Number recognition is based on the CNN model as shown in Fig. 5.

The CNN model used in this paper consists of two sets of a convolution layer and a sampling layer besides a fully connected layer. Relu is used as an activation function as it is often used in the field of image recognition, moreover, softmax function is used as activation function at an output layer and probability is calculated for each number. Learning session adjusts weight (parameters) with Adam using back propagation method. Cross-entropy is used as loss function to calculate the difference between the prediction and the truth. In testing session, the CNN model calculates probability for each number and extracts a number with the highest probability as a number output.

Number recognition using CNN is implemented with a machine learning library called TensorFlow[4] which Google developed and released as open source.

---

[3] OpenCV: http://opencv.org/opencv-3-2.html.
[4] TensorFlow: https://www.tensorflow.org/.

Fig. 6. "4", "5", and "7" drawn with one stroke.

Besides, the CNN model is trained 20,000 times in advance with the datasets of one-digit written numbers called MNIST[5]. In the process of number recognition, the user is asked to draw a number with one stroke even if it is "4", "5", and "7" as shown in Fig. 6 since the user draws a number without utilizing the button. In addition, feature point extraction is performed parallelly in number recognition. Then if the number of feature points is less than or equal to three, the drawing is recognized as unintended motion then ignored so to secure the redundancy.

Interactive Correction Mechanism. When recognition is conducted, GER-MIC provides the user voice feedback. For instance, when the recognition result is "○" GERMIC pronounces "circle", when the result is "1" GERMIC says "one". In that way, voice feedback enables the user to correct any faulty recognition on the fly without requiring the user to slow down in order to confirm the result on the computer screen.

To correct a recognition error, the user presses the button embedded in the pen-shaped mouse to trigger the correction mechanism. If the error relates to a diagram misrecognition, then the user can swap the diagram with the correct one by clicking. If the error relates to a number misrecognition, then the user can input the correct number by the number of clicks. For instance, if the intended number is "3" but is incorrectly recognized by the system, then the user can click the button three times to input the correct number.

4   Evaluation

We conducted grading task experiments to evaluate the effectiveness of GER-MIC. We recruited five subjects to serve as graders. They were given a tutorial and lesson to familiarize them with GERMIC. Subjects were then asked to draw three types of diagrams ("○", "△", and "/") and nine different numbers (numbers 1 to 9) for a total of 10 times per item. We then evaluated the recognition rate. Following that, subjects were asked to utilize GERMIC during the grading task. As shown in Fig. 7, subjects were given a paper to grade, which contained 10 sentences that were translated from Japanese to English. Subjects were asked to score the 10 translated sentences by comparing them against the correctly translated English sentences provided them for a maximum perfect score of 100. In

---

[5] The MNIST database of handwritten digits: http://yann.lecun.com/exdb/mnist/.

1. 私はペンを持っています I have a pen	1. 私はペンを持っています I have an pen
2. 私はサッカーをすることが好きです I like playing soccer	2. 私はサッカーをすることが好きです I like playing soccer
3. 私は京都へ行きました I went to Kyoto	3. 私は京都へ行きました I went at Shiga
4. 私はりんごを食べます I eat an apple	4. 私はりんごを食べます I eat an apples
5. あなたは先生ですか? Are you a teacher?	5. あなたは先生ですか? Are you a teacher?
6. 私は毎日英語を話します I speak English everyday	6. 私は毎日英語を話します I speak English everyday
7. これは私のバイクです This is my bike	7. これは私のバイクです This is my bike
8. 今すぐ手を洗ってください!! Wash your hands now!!	8. 今すぐ手を洗ってください!! Wash your hands now!!
9. 今日は晴れています It is sunny today	9. 今日は晴れています It are sunny yesterday
10. 今日は疲れました I am tired today	10. 今日は疲れました I are tire today

Correctly Translated English Sentences   **Translated English Sentences**

Fig. 7. Translated English sentences (right) are compared with the correct English sentences (left) in the grading task experiments.

addition, subjects were asked to tally their results on a spreadsheet. We measured the total amount of time it took for subjects to complete their grading tasks.

Two types of experiments were performed. In the first experiment, subjects were required to grade the sentences based on the following criteria. Each English-translated sentence consisted of four words. If the four words in the translated sentence matched all four words of the correct English sentence, subjects were to draw a "○" inside a square next to the sentence. If the number of un-matched words were greater than or equal to one, they were asked to draw "/". In the second experiment, if all four words of the translated sentence matched the words in the correct English sentence, they were to draw a "○"; if just one word did not match, they were to draw a "△"; and if the total number of unmatched words were greater than one, they were to draw a "/". Whenever they drew a "△", they were to draw a one-digit number as partial credit.

We compared the case that the subjects conducted grading without utilizing GERMIC with the case with utilizing GERMIC. In order to maintain a fairness in the comparison, we divided the subjects into the two groups: the group conducts grading with GERMIC after grading manually, the other group conducts grading manually after grading with GERMIC.

Table 1. Confusion matrix of diagram recognition for each subject.

I \ O	Subject 1			Subject 2			Subject 3			Subject 4			Subject 5			Accuracy
	O	△	/	O	△	/	O	△	/	O	△	/	O	△	/	
O	10			8	2		10			8	2		9	1		90%
△	2	8		1	9			10		1	9		3	7		86%
/			10			10			10			10			10	100%

Fig. 8. Case that drawn circle "O" misrecognized as triangle "△".

Fig. 9. Case that drawn triangle "△" misrecognized as circle "O".

4.1 Accuracy of Diagram Recognition

The results of diagram recognition for each subject compared to each subjects' diagram drawing is shown in Table 1. The recognition rate for "/" was 100% while recognition errors occurred between "O" and "△". It appeared that "O" tended to be misrecognized as "△" because the number of discernible feature points fell below 23 whenever the circle was drawn too small as shown in Fig. 8. In contrast, "△" tended to be misrecognized as "O" whenever the number of feature points were greater than or equal to 23 such that the triangle resembled more like a circle as shown in Fig. 9.

4.2 Accuracy of Number Recognition

The results of number recognition for each subject compared to each subject's number drawing is shown in Table 2. Correct recognition rates for "4," "5," and "7" are lower relative to the other numbers. It is assumed that users were not used to drawing such three numbers with one stroke: "4" tended to be misrecognized as "9" whenever the horizontal line was too short as circled in red in Fig. 10, "5" tends to be misrecognized as "3" or "6" when the lines shown in a red circle in Fig. 11 stick together, and "7" tends to be misrecognized as "9" when the entire number is drawn diagonally as shown in Fig. 12 and as "1" when the width of the number is too short. The accuracy rate is lower than the 99.3% accuracy of the CNN model. This is because GERMIC automatically reads trailing without

Table 2. Confusion matrix of number recognition for each subject.

I \ O	Subject 1									Subject 2									Subject 3									Subject 4									Subject 5									Accuracy
	1	2	3	4	5	6	7	8	9	1	2	3	4	5	6	7	8	9	1	2	3	4	5	6	7	8	9	1	2	3	4	5	6	7	8	9	1	2	3	4	5	6	7	8	9	
1	10									10									8		1						1	10									10									96%
2	1	9									9	1								10									9	1								10								94%
3			10								2	7						1			10									10								1	8	1						90%
4				8					2				8					2				4		1		3	2				8	1								8					2	72%
5				1	7	2							1	9							2		5	2	1							10							1	1	8					78%
6						10								1	9									10									10									1	9			96%
7	1						8	1		1						8									8	2								8								1	1	7	1	70%
8								9	1								10									10									10									9	1	96%
9			1					2	7									10									10								1	9							1	1	8	88%

Table 3. Comparison of the time taken to complete grading tasks only with "○" and "/" between the case without GERMIC and the case with GERMIC.

	Without GERMIC			With GERMIC
	Scoring (sec)	Tallying (sec)	Total Grading (sec)	Grading (sec)
Subject 1	258	216	474	309
Subject 2	243	197	440	277
Subject 3	248	148	396	385
Subject 4	183	230	413	284
Subject 5	204	139	343	301

pressing the button, thus, the beginning and the end of the trail tends to get limp. At this point, we can expect further improvement of recognition accuracy by removing such fluctuation of a line.

4.3 Effectiveness of GERMIC in Real Environment

We evaluated GERMIC in two different real environment simulations and measured its effectiveness. Hereafter, the results are described.

Effectiveness in Grading Tasks with "○" and "/" Only. The results of a GERMIC-based grading task when using only diagram types "○" and "/" for scoring is shown in Table 3. A grading task conducted manually without GERMIC involves scoring each sentence by marking a "○" and "/" and tallying the results in a spreadsheet; whereas a grading task using GERMIC only requires the scoring each sentence with a mark since GERMIC does the rest in terms of recognition, storage, and output of the results in a spreadsheet. This difference is reflected in the results, which shows that all of subjects completed their scoring task faster without GERMIC but on the whole completed their grading task faster (102 s or 24.7% faster on average) with GERMIC.

Effectiveness in Grading Tasks with "○", "/", and "△". The result of a GERMIC-based grading tasks when using diagram types "○", "/", and "△" for scoring is shown in Table 4. All subjects completed their scoring task faster without GERMIC but on the whole completed their grading task faster with GERMIC by 107.6 s or 14.9% on average.

Fig. 10. Case that drawn number "4" tends to be misrecognized as "9". (Color figure online)

Fig. 11. Case that drawn number "5" tends to be misrecognized as "3" or "6". (Color figure online)

Fig. 12. Case that drawn number "7" tends to be misrecognized as "1" or "9".

Table 4. Comparison of the time taken to complete grading tasks with "○", "/", and "△" between the case without GERMIC and the case with GERMIC.

	Without GERMIC			With GERMIC
	Scoring (sec)	Tallying (sec)	Total Grading (sec)	Grading (sec)
Subject 1	593	238	831	694
Subject 2	407	353	760	555
Subject 3	395	259	654	651
Subject 4	467	268	735	608
Subject 5	417	212	629	563

We also found that the subjects especially who were good at calculations could complete their grading tasks much faster than the others and the subjects especially who were good at operating the PC could complete their tallying tasks much faster than the others.

Feedback from Subjects. Subjects commonly reported that they would not have completed their grading tasks as quickly without GERMIC, and that they did not feel burdened by the interactive correction mechanism once they became familiar with using it. One subject felt he to wait a little while for voice feedback (feedback was given within 1 s after starting processing the handwritten character). We intend to continue improving GERMIC to reduce delay time. Another subject stated that she would have preferred voice over manual correction of a recognition error. We intend to look for a better interface to perform corrections and to find other applications for GERMIC.

5 Conclusion

The usage of conventional systems which support graders is limited from the view of environment and infrastructure e.g., automatic grading machines and tablet-based scoring systems require rich infrastructure. Besides, the system which supports manual grading hardly exists. When it comes to materializing such system, we must think of applying hand gesture recognition as there is a large number of systems perform gesture recognition. However, in such systems, recognition is performed on a user's consecutive motion without regard to retrial or alternation by the user even though that is likely to occur.

We proposed GERMIC as a gesture-based recognition system to assist with manual grading tasks. The important feature of GERMIC is its interactive correction mechanism, which is the integration of handwritten character recognition and voice feedback to enable users to correct recognition errors. We evaluated the effectiveness of GERMIC by conducting grading task experiments using the system. Subjects were asked to use GERMIC as they were grading a translation exercise. We found that all subjects completed their grading tasks much faster using GREMIC than when they were manually grading. In addition, handwritten diagrams and numbers were recognized by the system with high accuracy. Subjects indicated that they did not feel burdened by using the interactive correction mechanism once they became familiar with using it. Therefore, GERMIC significantly shortened the total time for completing the grading tasks without burdening the user and demonstrated the effectiveness of the interactive correction mechanism based on the gesture recognition model.

Acknowledgement. This research has been supported by the Kayamori Foundation of Informational Science Advancement.

References

1. Bulling, A., Blanke, U., Schiele, B.: A tutorial on human activity recognition using body-worn inertial sensors. ACM Comput. Surv. (CSUR) **46**(3), 33 (2014)
2. Ortiz, J.L.R., Oneto, L., Samá, A., Parra, X., Anguit, D.: Transition-aware human activity recognition using smartphones. Neurocomputing **171**(C), 754–767 (2016)
3. Ren, Z., Meng, J., Yuan, J., Zhantg, Z.: Robust hand gesture recognition with kinect sensor. In: Proceedings of 19th ACM International Conference on Multimedia, pp. 759–760 (2011)
4. Ren, Z., Yuan, J., Zhang, Z.: Robust hand gesture recognition based on finger-earth mover's distance with a commodity depth camera. In: Proceedings of 19th ACM International Conference on Multimedia, pp. 1093–1096 (2011)

5. Kuwahara, N., Kogure, K., Ohmura, A., Noma, H.: Wearable sensors for auto-event-recording on medical nursing - user study of ergonomic design. In: 2012 16th International Symposium on Wearable Computers, pp. 8–15 (2004)
6. Westerfield, G., Mitrovic, A., Billinghurst, M.: Intelligent augmented reality training for motherboard assembly. Int. J. Artif. Intell. Educ. **25**(1), 157–172 (2015)
7. Radkowski, R., Herrema, J., Oliver, J.: Augmented reality-based manual assembly support with visual features for different degrees of difficulty. Ind. Prod. Eng. **34**(5), 362–374 (2015)
8. Johnson, W., Jellinek, H., Klotz Jr., L., Rao, R., Card, S.: Bridging the paper and electronic worlds. In: Proceedings of INTERACT 1993 and CHI 1993 Conference on Human Factors in Computing Systems, pp. 507–512 (1993)
9. Bayar, G.: The use of hough transform to develop an intelligent grading system for the multiple choice exam papers. Proc. Karaelmas Sci. Eng. **6**(1), 100–104 (2016)
10. Benedito, J.L.P., Aragón, E.Q., Alriols, J.A., Medic, L.: Optical mark recognition in student continuous assessment. IEEE Rev. Iberoam. de Tecnol. del Aprendiz. **9**(4), 133–138 (2014)
11. Atasoy, H., Yildirim, E., Kutlu, Y., Tohma, K.: Webcam based real-time robust optical mark recognition. In: Arik, S., Huang, T., Lai, W.K., Liu, Q. (eds.) ICONIP 2015. LNCS, vol. 9490, pp. 449–456. Springer, Cham (2015). https://doi.org/10.1007/978-3-319-26535-3_51
12. Koile, K., Chevalier, K., Low, C., Pal, S., Rogal, A., Singer, D., Sorensen, J., Tay, K.S., Wu, K.: Supporting pen-based classroom interaction: new findings and functionality for classroom learning partner. In: Proceedings of International Workshop on Pen-Based Learning Technologies (PLT 2007), pp. 1–7 (2007)
13. Koile, K., Chevalier, K., Rbeiz, M., Rogal, A., Singer, D., Sorensen, J., Smith, A., Tay, K.S., Wu, K.: Supporting feedback and assessment of digital ink answers to in-class exercises. In: Proceedings of 22nd National Conference on Artificial Intelligence, pp. 1787–1794 (2007)
14. Tay, K.S., Koile, K.: Improving digital ink interpretation through expected type prediction and dynamic dispatch. In: Proceedings of 19th International Conference on Pattern Recognition, pp. 1–4 (2008)
15. Edwards, S.: Work-in-progress: program grading and feedback generation with web-CAT. In: Proceedings of 1st ACM Conference on Learning@ Scale Conference, pp. 215–216 (2014)
16. Caiza, J., Alamo, J.M.D.: Programming assignments automatic grading: review of tools and implementations. In: Proceedings of 7th International Technology, Education and Development Conference (INTED 2013), pp. 5691–5700 (2013)
17. Yamamoto, M., Umemura, N., Kawano, H.: Automated essay scoring system based on rubric. In: Lee, R. (ed.) ACIT 2017. Studies in Computational Intelligence, vol. 727, pp. 177–190. Springer, Cham (2018). https://doi.org/10.1007/978-3-319-64051-8_11
18. Liu, M., Li, Y., Xu, W., Liu, L.: Automated essay feedback generation and its impact in the revision. IEEE Trans. Learn. Technol. **PP**(99), 1 (2016)
19. Nguyen, D.M., Hsieh, J., Allen, G.D.: The impact of web-based assessment and practice on students' mathematics learning attitudes. Math. Sci. Teach. **25**(3), 251–279 (2006)
20. Rosten, E., Drummond, T.: Machine learning for high-speed corner detection. In: Leonardis, A., Bischof, H., Pinz, A. (eds.) ECCV 2006. LNCS, vol. 3951, pp. 430–443. Springer, Heidelberg (2006). https://doi.org/10.1007/11744023_34
21. Amma, C., Georgi, M., Schultz, T.: Airwriting: a wearable handwriting recognition system. Pers. Ubiquit. Comput. **18**(1), 191–203 (2014)

22. Ahmad, A.R., Khalia, M., Gaudin, C.V., Poisson, E.: Online handwriting recognition using support vector machine. In: Proceedings of 2004 IEEE Region 10 Conference TENCON 2004, vol. 1, pp. 311–314 (2004)
23. Doetsch, P., Kozielski, M., Ney, H.: Fast and robust training of recurrent neural networks for offline handwriting recognition. In: Proceedings of 2014 14th International Conference on Frontiers in Handwriting Recognition, pp. 279–284 (2014)
24. Suen, C.Y., Tan, J.: Analysis of errors of handwritten digits made by a multitude of classifiers. Pattern Recogn. Lett. **26**(3), 369–379 (2005)

SmokeSense: Online Activity Recognition Framework on Smartwatches

Muhammad Shoaib[1], Ozlem Durmaz Incel[2(✉)], Hans Scholten[1], and Paul Havinga[1]

[1] Pervasive Systems Research Group, University of Twente, Enschede, The Netherlands
{m.shoaib,hans.scholten,p.j.m.havinga}@utwente.nl
[2] Department of Computer Engineering, Galatasaray University, Istanbul, Turkey
odincel@gsu.edu.tr

Abstract. In most cases, human activity recognition (AR) with smartphones and smartwatches has been done offline due to the limited resources of these devices. Initially, these devices were used for logging sensor data which was later on processed in machine learning tools on a desktop or laptop. However, current versions of these devices are more capable of running an activity recognition system. Therefore, in this paper, we present SmokeSense, an online activity recognition (AR) framework developed for both smartphones and smartwatches on Android platform. This framework can log data from various sensors and can run an AR process in real-time locally on these devices. Any classifier or feature can easily be added on demand. As a case study, we evaluate the recognition performance of smoking with four classifiers, four features, and two sensors on a smartwatch. The activity set includes variants of smoking such as smoking while sitting, standing, walking, biking, as well as other similar activities. Our analysis shows that, similar recognition performance can be achieved in an online recognition as in an offline analysis, even if no training data is available for some smoking postures. We also propose a smoking session detection algorithm to count the number of cigarettes smoked and evaluate its performance.

1 Introduction

Human activity recognition using smartphones and smartwatches has enabled many novel, context-aware applications in different domains, especially healthcare [1]. Such devices were initially considered as resource-limited [2] such as the battery capacity, for running an activity recognition system over an extended period. It is also a challenging task to implement and evaluate different recognition systems on these devices. Due to these reasons, most of the research on human activity recognition using these devices is done offline (not on the device) in machine learning tools, such as WEKA or scikit-learn [3–8]. In recent years, smartphones and some smartwatch models have become capable of running such recognition systems. They have become more powerful in terms of

© ICST Institute for Computer Sciences, Social Informatics and Telecommunications Engineering 2018
K. Murao et al. (Eds.): MobiCASE 2018, LNICST 240, pp. 106–124, 2018.
https://doi.org/10.1007/978-3-319-90740-6_7

available resources, such as CPU, memory, and battery, so there has been a shift towards online activity recognition. In online recognition, the human activity recognition process is run on the device (smartphone or a smartwatch) in real-time. Offline analysis can be acceptable for applications where online recognition is not required [9]. For example, if the aim is to follow the sleeping patterns of a user, sensor data can be uploaded to a server and processed offline where real-time tracking is not necessary. However, if we aim to recognize smoking sessions of a user, online processing of the data on the watch or phone may be required. Online activity recognition on a local device (smartphone or smartwatch) does not depend on the internet connection all the time and also avoids the privacy concerns if users do not want their data to be uploaded to a server or cloud. It is important to note that "online activity recognition on smartphones" should not be confused with "online machine learning models". "Online machine learning models" are able to adapt themselves according to new data points, unlike offline or batch learning models [10]. We use the "online" term in a different way, for the practical implementation of activity recognition systems on mobile phones. These implemented systems can use either an online or a batch learning model.

There are a number of studies where activity recognition has been implemented on smartphones for real-time processing [11]. However, there are very few recent studies where such activity systems have been implemented and evaluated for their recognition performance as well as resource consumption on a smartwatch [12–14]. In most of these studies, especially on the smartwatch, it is very difficult to compare various aspects of an activity recognition system due to their different experimental setups. For example, they have used different classifiers, datasets, data features, platforms, performance metrics, validation methods, number of users, and implementations. Additionally, performance results of an online analysis and offline analysis can be different since conditions are usually idealized in an offline setting: there is no missing data, there is large size of training data, etc.

In this paper, we present SmokeSense, an online activity recognition framework for both smartphones and smartwatches. Our aim is to address the mentioned issues, validate the offline analysis results from our previous studies [15,16] and to compare various aspects of an activity recognition system in a similar environment and similar experimental setup. Based on this framework, we implemented a modular Android application for these devices where various classifiers, data features, sampling rates, and sensors can be evaluated for their recognition performance in an online maner. In this specific study, we evaluated the recognition performance of four commonly used classifiers on both a smartphone for recognizing seven physical activities[1] and on a smarwatch for recognizing the smoking activity. Smoking is one of the reasons for premature death and its reliable detection can enable tracking of smoking behavior [18,19]. Additionally, it can be used as an automated self-reporting tool in smoking cessation programs [18,19]. While performing these evaluations for smoking detection, we

---

[1] However, due to page size limitation we only present the results of smoking recognition. Interested readers can refer to [17].

consider two sensors, an accelerometer, a gyroscope and their combinations, considering both subject-specific training models and generic training models. Our results show that, similar recognition performance is achieved as in our offline analysis [16]. The use of the gyroscope besides an accelerometer has improved the recognition performance. Although subject-specific training models are observed to exhibit better performance, generic models also perform well at an acceptable level. Moreover, we learned that smoking while sitting is difficult to recognize compared to other postures due to its similarity to drinking while sitting. We also showed that smoking can be well recognized in different postures, such as while biking, from which no training data was available. Moreover, using a hierarchical classification approach for smoothing the results of windowing segments increased the recognition rates. We also evaluated the impact of various aspects (different classifiers, features, sampling rates, window sizes, activities, devices, sensors) of an activity recognition system on its resource consumption (CPU, memory, and battery) in [20]. We summarize our contributions as follows:

- From the system point of view, we developed a framework for online human activity recognition using smartphones and smartwatches. Compared to online recognition systems existing in the literature [], this framework can be used to detect any activity using smart watches and smart phones and it is an adaptive framework: any classifier, sensor, feature set can be added on demand.
- From the health care point of view, we proposed a rule-based smoking session detection algorithm where the aim is to detect the number of cigarettes smoked. This algorithm can be used as an automated self-reporting tool in smoking cessation programs.
- From the methodological point of view, we evaluated the recognition performance of the smoking activity on a smartwatch in real-time, considering different postures, such as while sitting, standing and in a group conversation. Compared to other studies in the literature where the analysis is done offline, all the analysis was performed for real-time recognition and even in a posture, smoking while biking, from which no training data was available.

The rest of the paper is organized as follows: In Sect. 2, we present the related studies and compare those with our study. We describe our framework for online activity recognition in Sect. 3. In Sect. 4, we present our performance evaluations. Finally, we present the conclusions, and future work in Sect. 5.

2   Related Work

Human activity recognition using smartphone sensors has been studied extensively for the last few years [1,11,21]. As mentioned, most of the work in this area is performed offline such that collected data is analyzed in machine learning tools, such as WEKA, Scikit-learn, R, and MATLAB. Activity recognition using smartwatch sensors is still relatively new, compared to smartphones. Most of the work using smartwatch sensors is also being done offline [22–26].

Recently, researchers have been moving towards online activity recognition in order to verify the offline results and to analyze the resource consumption of machine learning algorithms on mobile phones and other wearable devices such as smartwatches [27]. In a recent survey paper [11], we reviewed the studies that implement activity recognition systems on mobile phones. However, in these studies, only a few classifiers are tested, different platforms, datasets and experimental setups are used. Online activity recognition and in-device learning [28] on wearable device sensors is still relatively a new topic [12–14]. In these studies, battery consumption of sensor logging and online activity recognition process on smarwatches has been investigated. However, similar to the studies on mobile phones, different setups and use of different methods make it difficult to compare the results.

In this paper, our aim is to propose a conceptual framework and build an adaptive online activity recognition system that can run on smartphones and smarwatches where different classifiers, training methods, features, sensors can be added on demand. We aim to provide a testing platform also for other researchers to verify the results obtained in offline analysis.

Smoking recognition is one of the case studies that we performed for testing the framework, besides physical activity recognition. Most of the work on smoking recognition is done offline such that collected data is analyzed using machine learning tool on a desktop machine with no implementation on a smartwatch or smartphone. For example, studies in [18,29–31] follow such an offline approach for smoking recognition whereas in [32], the authors implemented the smoking recognition pipeline on the smartphone. However, to the best of our knowledge, none of these studies have evaluated online smoking recognition on a smartwatch. We previously published our results of offline analysis for smoking recognition using smartwatches and collected one of the largest smoking activity dataset [16]. In Table 1 in [16], we compare these smoking recognition studies in detail with our offline work and we also discuss the gaps in these existing studies. Unlike our work, most of these studies focused on an offline analysis, person-dependent evaluation, limited smoking postures, and combining other sensors with a smartwatch. Different than these studies, we perform an online smoking recognition analysis based on the proposed SmokeSense framework.

3   SmokeSense: A Framework for Online Activity Recognition

The activity recognition process can be divided into various components such as sensing, feature extraction, training, and classification. The generic activity recognition process is described in Fig. 1. It starts with sensing (step 1), if needed the collected sensor data can be preprocessed (step 2), features are extracted (step 3), a training model is created (step 4a) and in the final stage, the trained classifiers are used to classify new data instances into different activities (step 4b). This process can be divided into offline and online categories. In online activity recognition, the classification is done on the device (phone or wearable

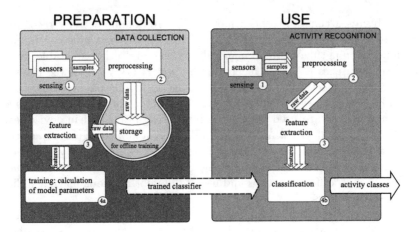

Fig. 1. Activity recognition process (The numbers (1, 2, 3, 4a, 4b shows the order of the steps involved in this process)

device). However, the training can still be done in two ways: online (on the device) and offline. The training can be very time and resource consuming, that is why it is usually done offline. We have opted for offline training in this work. We use offline training and then port these trained models to the mobile phone and the smartwatch.

3.1   Framework

We propose a conceptual framework for online activity recognition which integrates both smart phones and smart watches. These two devices are commonly used in combination and a lot of people already use/wear them. They are already connected with each other through Bluetooth. Therefore, we want to utilize sensing information from both these devices at different levels for richer context or activity recognition. For example, the smartwatch can send raw sensor information or extracted features to the smartphone where it can be combined with smartphone sensors for richer contextual information. However, we can also run the complete activity recognition process on the smartwatch and send the information about the recognized activities to the smartphone. In this case, models on smartwatch and smartphone can be trained to detect different activities, such as activities involving hand gestures can be detected using a smartwatch whereas the others can be identified using the smartphone. For example, the smartwatch can detect that a user is smoking or eating whereas the phone can detect the user's posture at that specific time such that if the user is doing this specific activity while sitting or standing or walking. We should note that, other wearable devices, such as smart glasses, that can run AR process can be integrated to the framework.

The framework consists of three main components: Activity recognition (AR) process on a smartphone, AR process on a smartwatch, and a machine learning tool (WEKA) for training models as shown in Fig. 2. In this framework, first a machine learning model is trained offline in WEKA. Then it is ported to the smartwatch and a smartphone in a serialized form. Afterwards, the AR process reads sensor data in real-time, preprocesses it, extract features over a segmented window (30 s) and then uses the trained model to predict the activity class of this segmented window. The smartwatch can also run the complete activity recognition process as well as sending raw sensor information or extracted features to the smartphone at the same time. For this purpose, we define the following modes of operation for this framework on how information can be processed and exchanged between the smartphone and the smartwatch.

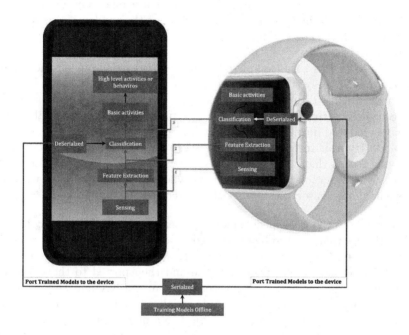

Fig. 2. Online activity recognition framework

– On phone only: In this mode, the whole AR process (sensing, feature extraction, and classification) runs on the phone and utilizes the phone sensors only. We do not utilize smartwatch in this mode. For example, if a user does not have a smartwatch, only this mode of operation can be used.
– On Watch only: In this mode, the complete AR process runs on the watch and utilizes the watch sensors only. It can send the predicted labels for the activities to the smartphone via Bluetooth for storing and displaying purpose. However, it can also store and display these on the watch.
– On both devices: In this mode, both smartphone and smartwatch are being used in the AR process. The smartphone always runs the complete AR process. However, we divide the AR process on the smartwatch into further modes of operation and these are shown with numbers (1, 2, and 3) in Fig. 2.

- Mode 1: In this case, only sensing is performed on the smartwatch such that smartwatch sends raw sensor information to the smartphone in real-time where they are combined with smartphone sensors before processing them for feature extraction and classification. Using this mode means more resource consumption because we will be using Bluetooth very frequently and will be sending a lot of data with each transfer. For example, we use 50 samples per second for reading sensor data.
- Mode 2: In this case, features are extracted from smartwatch sensors and these features are sent to the smartphone where they are combined with the features extracted from smartphone sensors before they enter into the classification phase. This mode should use relatively low resources because we will be sending only features after the window size is reached. However, if the number of features is very high then it may consume more resources as well.
- Mode 3: In this case, complete AR process is carried out on the smartwatch where only smartwatch sensors are used whereas in parallel smartphone runs its own AR process using its own sensors. We only send the recognized activities' labels to the smartphone. However, these labels can be stored and displayed on the watch too.
- Mode Hybrid: In this case, mode 3 can be combined with mode 1 or mode 2 such that smartwatch runs its own AR process and it also sends sensor information to the smartphone where it can be combined with the smartphone sensors for better activity recognition.

The decision to choose a specific mode of operation depends on many factors such as activities that need to be recognized, resources availability, and application requirements. For the training component, WEKA tool can be used where machine learning models are trained offline and then ported to these devices. After training these models, they are serialized in WEKA and stored in the relevant Android Apps where they are de-serialized at the time of their use. *Serialization* is the process of saving an object in a persistent form such as on a hard-disk as a byte stream. *Deserialization* is the reverse process where such serialized objects are converted back to its original form. This process is described in WEKA documentation [33].

We have implemented our Android app in a modular way based on the conceptual framework shown in Fig. 2, where the training is done offline in WEKA. For sensing, we have implemented the use of an accelerometer, a linear acceleration sensor, and a gyroscope. However, other sensors can easily be added to the implementation as per demand. For feature extraction, we have implemented min, max, mean and standard deviation. Other features can be added if needed. For classification part, the trained models from WEKA are used to predict the current window of sensor data and maps it to the relevant activity. These trained models can be placed in the asset or other folders in our app and they are ready to use. These three modules or parts are implemented as an Android service which runs in the background and does not need any user interaction. The app can be used in three modes: On phone only, on watch only, on both devices (only with option 3). Though we have implemented mode/option 3, the other options can be added a later stage. The current implementations are enough for the evaluation of the resources consumption and recognition performance of our use cases.

In our specific use case, we run smoking recognition process on the smartwatch. For training purpose, we used a dataset described in detail in [16]. We added an additional data of around 5 h to the data set in order to improve the null or other class, so smoking should not be confused with other activities. This additional data comes from a participant who took part in the evaluation of this study. He performed various activities such as drinking, eating, walking, biking, washing dishes, cooking, taking part in conversations, inactive (sitting, standing, laying in bed etc.) and others. We used WEKA tool for training the models because it is a java based toolkit which provides an easy to use serialization of these trained models. These serialized trained models can easily be ported to Android where we de-serialize them at run time to use them for real-time predictions.

We trained four classifiers in WEKA 3.7: decision tree (DT), support vector machine (SMO), random forest (RF), multilayer perceptron (MLP). We use these classifiers in their default settings except few changes. These changes were made for random forest. For random forest, we used two variants: one with 9 number of trees and other with 99. The default setting can easily be found in WEKA documentation [34]. For this specific study, we did not use any parameter optimization algorithms. These four classifiers were chosen because they have been previously shown to have reasonable recognition performance for recognizing various human activities [11]. Moreover, they were also chosen in a way that they represent various types of algorithms.

3.2 Smoking Session Detection Algorithm

It is important to detect the number of cigarettes smoked or smoking sessions. There are two ways to do so. One way is to sum the total number of smoking segments, convert that into total time spent while smoking and then divide it by the average smoking time per cigarette. This method works well if the underlying classification provides reasonable recognition performance for smoking. For example, it gives a higher number of smoking sessions if the false positive rate is high. Hence, it is important to correct as many as possible misclassified segments before we apply this method. The drawback with this method is that we cannot know the timing of each smoking session. If the underlying classification is poor, then it will lead to too many false positives. In the second method, smoking sessions can be calculated using a simple rule-based algorithm where it takes into account the neighboring segments for a specific amount of time and uses a threshold to decide if it is a smoking session or not. For this purpose, we developed a simple rule-based algorithm to detect these sessions. This algorithm is described in Fig. 3. We continuously monitor the prediction results of the classification function. We trigger a smoking session calculator as soon as we see a smoking segment. We also start counting the number of detected smoking segments after this trigger. We stop the session calculator in two cases:

- When an already defined session window size is reached. In our case, we use a window size of ten minutes as shown by *SWCthreshold* in Fig. 3.
- When there are no smoking segments for at least a specified amount of time. In our case, it was set to be at least 2 min as shown by the *OCthreshold* in Fig. 3. It helps in removing the random hand gestures classified as smoking.

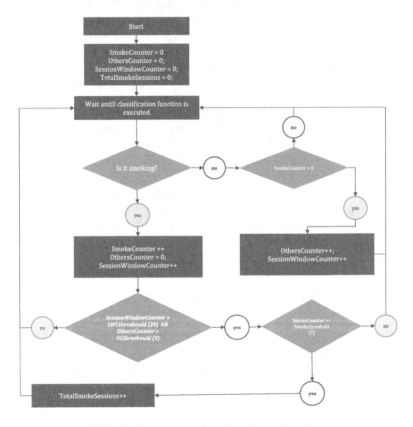

Fig. 3. Smoking session detection algorithm

After one these two conditions have been reached, then we see if there were at least seven segments of smoking in this session, shown in Fig. 3 by *Smokethreshold*. The average duration of a smoking session for our user in the testing phase was six minutes (12 segments). Therefore, we choose seven (7 segments: three and half minutes) as a threshold. If there are smoking predictions for more than half the average smoking session duration, then it should be classified as a smoking session. This value can be person-dependent. However, smokers can be asked at the start of using our app for their average smoking session duration. If we know that time, then this threshold can be automatically calculated for smokers according to their average smoking session duration. In Sect. 4.3, we evaluate the performance of this algorithm.

4   Performance Evaluation

For performance analysis, we trained four classifiers in WEKA: DT, SMO, RF, MLP. In this section, we first present the results of smoking recognition, using different sensors and different training models, namely subject-specific and generic training. Next, we evaluate the performance of smoking in a posture from which no training data was available. We also carried a resource consumption analysis while running online recognition algorithms. Our analysis show that the smartwatch's battery (LG R: 410 mAH) lasts for around eight hours while running a smoking recognition app using the accelerometer sensor only. The use of gyroscope in addition to an accelerometer decreases the battery life by almost an hour. The impact of classifiers' prediction task is very low on the battery except for KNN classifier because it runs through the whole dataset. In terms of memory usage, DT, MLP, SMO and RF (with 9 trees) classifiers occupy 12 to 13 MBs, while RF with 99 trees occupy 28 MBs. Model sizes are 19 KB for SMO, 137 KB for DT, 947 KB for MLP and RF (9 trees), while it is 10397 KBs for RF with 99 trees. The resource consumption analysis is discussed in detail in our other published work [20].

Finally, we analyze the performance of the proposed smoking session detection algorithm. Our evaluations involved a single participant and the results can be considered as indicative. However, these online results are found to be similar to our offline results from our previous study [16], and we expect it to be not so different if tested with a higher number of users. Additionally, in this paper our focus is more on the presentation of the framework and the smoking session recognition algorithm and the system can be tested with more participants for a more detailed performance analysis.

4.1   Smoking Recognition

For smoking recognition, we tested the four mentioned classifiers with one participant who also participated in the initial data collection phase presented in [16]. This participant wore a smartwatch (LG Watch R) at his right wrist and carried a smartphone (Samsung Galaxy S2) in his right pant's pocket for a couple of hours every day. The testing was spread over three weeks. He smoked 45 cigarettes over the testing period in various postures: 15 while standing, 15 while sitting, and 15 while walking. He also performed his daily activities during this testing time, such as working on a computer, taking lunch, drinking coffee, cooking, washing dishes, and many other activities.

In order to compare different scenarios, we created multiple versions of our app where each version was configured to run a specific scenario. Each scenario was defined by three components:

- Training Models: we trained the machine learning algorithms in two ways. (1) Using subject specific data: In this case, we only used data from this specific participant for training purpose who was taking part in our testing phase. (2) Using data from eleven participants: In this case, we used data from other nine participants and our current participant for training purpose. In this way, we can test both generic and subject-specific training models. In this dataset, we collected a dataset of 45 h for smoking and other similar activities such as eating and drinking coffee or tea. Out of these 45 h, the smoking activity was performed for 16.86 h in various forms such as smoking while sitting, standing, walking and in a group conversation. Each activity was performed multiple times by each participant on various days over a period of three months. Usually, the participants smoked 1–4 cigarettes (1 cigarette per session) in a day. In the meanwhile, they were also performing eating and drinking activities on different days according to their availability. Each participant wore a smart-watch (LG Watch R, LG Watch Urbane, Sony Watch 3) on the right wrist and a smartphone in the right pocket as all participants were right-handed. We collected data from multiple sensors from both smartwatch and smartphone, however, we only use accelerometer and gyroscope in this study. The data was collected at 50 samples per second from these sensors. For data collection, we developed our own Android application which can collect data from multiple sensors, both from the phone and smartwatch in real-time at a user-provided sampling rate. The details about this data is described in detail in [16]. We used 10-fold stratified cross-validation for evaluating our training models in WEKA.
- Sensor combinations: we used the accelerometer alone and also its combination with the gyroscope to see if there were any improvements due to such addition.
- Classifiers: For real-time activity recognition, we used four classifiers: SMO, RF9, MLP, and DT. Initially, we also tested with naive Bayes and KNN, however, we did not include them in this study because the recognition performance of naive Bayes was very low whereas running KNN was computationally expensive.

Each version of our app was running a specific scenario. These scenarios are shown in Table 1. For example, one version was running SMO classifier with the accelerometer alone whereas, the other was using the accelerometer with a gyroscope. In both these cases, the training data was coming from this specific participant who was doing the testing. However, at the same time, we were also running two other versions with similar configuration but the training data was coming from all ten participants. Similarly, four such versions were running for RF9. For MLP and DT, we used only its versions with accelerometer because we did not want to overload the CPU. All these different versions of our app were running at the same time.

As the performance metric, we choose F-measure as our classes are imbalanced. For example, the time spent during smoking was around 5 h whereas the rest of the activities were performed for around 38 h. This can also be seen

Table 1. Real-time smoking recognition scenarios

Scenario	Classifier	Sensors	Training method
1	SMO^A	Accelerometer	Subject-specific
2	SMO^{AG}	Accelerometer + Gyroscope	Subject-specific
3	RF^A	Accelerometer	Subject-specific
4	RF^{AG}	Accelerometer + Gyroscope	Subject-specific
5	DT^A	Accelerometer	Subject-specific
6	MLP^A	Accelerometer	Subject-specific
7	SMO^A	Accelerometer	Generic
8	SMO^{AG}	Accelerometer + Gyroscope	Generic
9	RF^A	Accelerometer	Generic
10	RF^{AG}	Accelerometer + Gyroscope	Generic
11	DT^A	Accelerometer	Generic
12	MLP^A	Accelerometer	Generic

Table 2. Confusion matrices of various classifiers for smoking activity

			SMO^A		SMO^{AG}		$RF9^A$		$RF9^{AG}$		DT^A		MLP^A	
			Smoking	Others	Smoking	Others	Smoking	Others	Smoking	Others	Smoking	Others	Smoking	Others
Actual	subject-specific Classifiers	Smoking	467	115	495	87	495	87	522	60	443	139	509	73
		Others	105	4366	106	4365	107	4364	98	4373	118	4353	124	4347
	Generic Classifiers	Smoking	459	123	496	86	475	107	504	78	462	120	499	83
		Others	254	4217	223	4248	224	4247	267	4204	275	4196	267	4204

(Predicted As)

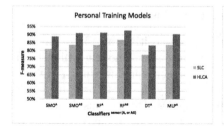

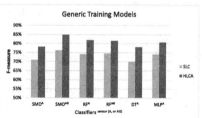

(a) Using subject-specific Training   (b) Using Generic Training

Fig. 4. Impact of various factors on recognition performance of smoking

from the confusion matrices in Table 2. However, we also use true positive rate or recall in some cases where we compare smoking in various postures because in such cases, true positive rate gives a better insight on their comparison. As shown in Table 2, when only accelerometer is used, MLP classifier performs the best in recognizing smoking, which is followed by RF both in subject-specific training and generic training. However, false positive rate of RF is lower (others recognized as smoking). When accelerometer is combined with gyroscope, missclassification rates decrease for all the classifiers.

In Fig. 4, we present the F-measure results obtained with different classifiers with either accelerometer or in combination with gyroscope. In Fig. 4a, results of using a subject-specific traning model are presented, while in Fig. 4b, results of using a generic training model are presented. Additionally, we ran single layer classification approach (mentioned as SLC in the figures) with our four classifiers in their default mode, as well as a hierarchical lazy classification algorithm (HLCA), proposed in [16]. Simply, HLCA is a rule based algorithm where classification results of activity recognition segments are smoothed/corrected by comparing with the results of neighboring data segments, considering the fact that human activities do not change instantly. In Fig. 4, results of using a single layer classification and HLCA are both presented. When we compare the results obtained with using a subject-specific model and a generic model, using a subject-specific model achieves better recognition rates, which is approximately 5% better. However, with generic models, still we achieve up to 85% F-measure with SMO and accelerometer and gyroscope combination. As mentioned, using gyroscope besides an accelerometer increases the recognition rates, however, this may increase the battery consumption on the devices, as we further investigated in [17].

When we compare the results of single layer classification with HLCA, as expected, we observed improvements in F-measure as observed also in our previous work [16] for offline recognition. Most of the misclassifications were corrected by taking into account the information among neighboring data segments. The observed improvements due to the addition gyroscope and due to the use HLCA can be seen in this figure.

4.2   Smoking Recognition with Different Postures

In Fig. 5, we present the recognition results (true positive rate) in different postures. We observe that it is relatively easy to recognize smoking while standing and while walking, but relatively difficult to detect smoking while sitting. The motion pattern of smoking while sitting can be very similar to drinking coffee or tea sometimes which makes it difficult to recognize. Due to this, it was mainly confused with drinking. Moreover, smoking can be done in many different ways while sitting compared to while standing and walking. Smoking while standing was recognized with the highest accuracy. We observed similar behavior when we calculated smoking sessions which we discuss in Sect. 4.3.

To see how well these trained models generalize, we also tested smoking while biking as we observed some smokers smoking while biking. It is important to note that these trained models had not included training data for smoking while biking. For this purpose, the participant smoked 5 cigarettes while biking from home to office on different days. We ran both SLC and HLCA for this detection and the results were reasonably well. HLCA outperformed the SLC approach. The F-measure and true positive for all twelve scenarios are given in Table 3.

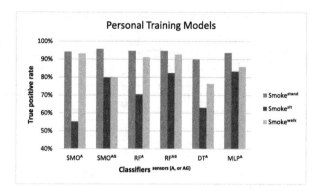

Fig. 5. Impact of smoking posture on its recognition performance

Table 3. Smoking[biking] recognition performance

		Generic Classifiers						subject-specific Classifiers					
		SMO^A	SMO^{AG}	RF^A	RF^{AG}	DT^A	MLP^A	SMO^A	SMO^{AG}	RF^A	RF^{AG}	DT^A	MLP^A
F-measure	SLC	69%	74%	70%	71%	73%	65%	71%	83%	65%	69%	78%	73%
	HLCA	79%	81%	79%	82%	86%	79%	84%	93%	85%	85%	85%	84%
True positive Rate	SLC	86%	86%	84%	86%	81%	78%	69%	86%	57%	59%	81%	72%
	HLCA	100%	95%	98%	97%	95%	91%	84%	91%	79%	76%	84%	88%

We observe that the recognition performance of smoking can be significantly improved by collecting more data for the null class (mentioned as others in our results). It is difficult to get a complete null class because we have to collect all possible hand gestures other than smoking for that. However, wearing the smartwatch for a few days should be sufficient for it. Initially, we tested our trained models with a limited null class which contained only drinking, sitting, standing, talking, and eating soup activities. The recognition results of smoking were relatively poor in terms of precision such that other random hand gestures were classified as smoking. After that, the participant who was involved in our testing process, collected more data for around 5 h while doing various activities such as washing dishes, laying in bed, working on computer, conversations, using stairs, walking, biking, drinking, watching TV etc. Using this additional data improved the overall recognition of the smoking activity. We believe collecting more data on daily activities can further improve the recognition of smoking.

4.3   Smoking Session Detection

We ran the smoking session detection algorithm, explained in Sect. 3.2 on the prediction results of all classifiers and compared its results with the ground truth. Based on this, we present the smoking sessions results in Table 4. It shows that this algorithm performs reasonably well for the subject-specific case. It can be seen from these results that the subject-specific classifiers provide better results than the generic ones as expected. Though the generic classifier performs

Table 4. Smoking sessions recognition

			Predicted as			
		Total predicted smoking sessions[a]	Smoking^{standing}	Smoking^{sitting}	Smoking^{walking}	Others classified as smoking (false positives)
Generic Classifiers	SMO^A	39	15	6	15	3
	SMO^{AG}	45	15	14	15	1
	RF^A	42	15	9	14	4
	RF^{AG}	46	15	14	13	4
	DT^A	40	15	8	15	2
	MLP^A	46	15	14	15	2
subject-specific Classifiers	SMO^A	40	15	10	15	0
	SMO^{AG}	45	15	15	14	1
	RF^A	42	15	11	15	1
	RF^{AG}	44	15	14	15	0
	DT^A	40	15	13	12	0
	MLP^A	45	15	14	15	1

[a] Actual smoking sessions = 45 where 15 while sitting, 15 while standing, and 15 while walking.

very well in some situations, it can lead to a higher number of false positives compared to a subject-specific classifier where a non-smoking activity is classified as smoking due to similar hand gestures. However, we expect this to improve when we add more data from these other participants in the context of the null class. Moreover, it is easy to identify smoking while standing whereas difficult while sitting as discussed earlier. In terms of sensors, the combination of an accelerometer and a gyroscope performs better than the accelerometer alone. In terms of classifiers, the support vector machine performs the best except for recognizing smoking while sitting using the accelerometer. We see higher recognition performance for support vector machine because it generalizes well and is resistant to over-fitting. However, it came at the cost of low performance for smoking while sitting because it is very similar to drinking tea or coffee.

We also ran this smoking session detection algorithm for the biking posture on top of our HLCA algorithm which corrects some of the misclassified smoking segments. We observed that the overall smoking session detection improved for all scenarios, however, in some cases, we had a higher number of false positives, especially for generic classifiers as shown in Table 5. It is an expected result as for HLCA to work better the underlying classification results should be reasonably high.

Finally, we ran of smoking session detection algorithm on top of SLC and HLCA and these results are shown in Table 6. It can be seen that we are able to recognize these smoking sessions with good accuracy even though there was no training data from such type of smoking. Our algorithm (HLCA) improves the smoking session recognition as well, however, occasionally it comes at the cost of false positives where a non-smoking session with random hand gestures or a drinking or eating session is classified as smoking. In the case of smoking session detection algorithm, running HLCA may not be very useful because both of them take into account the neighboring segments to improve the performance, making HLCA redundant.

Table 5. Smoking sessions recognition (HLCA)

			Predicted as			
		Total predicted smoking sessions	Smoking^{stand}	Smoking^{sit}	Smoking^{walk}	Others classified as smoking (false positives)
Generic Classifiers	SMO^A	39	15	6	15	3
	SMO^{AG}	45	15	14	15	1
	RF^A	42	15	9	14	4
	RF^{AG}	46	15	14	13	4
	DT^A	40	15	8	15	2
	MLP^A	46	15	14	15	2
subject-specific Classifiers	SMO^A	40	15	10	15	0
	SMO^{AG}	45	15	15	14	1
	RF^A	42	15	11	15	1
	RF^{AG}	44	15	14	15	0
	DT^A	40	15	13	12	0
	MLP^A	45	15	14	15	1

Table 6. Smoking^{biking} sessions recognition

		Actual Smoke^{biking} Sessions	Total predicted smoking sessions		Predicted as Smoke^{biking}		Others classified as smoking	
			SLC	HLCA	SLC	HLCA	SLC	HLCA
Generic Classifiers	SMO^A	5	5	6	4	5	1	1
	SMO^{AG}	5	5	5	5	5	0	0
	RF9^A	5	5	6	5	5	0	1
	RF9^{AG}	5	5	6	5	5	0	1
	DT^A	5	5	5	5	5	0	0
	MLP^A	5	5	5	5	5	0	0
subject-specific Classifiers	SMO^A	5	4	4	4	4	0	0
	SMO^{AG}	5	5	5	5	5	0	0
	RF9^A	5	3	4	3	4	0	0
	RF9^{AG}	5	3	4	3	4	0	0
	DT^A	5	5	5	5	5	0	0
	MLP^A	5	4	5	4	5	0	0

5   Conclusions and Future Work

In this paper, we presented a modular activity recognition system based on our conceptual framework, SmokeSense, for mobile phones and smartwatches where various classifiers, feature sets, and other parameters can be evaluated. As a case study, we analyzed the recognition performance of smoking on smartwatches and achieved an F1-measure of 92% for subject-specific classification and 85% for generic classification. In terms of recognition performance, we observed similar trends for online activity recognition as we observed previously in our offline analysis. For smoking recognition, the addition of the gyroscope to an accelerometer helped in improving recognition performance. Although, subject-specific training models are observed to exhibit better performance, generic models also perform well at an acceptable level. We learned that smoking while sitting is difficult to recognize compared to other postures due to its similarity to drinking while sitting. We also showed that smoking can be recognized in different postures, such as while biking, from which no training data was available. Finally, we proposed a smoking session detection algorithm and showed that it performs well in identifying the number of cigarettes smoked. Our evaluations involved a single participant, we are planning to test this system with more participants. We also plan to develop a context-aware activity recognition algorithm where sensors, sampling rates, window sizes are decided on demand.

Acknowledgements. This work is supported by Dutch National Program COMMIT in the context of SWELL project, by the Galatasaray University Research Fund under the grant number 17.401.004.

References

1. Lara, O.D., Labrador, M.A.: A survey on human activity recognition using wearable sensors. IEEE Commun. Surv. Tutor. **15**(3), 1192–1209 (2013)
2. Könönen, V., Mäntyjärvi, J., Similä, H., Pärkkä, J., Ermes, M.: Automatic feature selection for context recognition in mobile devices. Pervasive Mob. Comput. **6**(2), 181–197 (2010)
3. Fahim, M., Fatima, I., Lee, S., Park, Y.-T.: EFM: evolutionary fuzzy model for dynamic activities recognition using a smartphone accelerometer. Appl. Intell. **39**(3), 475–488 (2013)
4. Dernbach, S., Das, B., Krishnan, N.C., Thomas, B.L., Cook, D.J.: Simple and complex activity recognition through smart phones. In: 2012 8th International Conference on Intelligent Environments (IE), pp. 214–221. IEEE (2012)
5. Hall, M., Frank, E., Holmes, G., Pfahringer, B., Reutemann, P., Witten, I.H.: The weka data mining software: an update. ACM SIGKDD Explor. Newsl. **11**(1), 10–18 (2009)
6. Shoaib, M., Scholten, H., Havinga, P.: Towards physical activity recognition using smartphone sensors. In: Ubiquitous Intelligence and Computing, 2013 IEEE 10th International Conference on and 10th International Conference on Autonomic and Trusted Computing (UIC/ATC), pp. 80–87, December 2013
7. Shoaib, M., Bosch, S., Incel, O.D., Scholten, H., Havinga, P.J.: Fusion of smartphone motion sensors for physical activity recognition. Sensors **14**(6), 10146–10176 (2014)
8. Wu, W., Dasgupta, S., Ramirez, E.E., Peterson, C., Norman, G.J.: Classification accuracies of physical activities using smartphone motion sensors. J. Med. Internet Res. **14**(5), e130 (2012)
9. Kose, M., Incel, O.D., Ersoy, C.: Online human activity recognition on smart phones. In: Workshop on Mobile Sensing: From Smartphones and Wearables to Big Data, vol. 16, no. 2012, pp. 11–15 (2012)
10. Mohri, M., Rostamizadeh, A., Talwalkar, A.: Foundations of Machine Learning. MIT Press, Cambridge (2012)
11. Shoaib, M., Bosch, S., Incel, O.D., Scholten, H., Havinga, P.J.: A survey of online activity recognition using mobile phones. Sensors **15**(1), 2059–2085 (2015)
12. Rawassizadeh, R., Tomitsch, M., Nourizadeh, M., Momeni, E., Peery, A., Ulanova, L., Pazzani, M.: Energy-efficient integration of continuous context sensing and prediction into smartwatches. Sensors **15**(9), 22616–22645 (2015)
13. Poyraz, E., Memik, G.: Analyzing power consumption and characterizing user activities on smartwatches: summary. In: IEEE International Symposium on Workload Characterization (IISWC), pp. 1–2, September 2016
14. Liu, X., Chen, T., Qian, F., Guo, Z., Lin, F.X., Wang, X., Chen, K.: Characterizing smartwatch usage in the wild. In: Proceedings of the 15th Annual International Conference on Mobile Systems, Applications, and Services, MobiSys 2017, pp. 385–398. ACM, New York (2017)
15. Shoaib, M., Bosch, S., Incel, O.D., Scholten, H., Havinga, P.J.: Complex human activity recognition using smartphone and wrist-worn motion sensors. Sensors **16**(4), 426 (2016)

16. Shoaib, M., Scholten, H., Havinga, P.J., Incel, O.D.: A hierarchical lazy smoking detection algorithm using smartwatch sensors. In: IEEE 18th International Conference on e-Health Networking, Applications and Services (Healthcom), pp. 1–6. IEEE (2016)

17. Shoaib, M.: Sitting is the new smoking: online complex human activity recognition with smartphones and wearables. Ph.D. dissertation, cTIT Ph.D. thesis series no. 17–436, May 2017

18. Tang, Q., Vidrine, D.J., Crowder, E., Intille, S.S.: Automated detection of puffing and smoking with wrist accelerometers. In: Proceedings of the 8th International Conference on Pervasive Computing Technologies for Healthcare, pp. 80–87. ICST (Institute for Computer Sciences, Social-Informatics and Telecommunications Engineering) (2014)

19. Chen, G., Ding, X., Huang, K., Ye, X., Zhang, C.: Changing health behaviors through social and physical context awareness. In: 2015 International Conference on Computing, Networking and Communications (ICNC), pp. 663–667. IEEE (2015)

20. Shoaib, M., Incel, O.D., Scholten, H., Havinga, P.J.: Resource consumption analysis of online activity recognition on mobile phones and smartwatches. In: Proceedings of the 36th IEEE International Performance Computing and Communications Conference. IEEE, 10–12 December 2017

21. Incel, O.D., Kose, M., Ersoy, C.: A review and taxonomy of activity recognition on mobile phones. BioNanoScience 3(2), 145–171 (2013)

22. Gjoreski, M., Gjoreski, H., Luštrek, M., Gams, M.: How accurately can your wrist device recognize daily activities and detect falls? Sensors 16(6), 800 (2016)

23. Gjoreski, M., Gjoreski, H., Luštrek, M., Gams, M.: Recognizing atomic activities with wrist-worn accelerometer using machine learning. In: Proceedings of the 18th International Multiconference Information Society (IS), Ljubljana, Slovenia, pp. 10–11 (2015)

24. Attal, F., Mohammed, S., Dedabrishvili, M., Chamroukhi, F., Oukhellou, L., Amirat, Y.: Physical human activity recognition using wearable sensors. Sensors 15(12), 31314–31338 (2015)

25. Garcia-Ceja, E., Brena, R.F., Carrasco-Jimenez, J.C., Garrido, L.: Long-term activity recognition from wristwatch accelerometer data. Sensors 14(12), 22500–22524 (2014)

26. Knighten, J., McMillan, S., Chambers, T., Payton, J.: Recognizing social gestures with a wrist-worn smartband. In: 2015 IEEE International Conference on Pervasive Computing and Communication Workshops (PerCom Workshops), pp. 544–549. IEEE (2015)

27. Documentation for Google activity recognition API. http://developer.android.com/training/location/activity-recognition.html. Accessed 21 July 2014

28. Seneviratne, S., Hu, Y., Nguyen, T., Lan, G., Khalifa, S., Thilakarathna, K., Hassan, M., Seneviratne, A.: A survey of wearable devices and challenges. IEEE Commun. Surv. Tutor. 19(4), 2573–2620 (2017)

29. Scholl, P.M., Van Laerhoven, K.: A feasibility study of wrist-worn accelerometer based detection of smoking habits. In: 2012 Sixth International Conference on Innovative Mobile and Internet Services in Ubiquitous Computing (IMIS), pp. 886–891. IEEE (2012)

30. Varkey, J.P., Pompili, D., Walls, T.A.: Human motion recognition using a wireless sensor-based wearable system. Pers. Ubiquit. Comput. 16(7), 897–910 (2012)

31. Saleheen, N., Ali, A.A., Hossain, S.M., Sarker, H., Chatterjee, S., Marlin, B., Ertin, E., al'Absi, M., Kumar, S.: puffMarker: a multi-sensor approach for pinpointing the timing of first lapse in smoking cessation. In: Proceedings of the 2015 ACM International Joint Conference on Pervasive and Ubiquitous Computing, pp. 999–1010. ACM (2015)
32. Parate, A., Chiu, M.-C., Chadowitz, C., Ganesan, D., Kalogerakis, E.: RisQ: recognizing smoking gestures with inertial sensors on a wristband. In: Proceedings of the 12th Annual International Conference on Mobile Systems, Applications, and Services, pp. 149–161. ACM (2014)
33. https://weka.wikispaces.com/Serialization. Accessed Dec 2017
34. https://weka.wikispaces.com/Primer. Accessed Dec 2017

Machine Learning of User Attentions in Sensor Data Visualization

Keita Fujino$^{(\boxtimes)}$, Sozo Inoue, and Tomohiro Shibata

Kyushu Institute of Technology, Fukuoka, Japan
`fujino-keita@edu.brain.kyutech.ac.jp`, `sozo@mns.kyutech.ac.jp`,
`tom@brain.kyutech.ac.jp`

Abstract. In this paper, we propose a method for automatically estimating important points of large sensor data by collecting attention
points of the user when visualized, and applying a supervised machine-
learning algorithm. For large-scale sensor data, it is difficult to find
important points simply through visualization, because such points are
buried in a large scope of visualization. We also provide the results of
an estimation, the accuracy of which was over 80% for multiple visualizations. In addition, the method has the advantage that the trained
model can be reused to any other visualization from the same type of
the sensors. We show the results of such reusability for the new type of
visualization, which achieved an accuracy rate of 70–80%.

Keywords: Sensor data · Visualization · User attention
Attention points · Machine learning

1 Introduction

In recent years, the spread of smartphones and the miniaturization and price
reduction of sensor devices have significantly progressed. Accordingly, various
researches using sensors ongoing such devices are ongoing. Among them are
researches on sensing behaviors at home and in hospital by using infra-red, temperature, and humidity sensors [1], and researches on behavioural sensing using
position sensors and power consumption sensors [2]. As a method of utilizing
the enormous amount of data obtained through these sensors, visualization is
often conducted as the first step. Through visualization, important areas such as
the location of an accident, or areas that need improvement for better business
processes, can be found. In a hospital, for example, if any unusual movements
that a nurse may make during rounds can be found using a mobile sensor or
environmental sensor patterns, it becomes presumably possible to detect any
abnormalities and how critical they are.

However, although such observations may be possible by visualizing small-
scale data, it becomes difficult through human observation at a very large scale.
Methods on automatically finding important points in a large sensor data are
crucially required.

© ICST Institute for Computer Sciences, Social Informatics and Telecommunications Engineering 2018
K. Murao et al. (Eds.): MobiCASE 2018, LNICST 240, pp. 125–143, 2018.
https://doi.org/10.1007/978-3-319-90740-6_8

In this paper, we assume that the important points to be visualized can be learned from users' visual attention, and propose a method for realizing appropriate visualization by applying a supervised machine-learning. In the proposed method, we firstly extract feature values from sequential sensor data, and train the detection model of important points with training labels of user's attention. Using the trained model, the important points to be visualized (which we call *attention points*) of any sensor data of the same type can be extracted.

Furthermore, because our method uses the feature vectors from sensors— instead of visualization as input, the method has the advantage that the trained model can be applied to any other visualization from the same type of the sensors.

To evaluate the proposed method, we used several types of sensor data collected from a nursing home, as well as the attention point labels collected from an experiment with recruited observers. As a result, for all of the sensor data, the accuracy reached over 80%. We also evaluated whether the algorithms learned using a single visualization method can be applied to other visualization methods. As a result, even when the learning algorithms were replaced with both an illumination sensor and an acceleration sensor, an estimation accuracy of 70–80% could be obtained.

The contributions of this paper are as follows.

1. We propose a method for extracting only the sensor data that the user is able to pay attention to from an enormous amount of data, and evaluated them, which showed high accuracies with real sensor data.
2. Unlike learning from images, we propose a method that is applicable to different visualization methods from the original visualization.
3. We made a prototype system for collecting the users' attention points. A dataset was created through the system by employing various observers.
4. We discussed the validity and usefulness of our method through an analysis of the variable importance using ensemble learning, and by showing the results of visualization.

2   Background

Utilizing the enormous amount of sensor data obtained by smartphones and sensor devices, users can find important information, such as the location of an accident or an item of interest through visualization. For example, in a hospital, if it can be determined from a mobile or environmental sensor that a nurse acted in an unusual manner, it is possible to detect the abnormalities of round targets and to assume how critical such events are. In addition, if the sensor records the fact that the staff are conducting too many movements when carrying out their duties and office work, it can be inferred that the room layout and work procedures are inefficient.

Although such observations may be possible by visualizing small-scale data, they become difficult even for human observation at a large-scale. For example, Fig. 1 visualizes the acceleration data a 15 h work period of a staff member at

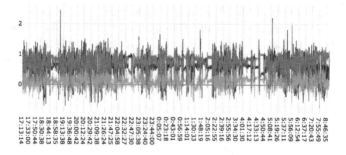

Fig. 1. An example of visualizing large-scale sensor data

a nursing facility. This figure does not reveal where individual work such as regular round was conducted, as well as what area we should focus on during an activity. Furthermore, when data becomes multivariate, manual search for optimal visualization may cause poor work efficiency. For this reason, technology to efficiently visualize sensor data and extract important areas from such data becomes very important.

With regard to such research, Wongsuphasawat et al. [7,8] proposed a system that automatically visualizes multiple objects and recommends a more useful visualization. This method, using several visualization methods, automates visualization by selecting the data variables, and recommends a useful visualization for the user. However, the system only presents various visualization methods and does not tell us where to put a focus. Therefore, it cannot be used for extracting useful sections from large data as shown in Fig. 1.

In addition, Walker et al. [9] proposed a system specialized for time series data. By specifying the attention points when observing the visualized time series data, the range can be enlarged and rendered. At this time, specified part is expressed in a tree. This allows an observation to be achieved while retaining the original information. Although such a visualization method can be easily displayed as long as it specifies attention points, there is no function for automatically detecting such points. Therefore, the problems of listing long-term data, such as in Fig. 1, and not knowing where to focus on remain.

As research on automating such attention points, a study by Bylinskii et al. [5] was considered. In addition, Bylinskii et al. proposed a method for estimating where to focus when viewing a graphic design or data visualization. Using a bitmap image in a graphic design or visualization data as input, the output is the attention points given as teaching data using click data, which can obtain the same result as gaze tracking, namely, a BubbleView [6], and learning and guessing using fully convolutional networks. As a result, the degree of importance is expressed as a heat map. As bitmap image of graphic design and visualization data as input, it makes output as an attention points given as training labels using click data which can obtain the same result as gaze tracking called Bubble-View [6] by learning and guessing using Fully Convolutional Networks. However, when trying to use the method proposed by Bylinskii et al. for visualization of sensor data, when multiple visualizations are performed on the same sensor data, or when switching to another visualization method in the middle of the analysis, it is necessary to prepare training data again for the new visualizaion method. If multiple visualizations are made for one type of sensor data, it is possible to estimate the attention points without preparing new training data, and the cost of constructing the estimation model is kept low.

Based on above, the following system that estimates attention points for sensor data is crucially required.

1. When the observer's visual attention is given as the training data of the sensor data, points to be visualized can be automatically estimated as *an attention point* and presented to the new sensor data or a new observer.
2. By learning a certain visualization method, it is possible to automatically estimate the attention points even if another visualization method is applied to the same type of sensor data.

3   Proposed Method

In this section, we propose a supervised machine-learning approach based on sensor and training data of the attention points, and propose a method for estimating and presenting such points for new sensor data, and even for a new visualization method.

In the following, we first show the basic usage in estimating the attention points from the sensor data X when the estimation algorithm f is given, and applying the training of the estimation algorithm f.

3.1   Estimation

Let $X_{1:n}$ be an input sensor data sequence. $1 : n = (1, 2, \cdots, n)$ represents the sample number proportional to the timestamps. $X_i \in X_{1:n}$ can be either a scalar or a vector. The method estimates the attention points with these sensor data $X_{1:n}$ using the proposed method, and the set of attention points is (Fig. 2)

$$f(X_{1:n}) = \{(b_1, e_1), (b_2, e_2), \cdots, (b_m, e_m)\}, \quad (1)$$

where $1 < b_i, e_i < n$. Using this set of attention points $\{(b_j, e_j)\}_{j=1}^m$, parts of the sensor data

$$\{X_{b_j:e_j}\}_{j=1}^m \quad (2)$$

are extracted and displayed.

An example of $m = 2$ is shown in Fig. 3. The upper-half of the figure shows the sensor data X visualized. The lower-half of the figure shows the attention points estimated using the proposed method.

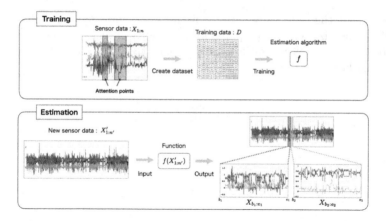

Fig. 2. Outline of the proposed method (At training, dataset D is created from the sensor data $X_{1:n}$ and the attention point set $\{Y_j\}_{j=1}^m = D$. From D, the estimation algorithm f is created by supervised machine-learning algorithm; At estimating, attention point set $\{Y'_j\}_{j=1}^{m'}$ is estimated by giving new sensor data $X'_{1:n'}$ as an input of the function f).

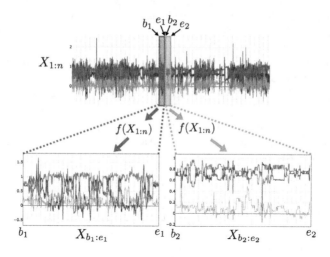

Fig. 3. An example of estimating attention points using the proposed method (upper half, visualizing sensor data X; lower half, attention points estimated using the proposed method).

3.2 Training

With the proposed method, we assume that the sensor data and the attention points of the viewers are collected. To obtain the training label of the attention points, we ask the user to observe the sensor series $X_{1:n}$, visualized as shown in Fig. 4, and to add a red frame to arbitrary areas where they focused their attention. At this time, the time at which the j-th red frame is attached is represented by the pair $y_j = (b_j, e_j)$ of the start point b_j and end point e_j. Actually, l visualizations are prepared for a plurality of sensor series $\{X_{1:n_k}^k\}_{k=1}^l$, and labeled for each visualization; for simplicity, however, only one series $X_{1:n}$ is described below.

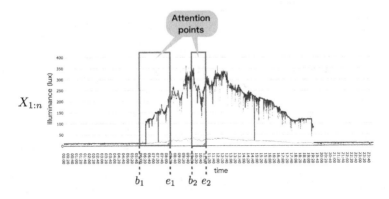

Fig. 4. An example of labeling attention points from visualized sensor data. The red frame indicates such points as labeled by the user. (Color figure online)

The procedure for training the attention points estimation algorithm from the dataset above is described below.

Algorithm

- Input: sensor series $X_{1:n}$, attention point set $\{Y_j\}_{j=1}^m$.
- Output: Function f to input a sensor series $X'_{1:n'}$ data, and output attention point set $\{Y'_j\}_{j=1}^{m'}$.

1. As shown in Fig. 5 B, sensor data are divided based on a fixed time width T, that is, a time window set $\{w(X_{1:n}, i)\}_{i=1}^N$ is obtained using a time windowing function $w(X_{1:n}, i) = ((i-1)T + 1) : (iT)$. The margins are skipped for simplicity. For the sake of simplicity, we hereafter represent $w(X_{1:n}, i)$ as w_i.
2. For each time window w_i, a vector $V_i = h(X_{w_i})$ is calculated using a feature vector calculation function h using statistics and frequency components. Specific feature vectors are described in Sect. 4.3.
3. Compare the time window w_i and the attention points (b_j, e_j) of $b_j \in w_i$ or $e_j \in w_i$ in the time window for each j, which are collectively labeled as $Y_j = T$ if more than one-half of the samples in the time window are focused on, and as $Y_j = F$ otherwise. Apply this to all time windows $w_i, \cdots, w_N$, and obtain the training data $D = \{(V_j, Y_j)\}_{j=1}^N$ with N samples.
   Fig. 5 D shows an example of training data D. A blue row in the figure shows V_j, and a red row indicates the label attached as the attention points Y_j.
4. Apply supervised machine learning with the attention points Y_j as an objective variable, and the feature variable V_j as an explanatory variable, to obtain an estimated model g.

5. Output the function f, which calculates

$$\{\tilde{Y}_i\}_{i=1}^N = \{g \cdot h(X_{w_i})\}_{i=1}^N \tag{3}$$

first, and then convert $\{\tilde{Y}_i\}_{i=1}^N$ into $\{(b_j, e_j)\}_{j=1}^m$ by converting the jth changing time from F to T and then b_j, and jth time from T to F and then e_j in the order of i.

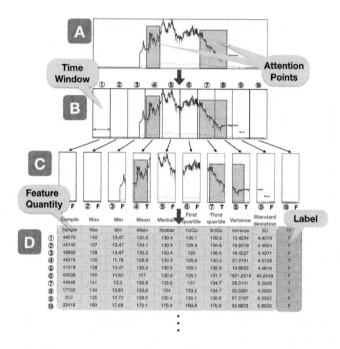

Fig. 5. Example of how to create a dataset. (A, the attention points labeled by the user; B, sensor data divided by a fixed time width T; C, calculation of the feature vector for each divided data, which are collectively labeled as $Y_j = T$ if more than one-half of the samples in the time window are focused upon, and as $Y_j = F$ otherwise; and D, example training data D. A blue row in the figure shows V_j, and a red row indicates a label attached as an attention point Y_j.) (Color figure online)

Using the function f obtained using the algorithm, the estimated attention points

$$\{(\tilde{b}'_i, \tilde{e}'_i)\}_{i=1}^{m'} = f(X'_{1:n'}) \tag{4}$$

are calculated for the new sensor series $X'_{1:n'}$.

This method is expected to be applicable to various visualization methods, because the feature vectors are calculated from the sensor data. Because Bylinskii et al. [5] create visualization data to be trained as an image, they do not expect to estimate the attention points from new visualization methods that have not yet been learned. With our method, because we use feature values from the sensor data, there is an advantage in that we can learn independently from visualization. Furthermore, if the sensor type is the same, any large-scale data can be handled.

4   Evaluation Experiment

In this section, to evaluate whether the attention points can be estimated using any visualization methods, we evaluate the following:

1. Can the proposed method estimate the attention points correctly?
2. Can we estimate for other visualization methods through the model trained by a certain visualization method?

Here, (1) is evaluated by the accuracy of the proposed algorithms. Regarding (2), we evaluate whether an estimation model trained by a certain visualization method can estimate correct attention points for other visualization methods for the same sensor type.

4.1   Sensor Data at a Nursing Home

In Japan, because of the declining birthrate and the increase in the elderly population, users of nursing care facilities are increasing, and there is a critical problem that the number of caregivers is insufficient. One way to solve this problem is to optimize the work for the staff in nursing care facilities. For this purpose, we are conducting research to sense the activities of the nursing staff. In doing so, the sensor data are collected using a smartphone or sensor device. Using the proposed method, we can expect that the data observations will become easier, and the data analysis more efficient.

We used SimpleLink SensorTag CC 2650 STK (Texas Instruments)[1] sensor devices, which were installed beside the beds in the individual rooms of the residents, or worn on the chests of the nursing staff. Smartphones with Android OS were installed in rooms where sensor tags were unavailable, and in shared locations. We used the illuminance sensor of the smartphone and the acceleration sensor of the sensor tag attached to the nursing staff.

At the same time, when the nursing staff carried out their work, they selected from about 25 action labels, including "patrol," "personal record (of their duties)," and "toilet assistance (of the residents)" from the smartphone app when they performed their activities. We extracted the acceleration sensor data from the time zones labeled "patrol" and "personal record." "Patrol" is a task of visiting the room of each resident and checking for abnormalities, which is an important activity to grasp the state of each resident. "Personal record" is a task to record such information as the body temperature and blood pressure of each resident, their physical condition, and other factors. It is also an important activity to improve the operational efficiency, such as how long it takes to record such information.

---

[1] http://www.ti.com/tool/cc2650stk.

4.2 Evaluation System

To conduct our experiments, we developed an evaluation system that operates on the Web, as shown in the Fig. 6. We used JavaScript as the applied language, namely, plotly.js[2] of the JavaScript library to visualize the data. In addition, Google Chrome was used as the applied browser. The center of the screen displays the visualized sensor data. The subject marks the attention points with a red frame for this visualized object. At this time, the coordinates of the red frame are also acquired. In addition, when a plurality of attention points exist, a red frame can be added by pressing "Add frame" button at the bottom of the screen, and marks can be applied as a focus points at a plurality of locations. When the subjects finish adding a red frame to all attention points, they can proceed to the next data by pressing "Next" button. The specific experiment method is described in the next section.

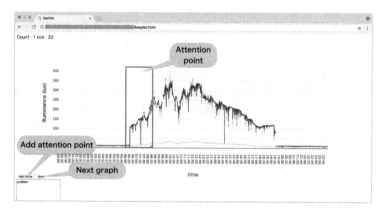

Fig. 6. Evaluation system (red frame, the attention points attached by the subject; "Add frame" button, addition of a red frame for the attention points; "Next" button, proceed to the next visualization data.) (Color figure online)

4.3 Evaluation Methods

The sensor data to be visualized are from the illuminance sensor and acceleration sensors and were obtained at the nursing home. We adopted these two types of sensor because the illuminance sensor data has a clear amount of changes, and the acceleration data has data of continuously fluctuate. The illuminance sensor data were visualized for one of 50 days of data, and the acceleration sensor data were randomly visualized from each of 20 data types labeled "patrol" and "personal record."

At that time, visualization was conducted using the two types of visualization methods considered for each sensor. For the illuminance sensor, as shown in

---

[2] https://plot.ly/javascript/.

Fig. 8, a box plot at 1 min intervals and a bar graph showing the average value at every 10 min were used, and for the acceleration sensor, as shown in Fig. 9, separate X-, Y-, Z-axis data and a three-axis composite value were visualized using a line graph. In the case of the illuminance sensor, by visualizing it with a box plot, it is possible to observe a change in data within a time zone. In addition, a bar graph is a commonly used visualization method in a wide range of fields [11].

The subjects marked the attention points on this visualized graph with a red frame. At this time, the illuminance sensor divides the time width of a fixed length described in Sect. 3 (1) into each hour, and the acceleration sensor divides it into 2 min intervals.

Calculation of the feature vectors in Sect. 3 (2) is based on "Maximum (Max)", "Minimum (Min)", "Mean", "Median", "First quartile (1stQu)", "Third quartile (3rdQu)", "Variance (Var)", "Standard deviation (Sd)", "Number of data (Sample)".

Following Sect. 3 (3), the coordinate of the red frame is acquired, and T or F is determined. This task was carried out by the subjects (five male students, 23 in age), and we collected data on the attention points. Figure 7 shows the actual experimental scenery.

As a result, the illuminance sensor recorded 6,000 data, and the acceleration sensor recorded 1,300 data. We divided this created dataset into learning and test data, and we learned the data through a random forest method with T/F as the objective variables, and another feature quantity as the explanatory variables. At this time, the test data are one visualization data from one subject, and the learning data applies 1-user-image-leave-out cross validation for everything else. Specifically, we used the R language randomForest package in this paper. The evaluation item (1) was evaluated using this created algorithm.

Fig. 7. Landscape actually experimenting

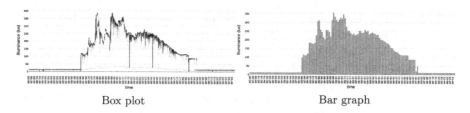

Box plot   Bar graph

Fig. 8. Example of visualization of illuminance sensor

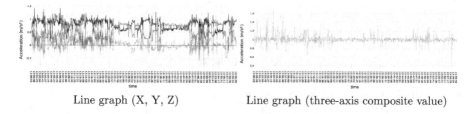

Line graph (X, Y, Z)   Line graph (three-axis composite value)

Fig. 9. Example of visualization of acceleration sensor

4.4 Results

Table 1 shows the results of item (1) with a cross validation for each visualization method of each sensor. When the illuminance sensor was visualized with a box plot, the accuracy was 85.7%, and when visualized with a bar graph the accuracy was 84.5%. When the acceleration sensor labeled patrol was visualized separately on the X, Y and Z axes, the accuracy was 85.0%, and when visualized with a three-axis composite value the accuracy was 87.9%. In addition, when visualizing the acceleration sensor data labeled as personal records separately for three axes, the precision was 76.6%, and the precision when visualized with a three-axis composite value was 80.8%.

Table 1. Accuracy for each visualization method. The "Sensor" column shows the sensor type, and the "Visualization Method" column shows the visualization method.

Sensor	Visualization method	Accuracy
Illuminance	Box plot	85.7%
	Bar graph	84.5%
Acceleration (patrol)	Line graph (X, Y, Z)	85.0%
	Line graph (three-axis composite value)	87.9%
Acceleration (personal record)	Line graph (X, Y, Z)	76.6%
	Line graph (three-axis composite value)	80.8%

Table 2 shows the result of item (2) with the estimation accuracy when applying the estimation model acquired by another visualization method. The first line shows the result of applying the model learned using the bar graph of the illuminance sensor to the box plot, where the estimation accuracy was 82.5%. The second line shows the opposite case of the first line, where the estimation accuracy was 81.8%. The third and fourth lines show the results of the acceleration sensor with "patrol" as the activity type. The third line shows the results of applying the model learned using the three-axis composite value as compared to those visualized separately on three axes, where the estimation accuracy is 70.9% and the estimation accuracy is higher than 50%, i.e., chance, for evaluation item (1), which is lower than the precision. The fourth row shows the opposite case, where the estimation accuracy is 71.6%, and the estimation accuracy is lower than the evaluation item (1). The fifth and sixth lines show the results of the acceleration sensor with "personal record" as the activity type. The estimation accuracy when applying the model learned using the three-axis composite value as compared to the three axes visualized separately was 68.8%. In the opposite case, the estimation accuracy was 69.9%, both of which are higher than chance; however, this is lower than the case of evaluation item (1). The reason for this lowering of the estimation accuracy will be discussed in the next section.

Table 2. Estimation accuracy when the estimation model of another visualization method is applied. The "Sensor" column indicates the sensor type. The "Training" column shows the visualization method for the training. The "Test" column shows the visualization method tested.

Sensor	Training	Test	Accuracy
Illuminance	Bar graph	Box plot	82.5%
	Box plot	Bar graph	81.8%
Acceleration (patrol)	Three-axis composite value	X,Y,Z	70.9%
	X,Y,Z	Three-axis composite value	71.6%
Acceleration (personal record)	Three-axis composite value	X,Y,Z	68.8%
	X,Y,Z	Three-axis composite value	69.9%

For the result of evaluation item (1), both the illuminance sensor and the acceleration sensor were able to obtain about an 80% estimation accuracy. For the result of evaluation item (2), with the illuminance sensor, the estimation accuracy did not decrease even when the learned model was replaced, whereas in the case of the acceleration sensor, the estimation accuracy was lower than that of evaluation item (1). The reasons for this decline in the estimation accuracy are discussed in the next section.

5   Discussion

In this paper, we applied two kinds of visualization using an illuminance sensor and an acceleration sensor, and evaluated the results using a random forest method applying the attention points as the object variable and the other feature vectors as the explanatory variable. With evaluation item (1), the illumination sensor and the acceleration sensor labeled "patrol" had an estimation accuracy of 80% or more. On the other hand, the acceleration sensor labeled "personal record" was slightly lower in estimation accuracy than the other two, which resulted from the user's attention points differing for each sensor.

Figures 10 and 11 show examples of which time zone the subject focused on in the data. With the illuminance sensor, it is understood that all subjects paid attention to places where the amount of change in data was large, as in Fig. 10.

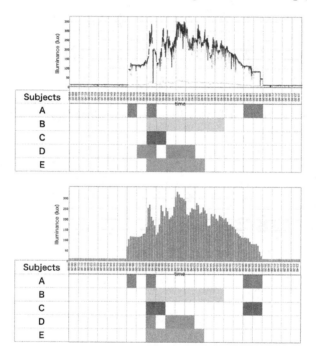

Fig. 10. Attention points for each subject (sensor type, illuminance sensor; upper half, visualization of the sensor data; lower half, attention points for each subject.)

Figures 12, 13 and 14 shows the importance of the feature vectors obtained when applying a random forest method. If we look at Fig. 12, we can see that the variance and standard deviation are particularly high. For the acceleration sensor labeled "patrol", we can see that all subjects paid attention to the same place, as shown in Fig. 11(Left). Therefore, it is considered that the estimation accuracy of the attention points increased. In the case of the acceleration sensor labeled "personal record", we can see that the attention points differ depending

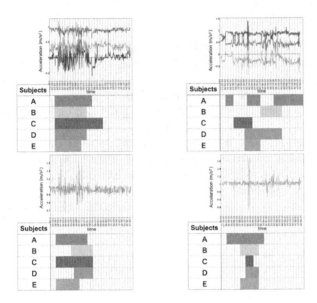

Fig. 11. Attention points for each subject (sensor type, acceleration sensor; left, patrol; right, personal record; upper half, visualization of the sensor data; lower half, attention points for each subject.)

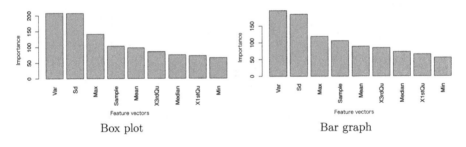

Box plot　　　　　　　　　　　　　Bar graph

Fig. 12. Importance of feature vectors (illuminance)

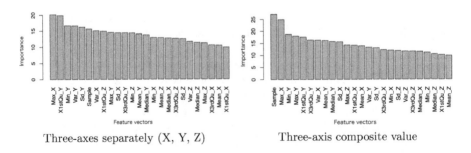

Three-axes separately (X, Y, Z)　　　　　Three-axis composite value

Fig. 13. Importance of feature vectors in case of patrol (acceleration)

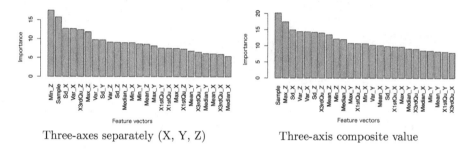

| Three-axes separately (X, Y, Z) | Three-axis composite value |

Fig. 14. Importance of feature vectors in case of personal record (acceleration)

on the subject when the three axes are different, as shown in Fig. 11 (upper right). Therefore, the estimation accuracy is considered to be less than 80%.

In addition, Figs. 15 and 16 shows a visualization of this estimation result. Figure 15 shows the result of visualizing the estimated portion of the illuminance sensor. It can be seen that the estimated range is wider than the attention points of the subject shown in Fig. 10. This is considered to be due to the conformity rates of 51.0% and 50.2% for the box plot and bar graph, respectively, and it is presumed that places other than the attention points were also estimated. Figure 16 shows the results of visualizing the estimated position of the acceleration sensor. In the case of the acceleration labeled "patrol", the precision of the three-axis composite value and the three separate axes are 75.8% and 78.3%, respectively, and most of the estimated points can be said to be attention points. The recall rates are 77.1% and 80.0%, and it is possible to estimate the majority of points that are actual attention points. In the case of acceleration labeled "personal record", the precision rates of the three-axis composite value and the three separately axes are 58.7% and 67.2%, and the positions where the

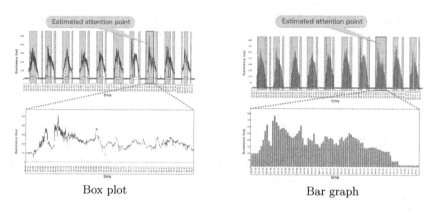

| Box plot | Bar graph |

Fig. 15. Example of visualizing estimated results (illuminance: for the upper half, the part surrounded by the red frame was a place estimated as attention points; lower half, visualized by zooming in on the estimated attention points.) (Color figure online)

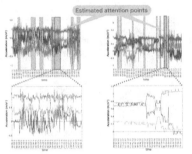
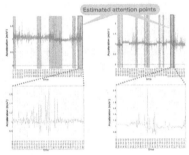

Three axes separately (X, Y, Z)   Three-axis composite value

Fig. 16. Example of visualizing estimated results (acceleration: in the upper half, the part surrounded by the red frame was a place estimated as the attention points; the lower half, visualized by zooming in on the estimated attention points.) (Color figure online)

three separate axes do not have more attention points are estimated. However, the recall rates are 67.4% and 76.7%, which shows that we can estimate many points that are actual attention points.

For the illuminance sensor used in evaluation item (2), even when the learning algorithm was replaced, there was not much change in the estimation accuracy for evaluation item (1). This is almost the same for both visualization methods and attention points, as shown in Fig. 10. Furthermore, because the importance of the feature vectors of both figures is the same in Fig. 12, it is considered that the precision did not decrease even when adapting to another visualization method.

On the other hand, for the acceleration sensor labeled "patrol", the estimation accuracy was about 70%, which was lower than for evaluation item (1). In the case of three separate axes, as shown in Fig. 11(left), the range of the attention points are wide for each subject, whereas in the case of the three-axis composite value, the range of the focus area differs for each subject. In addition, although the feature vectors such as the maximum value of the X axis and the minimum value of the Y axis are both high, as indicated in Fig. 13, the importance of the other feature vectors are different, and was considered to have decreased.

In the case of the acceleration sensor labeled "personal record", the estimation accuracy was less than 70%. As we can see in Fig. 11, this shows that the attention points are different for each subject compared with "patrol". In addition, as shown in Fig. 13, the importance of the "number of samples" is high for both cases, although the other features are different. Therefore, when the learning algorithm is replaced, the estimation accuracy is considered to be lower than for evaluation item (1).

In this way, when the change in data, such as from the illuminance sensor, is clear, it is possible to estimate the attention points with high accuracy. Furthermore, when the visualization method is similar, it was confirmed that the method can be applied to multiple visualization methods using a single learned algorithm. It was also confirmed that it is possible to estimate the attention points with high accuracy even when the data constantly change, such as with an acceleration sensor.

6   Related Works

Various studies on visualization methods regarding points of viewer attention have been conducted. In the following, in Sect. 6.1, we describe research gathering attention points data and estimating the design optimization and attention points. Section 6.2 also describes various studies on visualization methods.

6.1   Visual Attention on Design

Research using data on viewer attention points includes an optimization of the design of a Web page by collecting human gaze data [4]. An excellent web design includes how information can be efficiently conveyed to people in a manner intended by the designer to achieve a certain purpose. Therefore, it is necessary to predict and design the areas of interest so that people can efficiently collect information. With this method, by designing a Web page as an input, it is possible to create a design that can easily guide people's attention while maintaining as much of the design as possible. However, it takes a significant amount of time to collect human gaze data, and Web designs given as input must be completed to a certain extent. Bylinskii et al. [5] proposed a method for estimating where people focus on a graphic design and data visualization, and express such estimations through a heat map. Instead of tracking the viewer's line of sight through data collection, we use a method that can obtain similar results as gaze tracking using a mouse click, called BubbleView [6]. This makes it possible to collect data in an efficient manner. However, because this method estimates the attention point and expresses the result as a heat map, we have not conducted a design optimization based on the estimation result. In our research, even if switching to another visualization method can cope without the collection of new attention point data, in these studies, it is necessary to gather attention point data for each visualization method.

6.2   Visualization Methods

Systems that recommend which visualization is appropriate when visualizing data have been proposed [7,8]. Multivariate data are given as an input, and a plurality of visualizations are automatically performed through the selection of a certain variable. This type of system recommends a type of visualization combined with other non-selected variables. However, in the case of time series data such as sensor data, in general, a line chart is often used. It is not meaningful to use this type of system because its visualization method is limited. Because this system has a limitation regarding the amount of data that can be given as an input, it is incompatible with a large variety and quantity of data. Other systems specialized for time series data have also been proposed [9]. A line chart is visualized by providing the time series data as an input. When observing this type of visualization data, by zooming in on the area of interest, only that part is visualized, and the part of the original visualization data that is zoomed is expressed in a tree. With this system, it is easy to grasp which part of the original data the zoomed area shows. However, when the amount of data becomes too great, it becomes difficult to grasp what is being drawn, and zooming becomes difficult. To solve such a problem, a method of visualizing time-series data in a three-dimensional space has been proposed [10]. Using this method, it is possible to visualize enormous amounts of sensor data, but when expressed in a three-dimensional space, it becomes difficult to observe when compared with the case on a two-dimensional plane. In these studies, automatically estimating and visualizing the attention points, as achieved in our research, is not possible.

7   Conclusion

In this research, we proposed and evaluated a method to automatically estimate attention points for sensor data using supervised machine learning. As a result, the estimation accuracy of the illuminance sensor and the acceleration sensor labeled "patrol" was about 85%, but in the case of the acceleration sensor labeled "personal record" it was slightly lower at about 80%. We also evaluated whether the algorithms learned using a single visualization method can be applied to other visualization methods. As a result, it was possible to obtain an estimation accuracy of 80% or more with the illuminance sensor even if the learning algorithm is switched. In the case of the acceleration sensor, a slightly decreased estimation accuracy of around 70% was achieved. In the case of the illuminance sensor, all subjects focused their attention on almost the same place, but in the case of the acceleration sensor, it was considered that the estimation accuracy was lowered because the attention location of the subjects was slightly different for each visualization.

In the future, it will be necessary to search for different visualization methods and feature vectors that can improve the estimation accuracy for acceleration data. We will experiment with other sensor data and visualization methods, and apply them using a single learning algorithm, aiming at automatic visualization according to the users.

References

1. Chahuara, P., Fleury, A., Portet, F., Vacher, M.: On-line human activity recognition from audio and home automation sensors: comparison of sequential and non-sequential models in realistic smart homes. J. Ambient Intell. Smart Environ. **8**(4), 399–422 (2016)

2. Ueda, K., Suwa, H., Arakawa, Y., Yasumoto, K.: Exploring accuracy-cost trade-off in in-home living activity recognition based on power consumptions and user positions. In: 14th IEEE International Conference on Ubiquitous Computing and Communications (IUCC 2015), pp. 1131–1137 (2015)

3. Bikakis, N., Sellis, T.: Exploration and visualization in the web of big linked data: a survey of the state of the art. In: LWDM (2016)

4. Pang, X., Cao, Y., Lau, R.W.H., Chan, A.B.: Directing user attention via visual flow on web designs. ACM Trans. Graph. (TOG) **36**, 240 (2016)

5. Bylinskii, Z., Kim, N.W., O'Donovan, P., Alsheikh, S., Madan, S., Pfister, H., Durand, F., Russell, B., Hertzmann, A.: Learning visual importance for graphic designs and data visualizations. In: Proceedings of 30th Annual ACM Symposium on User Interface Software & Technology (2017)

6. Kim, N.W., Bylinskii, Z., Borkin, M.A., Gajos, K.Z., Oliva, A., Durand, F., Pfister, H.: BubbleView: an interface for crowdsourcing image importance maps and tracking visual attention. ACM Trans. Comput.-Hum. Interact. **24**, 36 (2017). (A Special Issue)

7. Wongsuphasawat, K., Moritz, D., Anand, A., Mackinlay, J., Howe, B., Heer, J.: Voyager: exploratory analysis via faceted browsing of visualization recommendations. IEEE Trans. Visual. Comput. Graph. **22**, 649–658 (2015)

8. Wongsuphasawat, K., Qu, Z., Moritz, D., Chang, R., Ouk, F., Anand, A., Mackinlay, J., Howe, B., Heer, J.: Voyager 2: augmenting visual analysis with partial view specifications. In: Proceedings of 2017 CHI Conference on Human Factors in Computing Systems (2017)

9. Walker, J., Borgo, R., Jones, M.W.: TimeNotes: a study on effective chart visualization techniques for time-series data. IEEE Trans. Visual. Comput. Graph. **22**(1), 549–558 (2016)

10. Imoto, M., Itoh, T.: A 3D visualization technique for large scale time-varying data. In: 14th International Conference on Information Visualisation (IV10), pp. 17–22 (2010)

11. Borkin, M.A., Vo, A.A., Bylinskii, Z., Isola, P., Sunkavalli, S., Oliva, A., Pfister, H.: What makes a visualization memorable? IEEE Trans. Visual. Comput. Graph. **19**, 2306–2315 (2013). (Proceedings of InfoVis 2013)

Measuring How We Play: Authenticating Users with Touchscreen Gameplay

Jonathan Voris$^{(\boxtimes)}$ (iD)

New York Institute of Technology, New York, NY 10023, USA
jvoris@nyit.edu

Abstract. Mobile devices are being used to access and store an ever-increasing amount of sensitive data. Due to their compact form factor, mobile devices can be easily lost or stolen. Yet users frequently choose not to enable authentication or select authentication methods which are insufficient to protect their devices, placing user information at risk. In this paper, we propose the use of a behavioral biometric based approach to authentication that functions by modeling the manner in which users interact wit mobile games, which are one of the most popular uses of mobile devices. We conducted an IRB approved study in which 30 participants were asked to play three popular Android games as well as utilize a mobile touchscreen without any gameplay prompting. We extracted features from users' touchscreen activity during these interactions, then applied a Support Vector Machine to classify users based on patterns which emerged from their usage during the game. Our results indicate that using gameplay as a behavioral biometric is an effective means of authenticating users to their mobile devices, but care must be taken to select a game which encourages users to make frequent distinctive gestures.

Keywords: Active authentication · Behavioral biometrics
Games for security · Gamification · Machine learning
Mobile authentication · SVM · Useful games

1 Introduction

Smartphone penetration rates have grown dramatically worldwide over the past decade. People have become accustomed to using their mobile devices to perform a greater variety of tasks, which has caused these devices to store and access an increasingly large amount of sensitive data. In many cases the data accessible via a mobile device is of greater value than the physical device itself. A recent study revealed that 50% of phone theft victims would pay $500 and 33% would pay $1,000 to retrieve their stolen devices; moreover, to regain their handset, 68% of victims would put themselves in danger [11].

Strong authentication is critically important to the process of securing the sensitive data stored on mobile devices. Unfortunately, many people underestimate the importance of the security of their devices. According to Consumer

© ICST Institute for Computer Sciences, Social Informatics and Telecommunications Engineering 2018
K. Murao et al. (Eds.): MobiCASE 2018, LNICST 240, pp. 144–164, 2018.
https://doi.org/10.1007/978-3-319-90740-6_9

Reports, 36% of American smartphone owners use simple 4 digit numeric passcodes to protect their devices, while 34% choose not to enable any authentication mechanism at all. [18]. Although multiple factors inform users' security decisions, one of the reasons for this missing layer of security is that many mobile authentication methods fail to take usability into consideration.

In an effort to provide users with more usable authentication to their mobile devices, we consider an alternative authentication mechanism which utilizes the process of playing a touchscreen game on a mobile device. Specifically, in order to unlock a device, users are required to play a particular game for which the proposed system has learned the user's behavior by constructing a model of inherent gameplay characteristics. The motivation behind the selection of games as a potential avenue for authentication is that the act of playing games is one of the most popular activities performed on mobile devices. As of 2016, 57% of mobile users have games installed on their phones [12]. Further, consumers spend 1.15 billion hours each month playing games, ranking them as the second most popular mobile activity following social media [12]. We thus explore applications of gameplay to the security task of authentication because of the natural usability benefits they confer as well as the fact that mobile device owners are already acclimated to playing them.

Note that unlike traditional authentication methods, such as passwords, our game-centric authentication solution is not knowledge-based; that is, users do not need to remember a pre-established secret in order to gain access to their mobile system. Instead, users are authenticated based on whether or not the patterns which emerge from how they interact with a game match or deviate from a model of how the legitimate device owner has played in the past. This provides several advantages over secret-based approaches to authentication, primarily that behavior cannot be lost, stolen, guessed, or brute-forced. Furthermore, using behavior to authenticate reduces the cognitive burden placed on users, thereby improving the usability of the authentication procedure. Although behavior has been explored as an authentication mechanism by previous researchers [3,4,21], this work is the first to explore the benefits of using gameplay to collect discriminative behavior on mobile touchscreen devices via a substantial user study.

To evaluate our approach we conducted a study with 30 participants who interacted with three pre-selected games and an application which did not involve any gameplay elements. This data was then processed to extract features which were useful in differentiating between users. We applied a multiclass Support Vector Machine (SVM) learning algorithm as well as a one-class SVM variant with different kernels and parameters to assess the discriminative power of the selected games. Our proposed system is capable of performing authentication in fewer than 5 s of gameplay with at most one false positive per day with 95% confidence and is not influenced by a user's skill or experience playing a particular game. These results suggest that using gameplay as a behavioral biometric is an effective means of authenticating users to their mobile devices. However, as not all games performed equal well in terms of authentication accuracy, care must be taken to select a game which is beneficial to the authentication process by encouraging users to make frequent distinctive gestures.

The remainder of the paper is organized as follows: Sect. 2 summarizes the related work. Section 3 discusses our threat model, study design, feature selection and data analysis. Section 4 presents the outcomes of data modeling and survey analysis, and Sect. 5 concludes the paper and presents potential future work.

2   Related Work

The most popular authentication methods are often the most straightforward to perform. This explains the widespread use of passwords, graphical patterns, and fingerprint recognition as authenticators. Since these mechanisms are the most broadly deployed, they are also some of the most studied and attacked. Weak passwords are vulnerable to guessing and dictionary attacks. To provide sufficient security, a lengthy combination of alphanumeric and special characters are required [22], which are difficult and tedious to enter on small touch devices [16]. Fingerprint recognition has recently gained popularity as scanning hardware has been included on more smartphones and the process offers fast user identification. However, it remains vulnerable to fingerprint spoofing attacks [10]. Graphical patterns are convenient for users but susceptible to shoulder surfing and other observation attacks [16].

Behavioral biometrics, which function by analyzing patterns of user activity, have recently been gaining traction in studies as an alternative authentication method for mobile devices. Previously proposed applications include continuous behavioral authentication on mobile devices via touchscreen usage [21] and application habits [15]. These methods apply machine learning to user interactions with the mobile device to generate a model which is then used authenticate users. For example, in [4], Frank et al. used k-nearest-neighbor clustering and SVMs to classify users while they performed reading and image-viewing tasks on a mobile device. Though the time-to-detection of their scheme is unclear, their results indicated that touchscreen biometrics were suitable as one component of a broader multi-modal authentication scheme.

Khan and Hengartner empirically evaluated the device-centric nature of implicit authentication schemes in [6] and concluded that application-centric implicit authentication schemes provide significant security improvements compared to their device-centric counterpart. However, this delegation increases the development overhead of the application provider. In [13], Neal and Woodard surveyed over a hundred biometric approaches to mobile security and found that physiological and behavioral modalities reduce the need for remembering passwords and PINs. They concluded that these methods offered improved security for mobile devices, even though biometric security remains a complex procedure due to hardware limitations, inconsistent data, and adversarial attacks.

Feng et al. incorporated contextual application information to improve user authentication for mobile devices in [3]. With extensive evaluation, they found that their context-aware implicit authentication system achieved over 90% accuracy in real-life naturalistic conditions with only a small amount of computational overhead and battery usage. Krombholz et al. evaluated a pressure sensitive authentication method for mobile devices in [9]. Their work demonstrated that using touch pressure as an additional dimension lets users select higher entropy PIN codes that are resilient to shoulder surfing attacks with minimal impact on usability and error rates. This is contrary to what Khan et al. presented in their study, however, as hidden features like finger pressure, angular velocity, and the finger width making contact with the screen are hard to imitate via shoulder surfing.

Khan et al. presented the results of their two-part study on usability and security perceptions of behavioral biometrics in [7] and found that 91% of participants felt that implicit authentication was convenient (26% more than explicit schemes). 81% perceived the provided level of protection satisfactory with only 11% concerned about mimicry attacks. On the other hand, false rejects were a source of annoyance for 35% and false accepts were the primary security concern for 27%. The authors concluded that implicit authentication is indeed a meaningful approach for user authentication on mobile devices with a reasonable trade-off in terms of usability and security.

In [1], Buscheck et al. discuss opportunities for improving implicit authentication accuracy and usability by including spatial touch features and using a probabilistic framework in their authentication scheme to handle unknown hand postures, showing a 26.4% reduction in the classification Equal Error Rate (EER) to 36.8%. Harbach et al. investigated users' mobile device locking and unlocking behavior in [5] and found that on average, participants spent around 2.9% of their smartphone interaction time authenticating their device. Participants that used secure lock screens considered it unnecessary in 24.1% of situations. In their study, shoulder surfing was perceived to be a risk in only 11 of 3410 sampled situations.

Khan et al. also studied shoulder surfing and offline training in [8], which they consider to be targeted mimicry attacks. The authors evaluate the security of implicit authentication schemes and demonstrate that it is surprisingly easy to bypass them, but only if the attacker is a malicious insider who is able to observe their victims' behaviors or if the device is compromised to collect and transmit a user's touch events which can then be used to train and mimic the victim's behavior. In [2], Cherapau et al. presented their investigation of the impact Apple's "TouchID" had on passcodes for unlocking iPhones. Their study revealed no correlation between the use of TouchID and the strength of users' passcodes. The researchers also found that the average entropy of passcodes was 15 bits, corresponding to only 44 min of work for an attacker to find the correct password by brute force.

A shortcoming of previously proposed biometric solutions is that they often require a long time window for model construction and user authentication. To address this issue, we propose the utilization of gameplay characteristics as an authentication method. The correct choice of game can be used to encourage users to perform more distinctive gestures at a faster rate, reducing training time as well as the overall time taken to complete the authentication process. Furthermore, unlike many traditional biometric authentication methods which require specific hardware to operate, our approach is applicable to any device with a touch-sensitive screen and is thus deployable to a broad array of mobile devices. The entertainment value provided by games encourages user engagement, which is useful for the training portion of the modeling process. An added benefit of using gameplay as an authenticator is that games do not typically involve revealing any potentially sensitive user information.

This work is a continuation of a previous pilot study intended to explore the potential of games as an authentication method [17] which found the approach to be promising, but lacked sufficient data to draw statistically relevant conclusions. In this paper, we expand the scale of the study to 30 participants and perform a more rigorous assessment of its viability. The reported accuracy of the multi-class models from the pilot study are higher than those reported in this research because the models were trained on a much smaller dataset for each game, resulting in overfitting. Moreover, in order to compare the classification performance of our gameplay models against activities that do not involve gameplay, we introduced a screen without any game-based prompting to our study process.

3   Evaluation

3.1   Threat Model

In this paper, we concentrate on the user-to-device authentication process which is used to protect the sensitive data stored on a mobile device in the event that it is acquired by an unauthorized individual, such as when a device is intentionally stolen, acquired by a co-worker, or forgotten in a public place. Our solution is to require potential users to play a short, specific touchscreen game on the "lock screen" to gain access to the device. The mechanism is intended to discriminate between an authentic user and an adversary, assuming that there is no vulnerability in the OS which may be exploited by the attacker to bypass the authentication procedure. Our threat model does not consider cases where an attacker has the time, access, and skill necessary to disassemble a device in order to manipulate its memory or directly access the data on its disk. Remote attacks via exploits and social engineering are also outside the scope of our proposed solution's threat considerations. Lastly, our model also assumes that an attacker is not able to observe or track a user's gameplay interactions and then effectively recreate them in order to impersonate the user's gestures. The issue of mimicry attacks will be addressed in future research.

3.2   Sensor Design

For our study, we developed a TouchScreen Monitor application to log users' touch interactions on Android devices. Because the Android Application Sandbox isolates data between different applications, touchscreen interactions with a particular application are not permitted to be recorded by other applications. To overcome this limitation, our proof-of-concept TouchScreen Monitor gathers raw touch screen data from the Android system using rooted access; in a practical deployment, the game used to authenticate users would be included as a built-in system lock screen. The sensor application has been developed using Java and the Android SDK framework.

The TouchScreen Monitor first executes the system command "su" to acquire root privileges. After permission is successfully granted, the application executes the system command "getevent" to record all touch events with the screen. Since raw touches are recorded at a fast sampling rate - less than 0.1 ms apart - during the logging process, they are buffered and written in bulk to the device's disk in order to minimize the number of writes performed. To improve reliability, the touchscreen log feature is implemented as a separate Android service on a different thread so it is automatically restarted to continue logging events if an error occurs in the main application. Using a separate thread for logging avoids interference with the application which is being monitored. The TouchScreen Monitor also supports uploading the collected data to a server for further analysis.

3.3   Experimental Study Design

We selected three popular games from the Google Play Store to conduct our experiments with: Angry Birds, Flow Free and Fruit Ninja. These games were chosen because they are popular unpaid games and demonstrated promising results in our pilot study [17]. Each of the three selected games also has relatively simple gameplay and gentle learning curves, which make them suitable for a diverse set of users. For the non-gameplay portion of our study, we asked users to make arbitrary gestures on a blank screen, allowing them make any type and number of interactions without any gameplay prompting. All experiments were conducted on the same Android device, which was a Samsung Galaxy S3 smartphone; exploring the applicability of games to establishing cross-device biometric profiles is another intended area of future research [14].

We designed our experiment as a within-subjects study in which volunteers were asked to play the three aforementioned games and use the blank screen sequentially, performing each activity for 5 min. Prior to each segment of a study session, if a participant had never played a particular game before, they would be allowed to play the game for a few minutes in order to acclimate themselves to the gameplay requirements and controls. During the experiment, the TouchScreen Monitor was run silently in the background to record all the user interactions which occurred during each activity. For Angry Birds and Flow Free, which require the user to play the game level by level, users were required to start from the first level of each game. Since each level has different scenarios and difficulty levels, this requirement ensured that differences between users' gestures are not caused by variations in level design, but are rather introduced naturally by users in response to the same game prompting. Fruit Ninja does not follow this pattern because users play the game until they fail and start again. In this game, a score is used to assess how well users play rather than level progression.

For the non-gameplay "blank screen" task, users could interact with the blank screen in any way they wanted, with nothing displayed in order to influence them towards making particular gestures. Users were asked to perform the study tasks naturally without pressure or monitoring from the study administrator. During each session, the administrator was careful not to mention the security implications of the study in order to avoid potential priming effects. After a participant performed each of the four activities, they were asked to complete a post-conditional questionnaire. This survey contained questions which collected basic demographic information as well as information pertaining to users' experience with smartphones, video games, and mobile games in general, as well as their prior experience with each of the mobile games used in the study.

The study was advertised at our institution via fliers and in-class announcements. We recruited 30 participants in total. Because our study was conducted at a university, our survey revealed a younger participant age than is representative of the broader population, with most of the participants being students between the ages of 18 and 34. A study with a more representative pool of volunteers is a target of future research.

3.4   Feature Extraction

The raw logs collected by the TouchScreen Monitor represent atomic, low-level user interactions with the touchscreen. We extracted higher-level features from those logs to create potentially distinctive characteristics for classification. There are two approaches to extract high-level features from touchscreen usage data: parse the continuous gesture into individual points, or combine them to form aggregate swipe gestures. As we experimented, the first approach gave inferior classification performance as it does not capture some of the important characteristics of a high-level swipe, such as the speed and initial and final coordinates of the gesture.

We followed the second approach and extracted seventeen high-level features of each swipe gesture which had been demonstrated to be conducive to user classification by previous work [4,17], including: (1) the initial X coordinate of the gesture, (2) the initial Y coordinate of the gesture, (3) the final X coordinate of the gesture, (4) the final Y coordinate of the gesture, (5) the time period during the gesture, (6) the average area covered by finger during the gesture, (7) the average finger width contacting the screen during the gesture, (8) the length of the gesture along the X axis, (9) the length of the gesture along the Y axis, (10) the distance traveled during the gesture, (11) the direction of the gesture, (12) the speed along X axis of the gesture, (13) the speed along the Y axis of the gesture, (14) the speed along the gesture's trajectory, (15) the velocity of the gesture, (16) the angular velocity of the gesture, (17) the finger orientation change during the gesture.

3.5   Feature Analysis

In practice, some features have more discriminative power than others features. In order to measure how well these features can discriminate between users, we utilize a measurement known as the Fisher function [19]. The scalar Fisher score for each feature is defined as the ratio between the between-class variance and the sum of all within-class variances:

$$f = \frac{\sigma_b^2}{\sum_{i=1}^{i=n} \sigma_i^2}$$

where σ_i^2 is the within-class variance. σ_b^2 is the between-class variance, which is defined as:

$$\sigma_b^2 = 1/n \sum_{i=1}^{i=n} (\mu_i - \mu_g)^2$$

where μ_i is the statistical mean for the feature values of user i, and μ_g is the grand mean of all mean values μ_i.

A higher between-class variance indicates that a feature is more distinctive for each user. A lower within-class variance implies that a feature's values are more consistent for the same user. Thus, features with lower relative Fisher scores can be considered potentially redundant and candidates for removal to optimize classification performance.

3.6 Data Modeling and Analysis

We implemented R language scripts to apply a multiclass Support Vector Machine (SVM) to the extracted feature set to classify participants using a variety of kernels and parameters. We choose to explore a SVM for gameplay authentication because it is a well-understood algorithm which had been successfully applied to behavioral authentication in the past, which allowed our experiments to focus on the question of the applicability of gameplay to the task of authenticating users. For the SVM implementation, we utilized the LibSVM based "e1071" R package. We conduct multiclass SVM classification with C-Support Vector Classification (C-SVC) using Radial Bias Function (RBF) and Polynomial kernel functions. To achieve multiclass classification, the classifier applied a "one-versus-one" technique in which binary classification is applied to each pair of users. 10-fold cross validation is used to conserve data while training and testing our model.

Some of the performance gains associated with a particular task could potentially be caused by the availability of larger quantities of training data. To prevent this factor from influencing our results, we do not train the model on each user's full dataset due to the fact that some activities cause users to make many more gestures than other activities and not all users performed precisely the same number of gestures during each task. For example, the Flow Free task resulted in nearly three times as many gesture samples to work with relative to Angry Birds. In our experiment, all users play the same initial levels for each game. However, since Flow Free does not consume as much time with animations as Angry Birds, users are able to play it at a faster pace and make more gestures. For an unbiased comparison, we construct the training dataset by choosing an equal number of samples per each user across all activities, in which the smallest amount of gestures generated by any user across all activities is the sample size for each user. For better classification performance, the data is standardized to have a mean of zero and a standard deviation of 1 before modeling.

To measure and compare the performance of each task and modeling technique, we plotted Receiver Operator Characteristic (ROC) curves and calculated the Area Under the ROC Curve (AUC). An ROC curve is a plot of a false positive rate (FPR) on the X axis against the classifier's true positive rate (TPR) on the Y axis which is generated by varying the acceptance threshold used in the classification process. The intersection point of the curve with the Y-Axis has a FPR of 0%, which causes classification to be highly restrictive in terms of FPR and does not allow any misclassification of illicit users as authorized users. Similarly, the point of the ROC curve which has a true positive rate of 1 will accept all authentic users but may decrease the rate of rejecting an unauthorized user. An ideal classifier is a model in which the FPR is 0% and the TPR is 100%, resulting in an AUC of 1. However, this ideal model is often impossible to achieve. Therefore, in practice, there is always a trade-off between the classifier's TPR and FPR; that is, a threshold that causes a classifier to have a lower FPR also has a lower TPR. On the other hand, a threshold that increases the TPR will also decrease the FPR. Our goal is to maximize the AUC, which represents the maximization of the chance of successfully authenticating a legitimate user while minimizing the rate of accepting unauthorized users.

Similarly, a Detection Error Tradeoff (DET) curve plots a classifier's FPR against its false negative rate (FNR), which is used to visualize the relationship between these errors. A classifier's FNR is related to its TPR via the equation: $FNR = 1 - TPR$. The Equal Error Rate (EER), which is the common value at which the FNR and FPR are equal, is used to express the balance between the false acceptance and false rejection performance of a classifier, with a lower EER corresponding to more accuracy in the classifier.

3.7   One-Class Classification

In addition to multiclass SVM classification, we also implemented a one-class SVM (oc-SVM) in R. With a multiclass classification approach, each user model is trained using both positive examples of their own data as well as negative examples from other users' data. In contrast, a one-class method only trains models using positive examples of each user's authentic data. A one-class approach is more appropriate to the task of user authentication, where the goal is to discern whether the legitimate device owner is using the device or any other user is, rather than determining which specific user is controlling it. Another practical reason why one-class modeling is more suitable for authentication is that a particular device would not have direct access to another user's model, and even if this information could be shared, the process would be difficult to scale.

For this purpose, we implemented a oc-SVM in R using the LibSVM library with a "one-classification" kernel type which accepts only positive data of an authentic user when training. The oc-SVM is applied for all three games as well as the "blank screen" task, just as with the multiclass modeling process. For each activity, we applied an oc-SVM to create a separate model for each user, in which 80% of their data is used to train the model. To validate the classifier, the remaining 20% of a user's data is combined with equal samples of every other users' data to create the validation set. As was the case with multiclass SVM classification, AUC and EER are again used as metrics to assess the accuracy of the oc-SVM models.

3.8 Survey Analysis

Users were asked to complete a survey at the conclusion of each experimental session. The post-conditional survey posed questions regarding demographic information, mobile device experience, video game experience, mobile game experience, and how engaged with each game people felt. The specific queries compromising the questionnaire are presented in Appendix A. Responses to these questions allowed us to categorize users according to different attributes in order to infer information about what aspects of participants' backgrounds may have an effect on gameplay based authentication accuracy. For example, users were asked how much experience they had which each of the three games used in our study: one week or less, one month, three months, six months, one year, or more than a year. This survey item provided insight into whether user classification, and thus authentication, was more or less accurate for users with a lot of experience playing a particular game as opposed to users who had not played the game very much, if at all. To answer this question, we grouped the oc-SVM AUC results according to gameplay experience and applied a one-way Analysis of Variance (ANOVA) test to assess how statistically significant differences in classification performance were between each gameplay experience group.

4 Results

4.1 Multiclass Classification

As detailed in Sect. 3.6, we implemented R scripts using the LibSVM library to perform multiclass SVM classification with the C-Support Vector Classification (C-SVC) training algorithm and tested both RBF and polynomial kernel functions. For the polynomial kernel, we conducted tests using different combinations of polynomial degrees and C parameter values, which control the size of the hyperplane margin. Based on our experiments, a C parameter of 10 resulted in the most accurate model. To optimize the performance using the RBF kernel, we applied hyperparameter optimization by varying the value of gamma from 0.1 to 0.9 and performed model training and testing for each gamma value. A gamma value of 0.51 produced the lowest error rates for this type of kernel.

After settling on modeling parameters, we plotted ROC curves which captured the classification performance for each user and activity. First, the classification probability that a validation instance belongs to a user is calculated.

Next, ROC curves are generated by varying the acceptance threshold applied to these probability values. These ROC curves were used to calculate the AUC for each user and activity. The individual per-user AUC values were averaged across all users to produce an aggregate AUC value for each task. We followed a similar process to derive average EER values for each study task. First, DET curves were plotted for each user and task. These DET curves were used to find the EER value for each user and task combination, and these per-user EER values were then averaged together to produce one overall EER per task.

We calculated the AUC and EER values to facilitate a comparison between how well our classifier was capable of distinguishing between users based on the touchscreen gestures they made while playing each game as well as the unprompted "blank screen" task. Table 1 presents the average AUC and EER of the three games - Angry Birds, Flow Free, and Fruit Ninja - as well as the "blank screen" activity. As shown in Table 3, the average AUC using a SVM with a RBF kernel is over 0.9 for Angry Birds and Fruit Ninja. The Angry Birds and Fruit Ninja gameplay resulted in better classification performance than the "blank screen" task, which had no gameplay context. Our hypothesis is that this was caused in part because users found making gestures without prompting from a game to be tedious, as our post-conditional survey responses revealed that only 12.5% of participants felt engaged during this activity.

Table 1. Multiclass SVM classification results for all activities

Activity	SVM kernel	Average AUC	Average EER
Angry Birds	Polynomial	0.870	20.38%
Angry Birds	RBF	**0.963**	**10.34%**
Flow Free	Polynomial	0.734	32.79%
Flow Free	RBF	**0.804**	**27.31%%**
Fruit Ninja	Polynomial	0.869	21.03 %
Fruit Ninja	RBF	**0.919**	**15.64%**
Blank Screen	Polynomial	0.847	23.53%
Blank Screen	RBF	**0.898**	**18.33%**

The activity which resulted in the highest classification error rates was Flow Free. We conclude that the most logical explanation for this result was due to the nature of Free Flow's gameplay, in which each level is a puzzle which typically has one specific solution. Thus, all users are required to make very similar gestures to complete each level, which made it more difficult to differentiate between each user's gameplay habits. The level of engagement among study participants may have also played a role in the relatively low modeling accuracy observed for Flow Free gameplay. According to our survey feedback, 59.4% of study participants felt engaged while playing Flow Free, whereas the percentage is 65.6% for Angry Birds. The most engaging game was Fruit Ninja with 78.10% of participants responding that they were engaged by its gameplay. When taken as a whole, these results imply that designs of Angry Birds and Fruit Ninja do the most to encourage users to make distinctive gestures. We also note that the accuracy of SVM classification is consistently higher when using a RBF kernel in comparison to a polynomial kernel for all four study tasks.

4.2   Feature Analysis

Table 2 contains a list of the 17 features we considered during our study and their corresponding Fisher scores. These values were calculated based on the gesture feature vectors extracted from all users across all activities. The features are arranged by Fisher score in descending order. Table 2 also lists another feature performance metric which we refer to as the "classification contribution," which is meant to capture the impact of omitting the feature on modeling performance. To determine the classification contribution of each feature, we implemented an R script to iterate over the feature set, remove each feature one at a time, apply multiclass SVM classification with the given feature removed, and calculate the AUC value produced when each feature is left out. The classification contribution value for each feature is obtained by subtracting the AUC after removing the feature from the AUC which is achieved when modeling is performed using all available features.

Table 2. Fisher scores for features across all gameplay activities

Feature	Fisher score	Classification contribution
Average finger width	0.003095	0.26%
Time period	0.002860	1.16%
Average area covered	0.002793	0.67%
Initial X coordinate	0.001341	0.51%
Initial Y coordinate	0.001184	0.63%
Angular velocity	0.000884	0.66%
Length along X axis	0.000764	−0.01%
Length along Y axis	0.000720	−0.11%
Distance traveled	0.000705	0.48%
Speed along Y axis	0.000416	−0.03%
Velocity	0.000416	−0.04%
Final Y coordinate	0.000351	0.21%
Speed along X axis	0.000343	0.05%
Finger orientation change	0.000302	0.74%
Final X coordinate	0.000271	0.17%
Trajectory speed	0.000078	−0.03%
Direction	0.000059	−0.12%

To verify the accuracy of our Fisher scores, we calculated the Pearson correlation coefficient between the Fisher scores and the classification contributions. The Pearson correlation coefficient measures the linear dependence between two variables, where a result of 1 indicates a complete positive linear correlation, while a value of −1 implies a totally inverse linear correlation, and a 0 implies no correlation between variables. The Pearson correlation coefficient between our features' Fisher scores and classification contributions is 0.6, which suggests that the classification contributions are highly correlated with Fisher scores. Thus, features with a lower Fisher score also tend to make less of a contribution to classification performance, which supports the accuracy of our estimates of each feature's discriminative power. In our dataset, features pertaining to gesture direction and speed tend to have the lowest Fisher score and classification contribution, which identifies these features as potentially redundant and therefore good candidates for removal in order to streamline our model.

4.3 One-Class Classification

After completing our multiclass modeling experiments, we repeated the classification process using a one-class modeling approach as described in Sect. 3.7. We again experimented with both RBF and polynomial kernel functions during our tests. Because one-class modeling is more appropriate to the application of mobile authentication, performance curves have been included in addition to a result summary. Figures 1, 3 and 5 present ROC curves for Angry Birds, Flow Free and Fruit Ninja gameplay classification. Figures 2, 4 and 6 present the DET curves which resulted from classifying users' touchscreen activity with these games. These figures were the result of using an RBF kernel during one-class modeling, which again produced models with lower error rates relative to the polynomial kernel function. Table 3 summarizes the performance of these

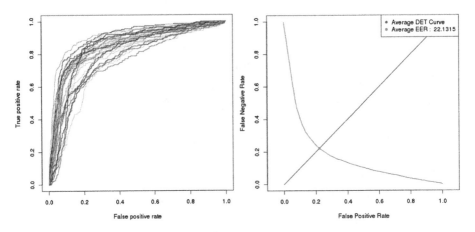

Fig. 1. Per-user ROC curves for oc-SVM model of Angry Birds gameplay

Fig. 2. Average DET curve for oc-SVM model of Angry Birds gameplay

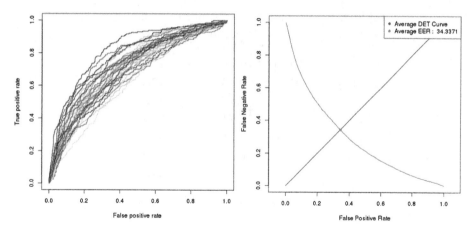

Fig. 3. Per-user ROC curves for oc-SVM model of Flow Free fameplay

Fig. 4. Average DET curve for oc-SVM model of Flow Free gameplay

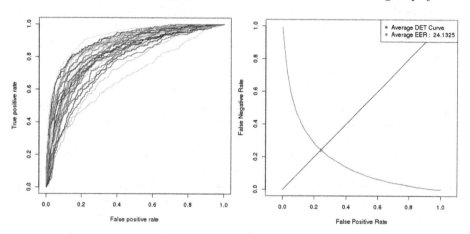

Fig. 5. Per-user ROC curves for oc-SVM model of Fruit Ninja gameplay

Fig. 6. Average DET curve for oc-SVM model of Fruit Ninja gameplay

models by presenting the average AUC and EER across all users for each study task and kernel type. We experimentally determined the model parameters which minimized the error rates of our classifier and found that a gamma value of 0.802, which controls the variance of the kernel, and a nu value of 0.1608, which controls the amount of permissible training errors, resulted in the best performance.

The oc-SVM classification results largely mirror those produced by multi-class classification. We observe that for all tasks and kernels, the oc-SVM produced less accurate classification results than the multiclass classifier. This is best explained by the removal of negative samples during the training process, which makes it more difficult for the model to learn the "boundary" between positive and negative instances. For both multiclass and one-class modeling, Angry Birds

Table 3. oc-SVM classification results for all activities

Activity	SVM kernel	Average AUC	Average EER
Angry Birds	Polynomial	0.521	49.85%
Angry Birds	RBF	**0.832**	**22.13%**
Flow Free	Polynomial	0.507	49.28%
Flow Free	RBF	**0.712**	**34.34%**
Fruit Ninja	Polynomial	0.493	51.39 %
Fruit Ninja	RBF	**0.831**	**24.13%**
Blank Screen	Polynomial	0.477	53.60%
Blank Screen	RBF	**0.806**	**39.12%**

and Fruit Ninja gameplay resulted in more accurate user classification relative to the unprompted "blank screen" task. However, Flow Free resulted in higher error rates than either other game or the unprompted gestures.

These results suggest that touchscreen patterns while playing computer games can be used to differentiate between users, and thus can be applied as an authentication mechanism for mobile devices. However, this result is not generalizable to all games. The style of gameplay must be considered when selecting a game to utilize as an authentication task. We hypothesize that Fruit Ninja and Angry Birds resulted in better classification performance because they prompted users to quickly make touchscreen gestures which were highly consistent for each user while being very distinctive between users. Both games encourage users to interact with the touchscreen in a very free-form fashion. In contrast, Flow Free demonstrated worse classification performance relative to the unprompted "blank screen" task because it forces users to make very specific touchscreen gestures in order to progress through the game. This resulted in study participants making very similar gestures to one another at a slower rate, which made it more challenging to distinguish users from each other. To summarize, gameplay characteristics must be taken into account when designing a behavioral authentication system which leverages a computer game to improve classification performance.

4.4   Effect of Experience

If a game is used to authenticate users, a natural question is the extent to which experience playing the game impacts its effectiveness. The authentication game should not require a particular amount of skill and should be capable of classifying novices just as well as experts. Conversely, getting better at playing a particular game should also not result in a degradation of classification performance. This could be possible if the gestures of experienced players converge to a optimal "solution" for a game. We attempt to explore this question using participant's responses to our post-conditional questionnaire. One of the questions posed was how much experience a user had with each of the three games that were tested. We divided our participants into groups based on how much experience they reported playing each game and found the average AUC from applying the oc-SVM model to each experience group. These results are presented in Table 4, which shows that classification accuracy does not vary much between experience groups.

Table 4. Average oc-SVM AUC categorized by amount of experience with each game

Experience	Angry Birds	Flow Free	Fruit Ninja
Never	0.843	0.723	0.823
One week or less	0.819	0.680	0.835
1 month	-	0.728	0.841
3 month	0.846	0.696	0.859
6 month	-	0.724	-
1 year	0.844	0.730	0.844
Over 1 year	0.848	0.660	0.841

We applied a one-way ANOVA test to the AUC values for these groups in order to determine if any statistically significant differences existed between users who have spent different amounts of time playing each game. Table 5 summarizes the results of this test. F represents the ratio of the variance between and within each gameplay experience group. F-critical is the threshold for determining if a significant different exists between the data groups under consideration, which we calculated using a 95% significance level. Since the F value is well below the F-critical value for each game, the null hypothesis of the ANOVA test can be accepted, which indicates that no statistically significant differences exist between the classifier's performance on each experience group. We therefore conclude that the amount of experience a user has playing a particular game does not effect the accuracy of using the game to authenticate them. Game-based authentication is thus equally applicable to users of all levels of experience with a game.

Table 5. ANOVA results for each game

Activity	F	F-critical
Angry Birds	0.623	2.759
Flow Free	0.929	2.528
Fruit Ninja	0.187	2.621

4.5   Time Taken to Authenticate

Since unlocking a mobile device is such a frequent activity, an important aspect of the usability of a mobile authentication scheme is the amount of time it takes to complete. To determine how long it takes to use a game to authenticate a user on a mobile device, we must first determine an acceptable threshold of false positives; that is, how frequently is the authentication scheme allowed to incorrectly identify a legitimate user as an attacker? We settled on one false positive per day as a reasonable threshold. According to the results of a recent study, an average smartphone user unlocks his or her mobile device an average of 110 times per day [20]. Allowing for one false positive per day would thus translate into a false positive rate of $1/110 = 0.91\%$ per each one second sample of touchscreen gameplay behavior. At this low false positive rate, using an oc-SVM based on Angry Birds as an authentication game would result in a true positive detection rate of 49.88% per sample. Thus, for each second of gameplay there is a 50.12% of failing to detect that the game is being played by someone other than the legitimate device owner. Detecting device misuse with 95% confidence would thus require 5 gameplay samples:

$$0.5012^x < (1 - 0.95)$$
$$0.5012^x < 0.05$$
$$x > 4.34$$

Thus, 5 s of Angry Birds gameplay activity can be used to authenticate users with 95% accuracy and at most one false positive per day. Though slower than authentication via traditional biometrics such as fingerprints, a 5 s time interval is reasonable in the context of mobile authentication. This suggests that gameplay can be utilized to reduce the time required to authenticate users via biometrics based on touchscreen behavior.

5   Conclusion

To summarize, this paper presented a novel approach to mobile authentication in which users are asked to play a game in order to authenticate themselves to their mobile devices. Computer games are potentially beneficial to the authentication process as they are usable by design and encourage players to rapidly make unique touchscreen gestures. To assess the viability of this proposed approach, a study was conducted in which 30 users were asked to play three popular mobile games as well as perform touchscreen gestures without gameplay prompting. Features which captured users' gameplay habits were extracted from these gestures and modeled using SVMs. Our results indicate that games are potentially useful authenticators. A multiclass model based on the Angry Birds game resulted in an AUC of over 0.95 and an EER of 10.34%. A more practical oneclass model of Angry Birds gameplay was shown to be capable of detecting device misuse in 5 s with 95% accuracy and one false positive per day. We conclude that authenticating users based on the manner in which they play a game can improve the performance of authentication relative to touchscreen tasks which do not involve gameplay. However, the game used as an authentication mechanism must be selected with care. Games which encourage users to make a wide variety of distinctive gestures were found to be beneficial, while those which required slow and specific gestures were not. Experience playing a game was found to not have an impact on the accuracy of authentication.

This work demonstrates the plausibility of using computer games for mobile authentication. However, future exploration is required to answer a number of remaining questions regarding gameplay-based behavioral biometric authentication. As future work, we intend to perform studies with larger, more representative volunteer groups in order to explore the susceptibility of gameplay authentication to mimicry attacks in which an adversary attempts to replicate a legitimate user's gameplay habits. We also plan to assess the extent to which gameplay behavior is affected by device hardware and firmware. We will further consider which characteristics of gameplay are conducive to user classification in order to more fully examine the usability of game-based authentication and the extent to which it can be generalized.

Acknowledgements. Many thanks to Graduate Assistant Tuan Ngyuen for his efforts performing the study reported in this paper and Graduate Assistant Sheharyar Naseer for his editing assistance.

A   Appendix: Study Questionnaire

Table 6 lists the survey questions that were used in our study in the order they were presented to participants.

Table 6. Post-conditional study questionnaire

Number	Question
1	What is your age?
2	What is your gender?
3	What is your ethnicity? (Please select all that apply)
4	What is the highest level of education you have completed?
5	Have you ever used a mobile device (such as smartphones, tablets, ebook readers, or portable game systems)?
6	How many different mobile devices (such as smartphones, tablets, ebook readers, or portable game systems) have you ever used?
7	How many different mobile devices (such as smartphones, tablets, ebook readers, or portable game systems) do you currently own?
8	In a typical day, how many hours do you spend using mobile devices (such as smartphones, tablets, ebook readers, or portable game systems)?
9	What mobile operating system have you used?

(continued)

Table 6. (*continued*)

Number	Question
10	In the past 30 days, have you used a mobile device (such as a smartphones tablet, ebook reader, or portable game system) to do any of the following activities?
11	I am an experienced mobile device user
12	How many apps are installed on your mobile device?
13	What method do you use to unlock your mobile devices? (Please select all that apply)
14	Have you ever played a video game?
15	In a typical day, how many hours do you spend playing video games?
16	How often do you play video games?
17	Please list some of your favorite video games
18	Have you ever played a video game on a mobile device?
19	In a typical day, how many hours do you spend playing games on mobile devices?
20	How often do you play video games on a mobile device?
21	Please list some of your favorite games for mobile devices
22	How long have you been playing Angry Birds?
23	How long have you been playing Flow Free?
24	How long have you been playing Fruit Ninja?
25	I felt engaged while playing Angry Birds
26	I felt engaged while playing Flow Free
27	I felt engaged while playing Fruit Ninja
28	I felt engaged while interacting with the blank screen
29	The mobile device was very responsive during the experiment
30	The touchscreen was very responsive during the experiment
31	I think that having to play a game before accessing my mobile device would be easier to use than my current authentication technique
32	I think that having to play a game before accessing my mobile device would be more secure than my current authentication technique

References

1. Buschek, D., De Luca, A., Alt, F.: Improving accuracy, applicability and usability of keystroke biometrics on mobile touchscreen devices. In: Conference on Human Factors in Computing Systems (CHI), pp. 1393–1402 (2015)
2. Cherapau, I., Muslukhov, I., Asanka, N., Beznosov, K.: On the impact of touch ID on iPhone passcodes. In: Symposium on Usable Privacy and Security (SOUPS), pp. 257–276 (2015)

3. Feng, T., Yang, J., Yan, Z., Tapia, E.M., Shi, W.: TIPS: context-aware implicit user identification using touch screen in uncontrolled environments. In: Proceedings of 15th Workshop on Mobile Computing Systems and Applications (HotMobile), p. 9 (2014)

4. Frank, M., Biedert, R., Ma, E., Martinovic, I., Song, D.: Touchalytics: on the applicability of touchscreen input as a behavioral biometric for continuous authentication. Trans. Inf. Forensics Secur. (TIFS) **8**(1), 136–148 (2013)

5. Harbach, M., Von Zezschwitz, E., Fichtner, A., De Luca, A., Smith, M.: It's a hard lock life: a field study of smartphone (un)locking behavior and risk perception. In: Symposium on Usable Privacy and Security (SOUPS), pp. 9–11 (2014)

6. Khan, H., Hengartner, U.: Towards application-centric implicit authentication on smartphones. In: Workshop on Mobile Computing Systems and Applications (HotMobile), p. 10 (2014)

7. Khan, H., Hengartner, U., Vogel, D.: Usability and security perceptions of implicit authentication: convenient, secure, sometimes annoying. In: Symposium on Usable Privacy and Security (SOUPS), pp. 225–239 (2015)

8. Khan, H., Hengartner, U., Vogel, D.: Targeted mimicry attacks on touch input based implicit authentication schemes. In: International Conference on Mobile Systems, Applications, and Services (MobiSys), pp. 387–398 (2016)

9. Krombholz, K., Hupperich, T., Holz, T.: Use the force: evaluating force-sensitive authentication for mobile devices. In: Symposium on Usable Privacy and Security (SOUPS), pp. 207–219 (2016)

10. Security Research Labs: Fingerprints are Not Fit for Secure Device Unlocking (2014). https://srlabs.de/bites/spoofing-fingerprints/. Accessed 12/18/17

11. Lana'i Lookout: Phone Theft in American, Breaking Down the Phone Theft Epidemic (2014). https://transition.fcc.gov/cgb/events/Lookout-phone-theft-in-america.pdf. Accessed 18 Dec 2017

12. Murdock, A.: Consumers Spend More than 1 Billion Hours a Month Playing Mobile Games (2015). http://www.vertoanalytics.com/consumers-spend-1-billion-hours-month-playing-mobile-games. Accessed 18 Dec 2017

13. Neal, T.J., Woodard, D.L.: Surveying Biometric Authentication for Mobile Device Security. Journal of Pattern Recognition Research **1**, 74–110 (2016)

14. Ngyuen, T., Voris, J.: Touchscreen biometrics across multiple devices. In: Who are You?! Adventures in Authentication Workshop (WAY) Co-located with the Symposium on Usable Privacy and Security (SOUPS) (2017)

15. Salem, M.B., Voris, J., Stolfo, S.: Decoy applications for continuous authentication on mobile devices. In: Who are You?! Adventures in Authentication Workshop (WAY) Co-located with the Symposium on Usable Privacy and Security (SOUPS) (2014)

16. Schaub, F., Deyhle, R., Weber, M.: Password entry usability and shoulder surfing susceptibility on different smartphone platforms. In: Conference on Mobile and Ubiquitous Multimedia (MUM) (2012)

17. Scindia, P., Voris, J.: Exploring games for improved touchscreen authentication on mobile devices. In: Who Are You?! Adventures in Authentication Workshop (WAY) Co-located with the Symposium on Usable Privacy and Security (SOUPS) (2016)

18. Tapellini, D.: Smart Phone Thefts Rose to 3.1 Million in 2013 (2014). http://www.consumerreports.org/cro/news/2014/04/smart-phone-thefts-rose-to-3-1-million-last-year/index.htm. Accessed 18 Dec 2017

19. Welling, M.: Fisher linear discriminant analysis. Technical report, Department of Computer Science, University of Toronto (2005)

20. Woollaston, V.: How Often Do You Check Your Phone? The Average Person Does It 110 Times a DAY (And up to Every 6 Seconds in the Evening) (2013). http://www.dailymail.co.uk/sciencetech/article-2449632/How-check-phone-The-average-person-does-110-times-DAY-6-seconds-evening.html. Accessed 18 Dec 2017

21. Xu, H., Zhou, Y., Lyu, M.R.: Towards continuous and passive authentication via touch biometrics: an experimental study on smartphones. In: Symposium on Usable Privacy and Security (SOUPS) (2014)

22. Yan, J., Blackwell, A., Anderson, R., Grant, A.: Password memorability and security: empirical results. IEEE Secur. Privacy **2**, 25–31 (2004)

vStore: A Context-Aware Framework for Mobile Micro-Storage at the Edge

Julien Gedeon[1]([⊠]) [iD], Nicolás Himmelmann[1], Patrick Felka[2], Fabian Herrlich[1], Michael Stein[1] [iD], and Max Mühlhäuser[1]

[1] Telecooperation Lab, Department of Computer Science,
Technische Universität Darmstadt, Darmstadt, Germany
gedeon@tk.tu-darmstadt.de
https://www.tk.informatik.tu-darmstadt.de
[2] Faculty of Economics and Business Administration,
Institute for Information Systems,
Goethe-Universität Frankfurt am Main, Frankfurt, Germany
felka@wiwi.uni-frankfurt.de
https://www.wiim.uni-frankfurt.de

Abstract. The way mobile users store and share their data today is completely decoupled from their current usage context and actual intentions. Furthermore, the paradigm of cloud computing, where all data is placed in distant cloud data centers is seldom questioned. As a result, we are faced with congested networks and high latencies when retrieving data stored at distant locations. The emergence of edge computing provides an opportunity to overcome this issue. In this paper, we present *vStore*, a framework that provides the capabilities for context-aware micro-storage. The framework is targeted at mobile users and leverages small-scale, decentralized storage nodes at the extreme edge of the network. The decision where to store data is made based on rules that can either be pushed globally to the framework or created individually by users. We motivate our approach with different use cases, one of which is the sharing of data at events where cellular networks tend to be congested. To demonstrate the feasibility of our approach, we implement a demo application on the Android platform, leveraging storage nodes placed at different locations in a major city. By conducting a field trial, we demonstrate the key functionalities of *vStore* and report on first usage insights.

Keywords: Mobile storage · Edge computing · Fog computing
Context-awareness

1 Introduction

Smartphones today have long surpassed their predecessors in terms of computing power, sensory capabilities and application diversity. Mobile phones nowadays feature a variety of different applications. Data captured by or sent to those

© ICST Institute for Computer Sciences, Social Informatics and Telecommunications Engineering 2018
K. Murao et al. (Eds.): MobiCASE 2018, LNICST 240, pp. 165–182, 2018.
https://doi.org/10.1007/978-3-319-90740-6_10

applications is usually stored at a distant server, i.e., in cloud computing infrastructures. In any case, this location is predetermined by that particular application. Furthermore, we see a plethora of different applications that serve the same or similar purpose (e.g., Dropbox, Google Drive and OneDrive for cloud-based data storage). Although users sometimes use different services to store the same data, the different applications remain isolated from one another and therefore hinder the sharing of data across them.

Recently, Cisco predicted that by the year 2020, 70% of the world population (i.e., 5.5 billion people) will be mobile users[1]. According to their predictions, 72% of those will use so-called smart devices, generating a traffic of over 30 exabytes every month. It is fair to assume that this will lead to highly congested core networks. This in part can be avoided if mobile data is stored closer to where it actually is retrieved. More generally, the way mobile data is stored and accessed today is completely decoupled from how the data is actually used and what the current usage contexts of users and their intentions are. Therefore, from the current state of the art, we can derive the following drawbacks and limitations:

1. High bandwidth utilization in the core network: Despite often being retrieved only in a locally restricted area, all data is first sent to the cloud, thus creating high bandwidth utilization and possible bottlenecks in the core network. This is going to worsen as more large-volume data, such as video, will be generated in the future.
2. High latency when retrieving data from a distant cloud. For data such as video, this has a direct impact on the perceived quality of service and therefore is undesirable.
3. No efficient sharing of data across different applications and users.

In this paper, we introduce *vStore* (virtual store), a framework that abstracts from concrete storage locations and—based on the current usage context and intentions of the user—chooses the most suitable storage location. From a networking point of view, *vStore* reduces the bandwidth utilization in the core network and the latency when retrieving nearby copies of requested data. From the user perspective, *vStore* provides context-awareness and facilitates the sharing and reuse of data across locations and applications. Furthermore, *vStore* enables network operators and businesses to provide better quality of experience for their customers by providing proximate cloudlet storage. Our novel framework takes into account the following when deciding on where to store data:

- **Type of data**, such as photo, video, contacts, etc.
- **Usage context** as provided by the mobile device. The context includes for example time, location, ambient noise level and network conditions.
- **User intention**, such as private use or sharing of data.

Instead of solely relying on either local (i.e., on the mobile device itself) or cloud-based storage, we also consider the use of cloudlets [4], small-scale micro-data

---

[1] https://newsroom.cisco.com/press-release-content?articleId=1741352.

centers located at the edge of the network that can be leveraged for computations. In the future, cloudlets on various kinds of network nodes, such as WiFi gateways, cellular base stations or middleboxes, could be used for storing small pieces of data (e.g., a photo taken at an event or point of interest). With *vStore*, we consider the heterogeneity of those network nodes in terms of the bandwidth and latency they can provide in order to optimize the placement decision. To this end, we implement our framework for Android devices and deploy storage nodes in a major city to demonstrate the feasibility of our approach. To the best of our knowledge, this is the first framework that provides the functionality to abstract storage locations and enables to perform storage decisions based on rules that take into account the current context of the user and heterogeneous edge infrastructures.

The remainder of this paper is organized as follows: In Sect. 2, we give an overview of the research topic and related work. Section 3 presents our idea of context-aware storage at the edge. We describe the design of our system and its components in Sect. 4. The results of our case study are presented in Sect. 5. Finally, we conclude the paper and given an outlook on future work in Sect. 6.

2   Background and Related Work

Before describing our approach to micro-storage at the edge, this section introduces the underlying concepts and reviews previous work related to ours.

2.1   Shifting the Focus from Cloud to Edge

While cloud computing has been the prevailing way for offloading data and computations [1–3], recent research has begun to identify the drawbacks of this approach [6,7]. Based on this, we can observe a shift from the cloud towards the edge of the network [5]. Known as fog computing [6,8] or edge computing [9,10], this new paradigm makes use of resources close to the users and their data. This includes leveraging opportunistic devices present in one-hop distance, such as standard WiFi routers [11,12]. Compared to cloud computing, the benefits of this approach include saving bandwidth in the core network and reduced latency. The concept of cloudlets [4] is promising to provide lightweight virtualization of applications for their deployment on resource-constrained devices. We argue that by applying this concept for the storage of data, we can reduce the amount of data stored in distant cloud infrastructures and at the same time provide better quality of service to mobile end users.

2.2   Context-Awareness

We aim to build a framework that makes storage decisions based on rules that take into account the current context of the user. Context is any information that characterizes a current situation [13] and according to Abowd [14], a system is context-aware if it uses context to provide relevant information and/or services to its users. In our system, contextual information should influence the storage decision. Examples of relevant context include from where the user retrieves the content, where one is located or what the network conditions are alike. In general, we can distinguish between low-level context (i.e. raw and unprocessed sensor data) and high-level context that is inferred from (often multiple) low-level context information.

As mobile phones today feature a multitude of built-in sensors, they are able to capture diverse contextual information. The most prominent contextual information is the location. However, it is easy to see how we can extend this to more sophisticated context. Especially fusing data from *hard sensors* (e.g., a GPS receiver or microphone) with data from *soft sensors* (e.g. one's calendar entries) can generate meaningful higher-level context. As an example, let's assume a user is located at a certain geo-coordinate. Adding a list of point-of-interests, we might derive that he or she is at a sports stadium. Further addition of microphone readings then might derive whether a sporting event is currently in progress. We will later describe how *vStore* uses this kind of context information to make storage decisions.

2.3 Mobile Storage

While offloading computations closer to the edge of the network has been studied previously, the possibility to store data at the edge has seldom been examined. Some previous works have proposed to complement cloud storage with an additional layer at the edge of the network. The decision where to store the data is often based on location alone [21], or data is synchronized with cloud storage infrastructures [20]. Using cloudlets for storage in a peer-to-peer fashion has been proposed by Yang et al. [22]. Other than location, network information and usage patterns of files have been taken into account to make storage decisions [23,24]. In our work we do not limit ourselves to these but provide a general framework that operates on rules, which can incorporate whatever contextual information can be gathered by the devices.

Several approaches have been proposed for caching data, either in a hierarchical way [17] or collaboratively determined by content popularity [18]. Other work combines caching with prefetching strategies based on predicted mobility [19]. By definition, caching is non-persistent and in our cases, we need higher retention times of the data (e.g., to enable sharing).

3   Context-Aware Storage at the Edge

We propose a novel approach to provide context-aware micro-storage to mobile users. Figure 1 compares our approach with the traditional way of having application-specific cloud resources for data storage (Fig. 1(a)). Contrary to that, we propose *vStore*, which makes decisions where to store data across application domains and takes into account heterogeneous storage nodes (Fig. 1(b)). Furthermore, our system takes into account contextual information to make the storage decision. We envision existing applications to use the framework as a middleware in order to facilitate the exchange of data between applications.

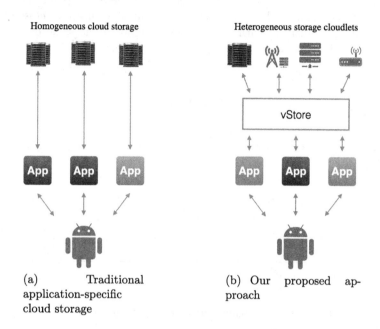

Homogeneous cloud storage

Heterogeneous storage cloudlets

vStore

(a)   Traditional application-specific cloud storage

(b) Our proposed approach

Fig. 1. Comparison of approaches

3.1 Use Cases

To further motivate the need for *vStore*, we describe three use cases that benefit from our approach. We base our observations partly on the results of a survey we conducted that had a total of 51 participants. Participants were aged 16–40 and mostly students and researchers.

Sharing Data at an Event. Especially during large-scale events, cellular networks are often congested [15]. A prominent example is football matches. Figure 2 shows measurements of the available cellular bandwidth during a match at the Commerzbank Arena, a stadium in Frankfurt, Germany with a capacity of 51,500 spectators. Compared to the average bandwidth available in the stadium when no match takes place, we can clearly see that the network quality decreases tremendously. At some distinct events, such as goals occurring in the match, the network collapses almost entirely. In such cases, edge cloudlets (that for instance are deployed on several WiFi access points) can be useful to provide users with storage services. Besides the obvious use case of storing data in the cloud for later use or sharing with people not present at the event, a more interesting use case for edge storage arises when data is to be shared among people present at the very same event. This type of sharing has been examined before in the context of video streaming [16] but not in consideration of infrastructural support of edge computing architectures. In our survey, over 50% of the participants stated that they at least occasionally share data such as pictures at an event; close to 20% of those almost exclusively with other people attending the same event. Only 4% of our participants have never experienced congested connections during events.

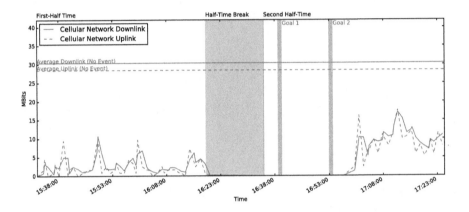

Fig. 2. Cellular bandwidth during a football match

Context-Aware Storage Across Applications. In our survey, we questioned participants whether the storage services they choose to use depend on (i) whether the data is intended for private or public use, (ii) their current location and (iii) the date and time of data capture. The results of those questions are depicted in Fig. 3(a). We can clearly observe that the majority of users bases the decision on where to store their data to a great extent on these three contextual properties. Thus, we will consider them among other properties in *vStore* to make context-aware storage decisions. Furthermore, some users upload the same data to more than one storage service (Fig. 3(b)). With the introduction of *vStore*, we aim to provide a unified way to make this decision for the user.

Getting Suggestions for Data Related to One's Current Context. When at a certain location or when performing a certain activity, users often search for information related to that specific context. With the capability to query our framework for data that is similar to one's usage context, we can provide users with such kind of information. Coming back to the example of an event, over 78% of our surveyed participants at least sometimes retrieve data related to an event they attend.

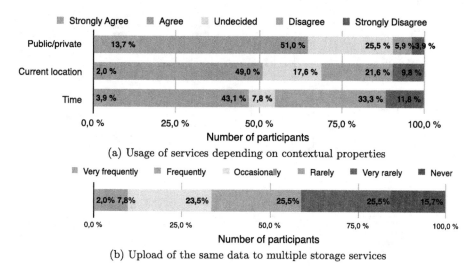

(a) Usage of services depending on contextual properties

(b) Upload of the same data to multiple storage services

Fig. 3. Survey results about the usage of multiple storage services

3.2 Problem Definition and Requirements

From the use cases motivated above, we define the problem we want to tackle as follows: Given data that mobile users want to store and contextual information, find the most suitable storage location. In order to provide context-aware micro-storage as we envisioned, the system should fulfill the following requirements: (i) storage location agnosticism, (ii) openness to extensions and third-party applications, and (iii) extensibility to implement new rules for storage decisions. In the next section, we will describe the design of our system in detail and how it fulfills these requirements.

4 System Design and Implementation

In this Section, we describe the design of our system and its individual components. Figure 4 shows a high-level overview of our system. In the following subsections, we will explain in detail the most important parts of our system, including a demo application that makes use of *vStore* on Android phones.

4.1 Virtual Storage Framework

The storage framework is the main contribution of this paper. It provides interfaces to applications in order to store and retrieve data while abstracting from a concrete storage location. The framework collects current contextual information, maintains a list of available storage nodes and—based on a set of rules—makes the decision where to store the data. For each data item to be stored, a unique identifier is generated that is later used to retrieve specific data across storage nodes.

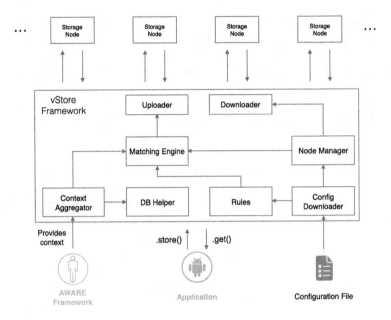

Fig. 4. System architecture

Context Aggregator. The task of the context aggregator is to collect the different kinds of contextual information. In Fig. 5, the architecture of this aggregator is summarized. To gather contextual information from the mobile phones, we rely on three providers of such information: First, we make use of AWARE[2], an open source framework for context instrumentation on Android phones. Second, the Google Places API provides a list of places that surround the user, their type and the likelihood of the users being located at those places. Third, the Android Connectivity API provides information about the network connectivity of the device. In detail, we collect the following contextual information:

- Location: A plugin for AWARE provides location information using the Google Fused Location API.
- Places: Each time a new location is available, we query the Places API for a new list of places. We group the large amount of place types provided by this API into three groups, namely points of interest (POI), event (such as stadiums, city halls and night clubs) and social (such as restaurants, cafes and bars).
- Noise: The ambient noise level is measured by an AWARE plugin through the phone's microphone. By configuring a threshold, we can determine if the current environment should be considered as loud or silent.
- Activity: The user activity is provided by another plugin that internally uses the Google Awareness API to identify the user's current activity (e.g., still, driving or walking).

---

[2] https://www.awareframework.com.

- Network: We use Android's *ConnectivityManager* and *TelephonyManager* to fetch details about the user's current connectivity situation (e.g. to what kind of network the user is currently connected to).
- The time and date as reported by the phone's operating system.

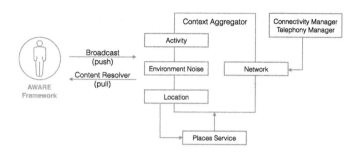

Fig. 5. Context aggregator

Node Manager. The node manager maintains a list of all available storage nodes. When storage nodes are added to the framework, their type, location and bandwidth need to be specified. Available nodes can then be queried according to these properties. Before a node is stored in the internal database of *vStore*, the node manager checks if the node is reachable. Node information can be updated and deleted through an API.

Rules. In our framework, rules are used to make the storage decision and are evaluated by the matching engine, as described later. In *vStore*, rules can either be defined globally or created individually by the users. A rule specifies certain conditions that have to be fulfilled in order for that rule to be triggered. We specify our rules to consist of three parts:

- Metadata properties: These denote for which MIME type and file size the rule should be taken into account during the matching process.
- Context triggers: These properties determine under which contextual conditions a rule is triggered. Any of the aforementioned contextual information can be specified here. All of the configured contextual properties have to match the context that is given at the time of evaluating the rule.
- Decision layers: The decision layers determine which storage nodes are chosen. A rule can consist of several layers where each layer represents a possible decision outcome. A layer can either be configured to match storage nodes that are of a certain type or that match certain constraints such as bandwidth or distance to the user. A decision layer can also point to one specific storage node. In this case, the file will be stored on this particular node. The decision layers are evaluated only if the first two tiers of the rule (i.e. metadata properties and context triggers) are fulfilled.

The way we define rules follows the *Event Condition Action* (ECA) paradigm. Mapped to our implementation, the event is the request to store a file, the conditions are the triggers that have to be fulfilled, and the action is the execution of a decision layer and, thus, the storage of a file on a storage node.

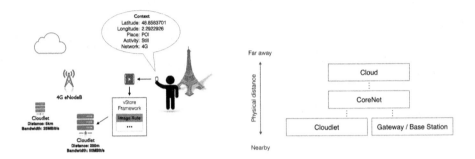

Fig. 6. Example of storage location matching

Fig. 7. Storage node hierarchy

Matching Engine. The matching engine is the main part of the framework. It makes the decision where to store data, given user data, contextual information, a set of available storage nodes and rules as input. The matching process consists of two steps: First, all rules are evaluated with respect to the configured trigger conditions and the type of data. We only consider rules where these two parts match the input. For instance, a rule that only applied to image files would not be evaluated further if the data the users wants to store is a document. Similarly, for the contextual information, let's assume the rule specifies that it only applies to files of a certain size and is restricted to a specific location or within a range from a point of interest. If these properties do not match with the file that is to be stored, this particular rule is discarded. In the second step of the matching process, for each of the remaining rules that satisfy the metadata and context triggers of the input data, a score $s, 0 \leq s \leq 100$ is computed to determine the most detailed rule, meaning the rule that incorporates the most contextual information. For instance, a rule that triggers within 150 m of a point of interest would be assigned a higher score than one triggering within 500 m. We apply different weights $\alpha \in \{0.1, 0.15, 0.2\}$ to put more emphasis on contextual information that is based on location. The rule with the highest score is then chosen, and according to its decision layers (see previous section), a storage node is then selected. In cases where the decision layers do not lead to a feasible solution, for instance because no nodes that fit the constraints are available, the rule with the second highest score is chosen and evaluated next. Figure 6 shows an example of a storage decision, in which a user takes a photo near a point of interest. A rule triggers because the user is currently still and not in motion, is connected to a 4G cellular network and at a point of interest. In this example, this rule (labeled *Image Rule* in the figure) is the one with the highest score, and in its decision layer, a cloudlet with a maximum distance of 200 m and at least 50 MBit/s of bandwidth is chosen to store the photograph.

4.2 Storage Nodes

Storage nodes are the devices that are available to store the data. In a real-world deployment, a storage node could be hosted on a variety of devices, either close-by or distant to the user. To take into account this heterogeneity, we define different types of storage nodes as outlined in Fig. 7. Besides cloud nodes, we consider cloudlets, gateway nodes and nodes in the core net. The latter could be represented by network layer middleboxes, which could have additional capabilities to store data as it passes through those devices. Gateway nodes on the other hand are devices to which users have a direct wireless connection to, such as WiFi access points or cellular base stations.

In addition, we also consider private clouds as a type of storage nodes, for instance systems such as ownCloud[3] that are owned by end users themselves. Including this kind of nodes allows to define storage rules for the storage of private data, i.e., data that is not shared among different users of the framework.

4.3 Configuration

The *vStore* framework can be configured externally. This mainly serves two purposes: (i) initially retrieving available storage nodes and (ii) including global rules for the placement decision. Defining global rules that are available on all devices is important for users who do not wish to specify custom rules. This ensures that at least some basic storage decisions can be made. To this end, the framework relies on a central configuration file that is regularly retrieved and updates available storage nodes and rules. However, in the future, we envision the configuration of the framework to be managed in a distributed way. This would for instance enable users who have the same or similar context to share custom rules they have defined.

4.4 Demo Application

As a case study and to demonstrate the integration of the framework on a mobile platform, we developed a demo application on Android phones. With this application, users are able to (i) store their data on a storage node determined by the matching engine of the framework, (ii) mark this data as either private or public, (iii) create custom storage mapping rules that are then used by the mapping engine and (iv) get context-related data from other users. The application's main screen shows a summary of all current contextual information available (Fig. 8(a) and (b)). Users can view their own files (Fig. 8(c)) and are able to upload files on this screen. This can be done for public files (right pink button) and private files (left pink button). To demonstrate the framework's ability to retrieve files

---

[3] https://owncloud.org.

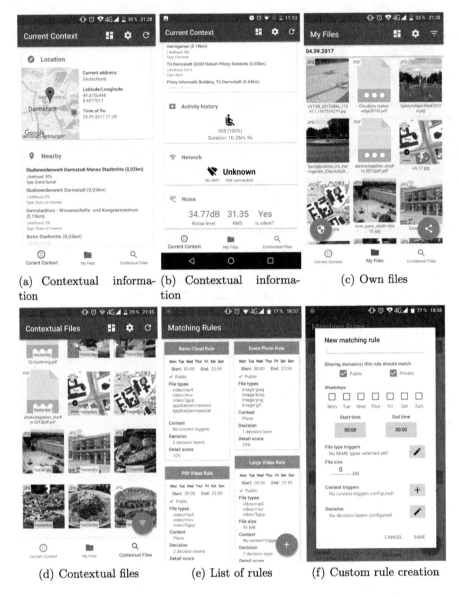

(a) Contextual informa-
tion

(b) Contextual informa-
tion

(c) Own files

(d) Contextual files

(e) List of rules

(f) Custom rule creation

Fig. 8. Screenshots of the demo application (Color figure online)

based on context, users can retrieve files with a similar context to their current
one (Fig. 8(d)). Furthermore, the app shows all currently active storage rules
(Fig. 8(e)) and allows for the creation of custom rules by the user (Fig. 8(f)).

We will use this application for our user study to conduct preliminary experiments on storage rules in a heterogeneous city-scale environment. Details of this
evaluation are described in the next section.

5   Preliminary Results

In this section, we report on preliminary experiments we conducted using the demo application we described in Sect. 4.4. We show the feasibility of our approach by deploying several storage nodes in a major city and conduct a user study by defining sample rules and evaluating the resulting storage decisions that *vStore* made. We conclude the section by providing a discussion about our findings.

5.1   Experimental Setup

We deployed a total of six storage nodes in the area of Darmstadt, Germany. The maps shown in Fig. 9 visualize our deployment. Figure 9(a) shows an overview of the area with the location of the storage nodes and Fig. 9(b) zooms in on the city center with a heatmap depicting where most of the data was captured. For a quick deployment, we use Raspberry Pis running mongoDB as data storage. A NodeJS server implements the storage service and acts as an interface between the data storage and the *vStore* framework. To simulate different types of storage nodes we would have in a large-scale deployment, we set different node types in our system: two cloudlets, one gateway, one cloud node, one core net node and one private cloud.

We defined several global rules that were pushed to the phones in our field trial of *vStore*. They are described in Table 1. The *POI Photo Rule* will be executed when the user is detected to be close to a point of interest and takes a photo. It matches any file size, day and time, and only applies to photos the user wants to share. With the configured context, a detail score of 25% is reached. The decision is divided into two layers. The first layer tries to save the file on a gateway if one is available within 5 km from the POI. If none is available, it tries to find a cloudlet in a radius of 20 km. The *Social Photo Rule* will be executed in places that we consider to be social according to our places context. Here, the same conditions apply as for the POI Photo Rule. We define two rules to be able to evaluate them separately, according to the different place context. The *Driving Rule* takes into account the activity context, as reported by the context aggregator. If the user's current activity is driving, it does not mean that he is driving the car himself. This rule would also apply in trains or taxis. Any file uploaded in this context will not be stored on nearby cloudlets since he might only drive by a nearby POI without the intention of sharing or retrieving related data. The *Event Photo Rule* applies in the context of a place that is of the type event and a noise level of at least 20 dB. We determined the value for this empirically by evaluating the behavior of the AWARE Noise plugin, even though this value seems highly inaccurate. If this context is given, the rule will store shared photos on a cloudlet within a radius of 30 km. The *Basic Cloud Rule* will be used as a fallback due to the low detail score, should no other rule yield a result. It then checks if a core net node with a bandwidth of 10 GBit/s is available to upload the data. If this is not the case, the file will be stored in the cloud.

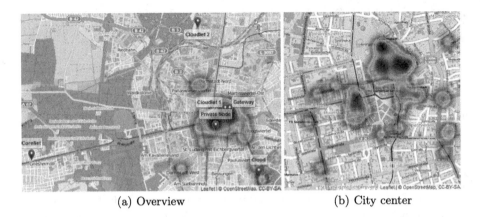

(a) Overview   (b) City center

Fig. 9. Node locations and usage heatmaps

Finally, to also evaluate the storage of private files, we created a *Basic Private Rule*. This rule matches everything the user wants to store for private use.

We distributed the demo application to six participants and configured the framework with the aforementioned rules. The participants were asked to use the application to capture various kinds of data (e.g. photos, videos, contacts) and store them using the demo application described in Sect. 4.4. The map in Fig. 9 shows on a heatmap where users were most active.

5.2 Usage Patterns and Storage Decisions

We now look at how users used their devices, i.e., which types of data they stored and which storage decisions were made based on the rules we defined. The bottom row of Table 1 shows how many times each rule was triggered. We can observe that the *Basic Cloud Rule* was triggered the most, however, data was stored on cloud nodes only for 29.3% of all data. This is because the cloud rule has a very low detail score. In many cases, other rules that relate to the user's location or define a proximity to a point of interest, have a more detailed score and therefore those are the ones that determine the placement. We can think of the cloud rule as a fallback, in case there is no most likely place (e.g., when we are not sure where the user is).

The resulting placement decisions for the different file types that were used during our study are shown in Table 2. In total, users stored 178 files using *vStore*, most of which were photos. Out of those, 35.9% were stored on cloudlets, 19.3% on gateway nodes and 2.7% on core net nodes. These numbers confirm the benefits that can be obtained in future edge computing environments. In contrast to this, without *vStore*, users would likely have all their photos uploaded to distant cloud infrastructures. The table furthermore depicts the sharing ratio for each type of data, i.e., whether users marked the data to be publicly shared on the storage nodes or for their private use. From the results, we can observe

Table 1. Placement rules

	POI Photo Rule	Social Photo Rule	Driving Rule	Event Photo Rule	Basic Cloud Rule	Basic Private Rule
Context	Place: POI	Place: Social	Activity: Driving	Place: Event, Noise: > -20dB	None	None
File Size	Any	Any	Any	Any	Any	Any
File Types	JPG, BMP, PNG, GIF	JPG, BMP, PNG, GIF	Any	JPG, BMP, PNG, GIF	Any	Any
Sharing Domain	Public	Public	Public	Public	Public	Private
Weekdays	Mon-Sun	Mon-Sun	Mon-Sun	Mon-Sun	Mon-Sun	Mon-Sun
Time	Any	Any	Any	Any	Any	Any
Decision Layers	**Layer 1** Gateway $\leq$ 5km **Layer 2** Cloudlet $\leq$ 10km	**Layer 1** Cloudlet $\leq$ 5km **Layer 2** Cloudlet $\leq$ 10km	**Layer 1** Cloud	**Layer 1** Cloudlet $\leq$ 30km	**Layer 1** CoreNet with ↑ 10GBit/s, ↓ 10GBit/s **Layer 2** Cloud	**Layer 1** Private Node
Detail Score	25 %	25 %	20 %	35 %	10 %	10 %
Times executed	36	34	18	5	47	5

that this heavily depends on the data type. While users were willing to share over 80% of their images, for more sensitive information such as contacts this number drops down close to 3%. With the set of rules we defined, we are able to capture the user's intention, as the sharing domain influences the placement decision *vStore* makes.

Table 2. Placement results

	Node Type							Total	Sharing Ratio
	Gateway	Cloudlet 1	Cloudlet 2	CoreNet	Cloud	Private Node	Phone		
Images	28	35	17	4	43	4	14	145	81.46%
Videos	3	6	1	1	3	0	3	17	9.55 %
Documents	0	1	0	2	7	1	0	11	6.18 %
Contacts	2	0	0	0	3	0	0	5	2.81 %

5.3 Discussion

With our preliminary experiments outlined in this section, we were able to show how we can make context-aware storage decisions that include heterogeneous storage nodes by using rule-based matching. However, the accuracy of contextual descriptions remains an issue. For instance, files were sometimes saved using a wrong context, due to the fact that the context is not updated in real time. Keeping an accurate context on a mobile phone is always a trade-off between accuracy and energy consumption. In addition, much work still needs to be done in order to correctly recognize higher-level context. However, our user study motivated the use cases of using cloudlets, especially if they are located at the edge of the network and close-by to mobile users. This is especially true in the context of sharing data locally. For this use case, *vStore* offers the possibility to define rules that are triggered when a user is at a certain location or point of interest. As outlined in Sect. 3.1, many people today share data at events, some of them even with people present at the same event. For the future, we envision storage cloudlets to be deployed throughout city areas, some of which are co-located at the radio access network or act as gateway nodes themselves (e.g., WiFi hotspots during events).

Of course, appropriate rules are required to make the framework beneficial in practical use. We enable users to define custom rules that they can represent their usage intentions with. In addition to custom rules, the framework allows for global rules to be configured. In our field trial, we could see that even with just a basic set of global rules, these were often executed when making the placement decisions. In future use of the system, infrastructure providers could set these global rules, e.g., to specify local cloudlets on gateway nodes when regular networks are overloaded.

6   Conclusion and Future Work

In this paper, we presented *vStore* (virtual store), a framework that enables micro-storage at the edge of the network and abstracts from predefined storage locations for data captured by mobile users. This enables (i) decoupling of storage locations from specific cloud infrastructures and therefore facilitates the exchange of data across applications and (ii) leveraging small-scale cloudlets at the edge of the network to provide better quality of service to mobile users. An example use case for the latter is the sharing of data when cellular networks are congested, e.g., during large-scale events. *vStore* allows different stakeholders (e.g., mobile users or infrastructure providers) to define custom rules that are evaluated when making the decision where to store the data. We showed the viability of our system with a user study using a demo application that users could use to capture and upload data. Furthermore, users were able to retrieve related data related to their current usage context. We deployed different storage nodes in a major city and through the implementation of example decision rules we were able to show how this framework can complement existing cloud-based storage infrastructures.

vStore provides an extensible framework we encourage other researchers to use in order to test new approaches to decide storage locations. The rule framework allows for custom definition and evaluation of decision algorithms. We especially envision the emerging research on machine learning to be able to contribute interesting insights on this. In future work, we will investigate optimizations on the network layer as well as suitable replication mechanisms that are required for a larger-scale deployment of our system. Furthermore, we plan to include mechanisms to include the dynamic discovery of storage nodes into the framework.

Acknowledgements. This work has been co-funded by the German Federal Ministry for Education and Research (BMBF, Software Campus project DynamicINP, grant no. 01IS12054) and by the German Research Foundation (DFG) as part of the Collaborative Research Center (CRC) 1053 - MAKI.

References

1. Jadeja, Y., Modi, K.: Cloud computing - concepts, architecture and challenges. In: International Conference on Computing, Electronics and Electrical Technologies (ICCEET), pp. 877–880. IEEE (2012)
2. Chun, B., Ihm, S., Maniatis, P., Naik, M., Patti, A.: Clonecloud: elastic execution between mobile device and cloud. In: 6th Conference on Computer Systems, EuroSys, pp. 301–314. ACM (2011)
3. Flores, H., Hui, P., Tarkoma, S., Li, Y., Srirama, S., Buyya, R.: Mobile code offloading: from concept to practice and beyond. IEEE Commun. Mag. **53**(3), 80–88 (2015)
4. Satyanarayanan, M., Bahl, P., Caceres, R., Davies, N.: The case for VM-based cloudlets in mobile computing. IEEE Pervasive Comput. **8**(4), 14–23 (2009)
5. Satyanarayanan, M.: The emergence of edge computing. IEEE Comput. Mag. **50**(1), 30–39 (2017)
6. Yi, S., Li, C., Li, Q.: A Survey of fog computing: concepts, applications and issues. In: Workshop on Mobile Big Data (Mobidata), pp. 37–42. ACM (2015)
7. Yi, S., Hao, Z., Qin, Z., Li, Q.: Fog computing: platform and applications. In: 3rd IEEE Workshop on Hot Topics in Web Systems and Technologies (HotWeb), pp. 73–78. IEEE (2015)
8. Bonomi, F., Milito, R., Zhu, J., Addepalli, S.: Fog computing and its role in the internet of things. In: 1st Edition of the MCC Workshop on Mobile Cloud Computing, pp. 13–16. ACM (2012)
9. Chandra, A., Weissman, J., Heintz, B.: Decentralized edge clouds. IEEE Internet Comput. **17**(5), 70–73 (2013)
10. Beck, M., Werner, M., Feld, S., Schimper, T.: Mobile edge computing: a taxonomy. In: 6th International Conference on Advances in Future Internet (AFIN), pp. 48–54. IARIA (2014)
11. Meurisch, C., Seeliger, A., Schmidt, B., Schweizer, I., Kaup, F., Mühlhäuser, M.: Upgrading wireless home routers for enabling large-scale deployment of cloudlets. In: Sigg, S., Nurmi, P., Salim, F. (eds.) MobiCASE 2015. LNICST, vol. 162, pp. 12–29. Springer, Cham (2015). https://doi.org/10.1007/978-3-319-29003-4_2
12. Gedeon, J., Meurisch, C., Bhat, D., Stein, M., Wang, L., Mühlhäuser, M.: Router-based brokering for surrogate discovery in edge computing. In: International Workshop on Hot Topics in Planet–Scale Mobile Computing and Online Social Networking (HotPOST). IEEE (2017)
13. Dey, A.K.: Understanding and using context. Pers. Ubiquit. Comput. **5**, 4–7 (2001)
14. Abowd, G.D., Dey, A.K., Brown, P.J., Davies, N., Smith, M., Steggles, P.: Towards a better understanding of context and context-awareness. In: Gellersen, H.-W. (ed.) HUC 1999. LNCS, vol. 1707, pp. 304–307. Springer, Heidelberg (1999). https://doi.org/10.1007/3-540-48157-5_29
15. Frömmgen, A., Heuschkel, J., Jahnke, P., Cuozzo, F., Schweizer, I., Eugster, P., Mühlhäuser, M., Buchmann, A.: Crowdsourcing measurements of mobile network performance and mobility during a large scale event. In: Karagiannis, T., Dimitropoulos, X. (eds.) PAM 2016. LNCS, vol. 9631, pp. 70–82. Springer, Cham (2016). https://doi.org/10.1007/978-3-319-30505-9_6
16. Dezfuli, N., Huber, J., Olberding, S., Mühlhäuser, M.: CoStream: in-situ co-construction of shared experiences through mobile video sharing during live events. In: CHI Extended Abstracts on Human Factors in Computing Systems, pp. 2477–2482. ACM (2012)

17. Duro, F., Blas, J., Higuero, D., Perez, O., Carretero, J.: CoSMiC: a hierarchical cloudlet-based storage architecture for mobile clouds. Simul. Modell. Pract. Theory **50**, 3–19 (2014)
18. Cao, Z., Papadimitriou, P.: Collaborative content caching in wireless edge with SDN. In: 1st Workshop on Content Caching and Delivery in Wireless Networks (CCDWN). ACM (2016)
19. Zhang, F., Xu, C., Zhang, Y., Ramakrishnan, K., Mukherjee, S., Yates, R., Thu, N.: EdgeBuffer: caching and prefetching content at the edge in the MobilityFirst future internet architecture. In: World of Wireless, Mobile and Multimedia Networks (WoWMoM), pp. 1–9. IEEE (2015)
20. Hao, Z., Li, Q.: EdgeStore: integrating edge computing into cloud-based storage systems. In: Symposium on Edge Computing, pp. 115–116. IEEE/ACM (2016)
21. Stuedi, P., Mohomed, I., Terry, D.: Wherestore: location-based data storage for mobile devices interacting with the cloud. In: 1st ACM Workshop on Mobile Cloud Computing & Services: Social Networks and Beyond. ACM (2010)
22. Yang, Z., Zhao, B., Xing, Y., Ding, S., Xiao, F., Dai, Y.: AmazingStore: available, low-cost online storage service using cloudlets. In: 9th International Workshop on Peer-to-Peer Systems. USENIX (2010)
23. Bazarbayev, S., Hiltunen, M., Joshi, K., Sanders, W., Schlichting, R.: PSCloud: a durable context-aware personal storage cloud. In: 9th Workshop on Hot Topics in Dependable Systems. ACM (2013)
24. Han, D., Yan, Y., Shu, T., Yang, L., Cui, S.: Cognitive context-aware distributed storage optimization in mobile cloud computing: a stable matching based approach. In: 37th International Conference on Distributed Computing Systems (ICDCS). IEEE (2017)

A System for Training Stuffed-Suit
Posing Without a Suit

Ryo Nakayama[1]([✉]), Tsutom Terada[1,2], and Masahiko Tsukamoto[1]

[1] Graduate School of Engineering, Kobe University, Kobe, Japan
nakayamaryou@stu.kobe-u.ac.jp, tsutomu@eedept.kobe-u.ac.jp,
tuka@kobe-u.ac.jp
[2] PRESTO JST, Japan Science and Technology Agency, Kawaguchi, Japan

Abstract. People who perform while wearing stuffed suits are popular among people of all ages; however, the performers need to train themselves stuffed-suits on their posing before performing. Many performers are forced to train themselves to pose without wearing a stuffed suit because there are few environments where they can train with a stuffed suit, which makes pose training difficult for them. This paper describes a system we propose that enables performers without a stuffed suit to pose train themselves by observing images of the same type of stuffed suits that performers actually wear. Using our system enables users to train themselves with the same sensations they would feel when wearing stuffed suits, which enables them to perform the posing smoothly in a stuffed suit. We carried out a preliminary study to verify the difficulties performers face when wearing a stuffed suit and implemented a prototype of our proposed system. Evaluation results confirmed that using our system enabled performers to improve their posing skills compared with conventional training methods.

Keywords: Stuffed suit · Training · Motion capture system
Visually feed back

1 Introduction

Stuffed suits have been widely used in various theme parks and events because people wearing stuffed suits provide performances popular among people of all ages and make them smile and be happy. Performers wearing stuffed suits need to perform as the character they play because stuffed suits have a role to make the characters in the virtual world appear in the real world.

To perform in an expert manner, performers need to perform the posing like the character they portray. Stuffed suits alone cannot change their voices or facial expressions. If the stuffed suits do not correctly portray the character being represented, the people watching will feel uncomfortable. Therefore, before each performance performers need to thoroughly practice their posing for the stuffed suit they will wear.

© ICST Institute for Computer Sciences, Social Informatics and Telecommunications Engineering 2018
K. Murao et al. (Eds.): MobiCASE 2018, LNICST 240, pp. 183–200, 2018.
https://doi.org/10.1007/978-3-319-90740-6_11

In training while wearing a stuffed suit, many performers are forced to train without wearing one because there are few environments where they can train while wearing one. In general training environments, they imagine the appearance of the suits and imitate the appearance they will convey by posing in front of a mirror. However, it is difficult for them to imagine how they will perform without wearing a stuffed suit because of the differences between their own bodies and those that people will see when they are wearing a stuffed suit.

To address this issue, we propose a system that enables performers who are not wearing a stuffed suit to be trained in stuffed-suit posing by visually presenting them with the same type of stuffed-suit images that they would use as performers. In our system, the user first needs to create a database that consists of several images of stuffed-suit posing and user's skeleton data in the stuffed suit. Then, the user uses the database and trains himself or herself in stuffed-suit posing in front of a Kinect device and a display. Our system visually presents images of stuffed-suit posing that matches those with the database on the display in real time, based on the user's skeleton data measured by Kinect. In addition, we implemented a function that enabled users to learn whether or not they could pose in the same way as they could when wearing a stuffed suit. More specifically, we implemented a function to feed back to users which body parts were out of the range of motion that stuffed suits allow when they posed in a manner that they could not have done without wearing a stuffed suit. We carried out a preliminary study to verify the difficulties in training stuffed-suit posing and implemented a prototype application of our proposed system. The evaluation results indicated that our system is effective for enabling users to pose without wearing a stuffed suit.

2   Related Work

There are several studies on improving stuffed-suit performances. Okazaki et al. proposed a system for performers in stuffed suits [1]. The system has two functions, i.e., posing support and vision extension. In the posing support system, users can pose like the character they wish to portray by using displayed images of stuffed suits they get in a head mounted display (HMD). In the vision extension system, they can see the camera images the HMD gets around the eye level of the user wearing a stuffed suit. The system enables performers to check the surroundings easily and react to the action of surrounding people quickly. Tei et al. proposed a multimodal interface that supports stuffed-suit performance by visual information using an HMD as well as auditory information using speaker and tactile information from a vibration motor provided to the user according to circumstances [2]. Slyper et al. proposed a system in which a person wearing a stuffed suit can talk with other people [3]. Users wearing stuffed suits can talk to others by operating a mouth input device with their tongue and selecting the sound of the character's voice. Although many studies have been reported that support stuffed-suit performances, none have been reported that support the training of users not wearing a stuffed suit, as our proposed system does.

Kinect [4] is widely used for measuring body motion in systems that support human motion acquisition. Since Kinect is relatively inexpensive and users do not need to wear any sensors on their body when using it, they use it in several motion acquisition systems such as those reported by Kyan et al. ([5], Dimitrios et al. [6], and Saha et al. [7]). Because of Kinect's high versatility, we used it in our study to measure the data obtained for users when they were training while wearing a stuffed suit. In such cases, however, Kinect cannot effectively measure data. Since we needed to measure the data for users wearing stuffed suits, we sought measuring methods other than those from Kinect.

Motion capture systems are frequently used for measuring body motion. They measure and record movements in time sequences in accordance with position information in spaces for human body parts. Van der Linden et al. proposed a system that supports the learning of dance skills by mimicking the movement of avatars created on the basis of familiar motion data acquired using an inertial motion capture system [8]. Tommi and Marc are trying to convey South African traditional dances to people of different cultures using an optical motion capture system [9]. Van der Linden et al. proposed a system that helps to improve violin playing skills by showing beginners how to hold the violin and how to improve their bowing technique by using an inertial motion capture system [10]. In this way, motion capture systems have been effectively used in extraction, storage and inheritance of human motions. Using an inertial motion capture system makes it possible to measure human motion data obtained inside stuffed suits.

In our study, we aimed to construct a highly versatile system by separately using Kinect, which is widely popular and easy to use, and an inertial motion capture system that can measure human motion data obtained inside stuffed suits.

3   Preliminary Study

In general, many performers have to train to perform without wearing a stuffed suit because they cannot always prepare the suit in advance. When training, they imagine their appearance in the suit and imitate the pose they wish to convey in front of a mirror. However, in many cases, when they actually wear the stuffed suit, they cannot pose like they did in the training. In this section, we describe an experiment we conducted to explore why they are unable to do so and how to solve the problem. In the experiment we investigated two types of stuffed suits with a large head (Fig. 2). Stuffed suits of this type are the most often used. Suits A and B comprise three parts: the head, torso and leg parts. Suit A is larger in size and heavier than suit B because it is for a male character while suit B is for a female one. We used these suits because we felt the differences between them might affect the obtained results (Fig. 1).

3.1   Experiment Environment

In this experiment, we measured the skeleton data by using a motion capture system when the subject posed with the same appearance in three states: non-

Stuffed suit A   Stuffed suit B

Fig. 1. Two types of stuffed suits.

wearing, wearing-A and wearing-B (Fig. 2). The experiment subject had had no previous experience in wearing a stuffed suit. His actions were adjusted so that they would be the same for all three states. The motion capture system we used to measure the skeleton data was 3-Space Sensors, which enables measurements to be taken through 17 inertial sensors attached to the subject with a band and enables skeleton data to be visualized by using dedicated software [11]. Using a camera enabled us to obtain the appearance image of each state at the same time as we obtained the measured skeleton data. After the measurements, we compared the obtained skeleton data.

Fig. 2. Identical pose for non-wearing, wearing-A and wearing-B states.

3.2   Results and Discussion

Figure 3 shows the skeleton data measurement results obtained with the dedicated software and the subject's appearance image in each state. Clear differences were found in the skeleton data between the wearing and non-wearing states. The difference from the right shoulder to the elbow was especially clear; when wearing a suit the subject was unable to raise the shoulder as well as he could when not wearing one. We consider that this is because the head part of the suit covers the shoulder and makes it harder for the subject to lift it. There were also clear differences in the skeleton data between the wearing-A and the wearing-B cases. That is, it was harder for the subject to raise the shoulders and

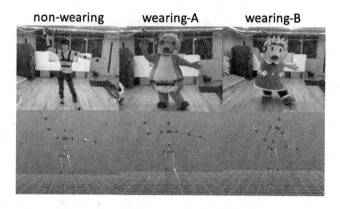

Fig. 3. Skeleton data measurement results for the non-wearing, wearing-A and wearing-B states

upper body in the latter case. We consider that this is because the smaller suit B restricts the range of movement more than for suit A. From this, we concluded that the type of suit will affect freedom of movement, even for suits having the same shape.

In this way, we concluded that performers cannot effectively make the motions of the stuffed suit's character because of the differences between the suit's appearance and the actions the performer makes when wearing it. Therefore, in actual performances they cannot pose in the same manner that they could when wearing a stuffed suit in training. Thus, in actual performances their poses do not come across effectively and this has a negative effect on the popularity and reliability of people wearing stuffed suits. We also concluded that the type of suit worn brings about differences in the performer's range of motion. That is, even performers who have worn suit A may not be able to perform in the same manner when wearing suit B because of the differences in the range of motion the suits allow them.

These results indicate that it is important for performers to understand the range of motion that suits will allow them during the time they are training. It is hard for performers who have never worn a stuffed suit to judge from the suit's appearance how it will restrict their freedom of movement. Even performers who have worn stuffed suits previously find it hard to imagine how a suit they have never worn will affect their freedom of movement. Beginning with the next section, we will describe the differences between the appearance of a stuffed suit and the actions the performer makes when wearing it. These differences make it difficult to train people on how to perform when wearing a stuffed suit when they are not actually wearing one.

4 Proposed System

In our study, we designed and here propose a system that enables performers not wearing a stuffed suit to be trained as if they were wearing one, by visually presenting them with images of performers wearing stuffed suits posing in the same way as they will. The system enables users not wearing a stuffed suit to feel the same sensations in training as they would when wearing one. The results we obtained in a preliminary study confirmed the need to provide two system requirements for training purposes.

Requirement 1: users can learn the range of motion stuffed suits provide them. Posing training by watching one's image in a mirror induces users to train themselves in posing that cannot be performed when wearing a stuffed suit because the users imagine their appearance in wearing a stuffed suit during training. In such training, the users perform incomplete posing when wearing the stuffed suit because they cannot pose in the same way as they could during training. Therefore, in the posing training without a stuffed suit, if users perform posing that they could not while wearing the stuffed suit, the system needs immediate presentation to the user. For example, when the users train themselves in stuffed-suit posing B (Fig. 2), if they raise their shoulder, the system visually tells them they cannot perform this pose when wearing stuffed suit B. Through a trial-and-error procedure this enables users to find poses they can perform with a stuffed suit and learn the range of motions the stuffed suit will allow them.

Requirement 2: users can in real time see how they perform when wearing a stuffed suit. In several training systems, such as those for sports and dances, there are many ways to feed users' training data, such as graphs and video, back to the user after training. However, in this method, we considered that it is hard for performers to memorize their body sensations in posing by associating them with their training data. Therefore, our proposed system visually presents stuffed-suit posing to users in real time, which enables them to memorize the posing by associating it with their own body sensations.

4.1   System Structure

The structure of our proposed system is shown in Fig. 4. The system consists of a Kinect device, a motion capture system, a PC and a display. The system consists of two phases: a database-creation phase and a posing-training phase. In the database-creation phase, an expert performer with experience in wearing stuffed suits will acquire the appearance image of the stuffed suits and his/her skeleton data and will save them in a PC database. In the posing-training phase, users use the database and train themselves on how to pose in front of the Kinect device and a display. In the posing training, our system visually presents stuffed-suit posing to the user in real time.

4.2   Database-Creation Phase

It is desirable for an expert performer to carry out this Database-Creation phase because abundant databases cannot be created from the performances of beginners wearing stuffed suits. In this phase, expert performers wear a stuffed suit

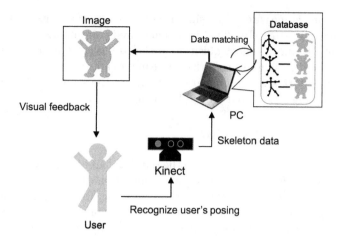

Fig. 4. System configuration.

and their skeleton data are measured by using the motion capture system. The use of a camera simultaneously enables them to see the images of themselves wearing the stuffed suit. Data measurement and appearance image acquisition are performed in synchronism with each other. After the measurements, the users create a database by associating the skeleton data with the appearance image as shown in Fig. 5, then saves them in the PC. The skeleton data is three-dimensional coordinates of 17 joints' position of the human body. The data is $17 * 3 = 51$-dimensional data. The procedure of this phase is shown below.

1. An expert performer wears a stuffed suit and inertial sensors of a motion capture system and performs various poses.

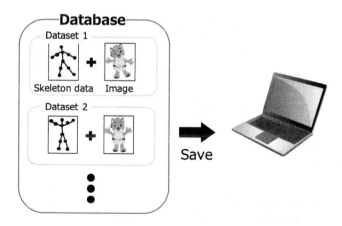

Fig. 5. Database-creation phase.

2. Skeleton data is measured by using a motion capture system with the sampling number set to 10 Hz. The data is acquired continuously.
3. At the same timing as the acquisition of skeleton data, appearance images of the stuffed-suit posing are recorded by using a camera.
4. The skeleton data and the appearance image of the stuffed suits acquired at the same timing were saved on the PC as a database.

4.3   Posing-Training Phase

In the posing-training phase, users use the database and train themselves on the posing in front of a Kinect device and a display. If another person conducts the database-creation phase, the user uses that database. In the training of stuffed-suit posing without a stuffed suit, the display visually presents stuffed-suit posing images that match those in the database. The procedure of this phase is shown below.

1. The user gets posing training without a stuffed suit in front of a Kinect device and a display.
2. User's skeleton data is measured by using Kinect.
3. The measured skeleton data is matched with skeleton data in the database.
4. Stuffed-suit images corresponding to skeleton data in the database presented to the user on the display.

Recognition Method. The flow of data processing was as follows. Figure 6 shows the data processing flow. First, we used the nearest neighbor method to search for the data in the database that was closest to that in the Kinect device. We set the learning data as the skeleton data acquired in the database-creation phase. The test data was set as the skeleton data acquired from Kinect in the

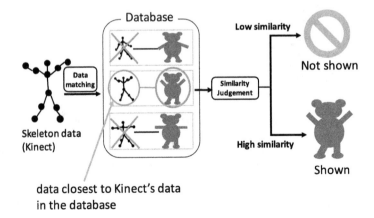

Fig. 6. Recognizing the processing flow of the posing-training phase.

posing-training phase. One label was assigned to one dataset with the skeleton data in the database and the appearance image of the stuffed suits. We allocated the labels so that they would match the number of skeleton data elements in the database. Therefore, the number of labels depended on that of the datasets in the database. For determining labels, we calculated the distance between the learning data and the test data at each joint and took the total of the distances as the total distance of data for one label. Skeleton data of the label with the smallest total calculated distance was selected as the skeleton data closest to that from Kinect. Next, we judged the similarity between the skeleton data from Kinect and the selected data. If there was even one joint whose distance was at least 10 cm longer than the skeleton data from Kinect in the selected data, we regarded it as having low similarity and so did not display the appearance image of the stuffed suit. If there were no joints whose distance was at least 10 cm longer than the skeleton data from Kinect, we regarded them as having high similarity and displayed the image of the stuffed suits. This function enables users to determine whether they could perform the posing they intended whether or not they were wearing the stuffed suit.

5 Implementation

On the basis of what we reported in the previous section, we implemented a prototype of our proposed system. In the database-creation phase, we used the Xsens MVN motion capture system [12] and logicool HD PRO WEBCAM C 920 R [13]. This motion capture system can measure a user's motion data by wearing a dedicated suit with 17 motion sensors on the body. The camera can acquire the appearance images of the stuffed suits at the same time it acquires the motion data by connecting to a PC. The sampling frequency of the motion sensor was set to 10 Hz and the PC used Lenovo's ThinkPad X1 Carbon (CPU: COREi 7-4600 U 2.10 GHz, 2.69 GHz, memory: 8 GB). As the software for the motion capture system and the camera, we used Microsoft's Visual C ++ 2013 and OpenCV [14]. In the posing-training phase, we also developed applications using Microsoft's Kinect and Visual C ♯ 2013. The sampling frequency of Kinect was set to 30 Hz.

5.1 Application

The application displays the appearance image of the stuffed suits that is the closest to a user's posing in real time. If the user performs posing that cannot be performed with the stuffed suit, the application immediately presents this information to the user. In the posing training, the user performs the posing in front of a display and the Kinect device as shown in Fig. 7. In this application, we implemented a skeleton correction function for users to use our system with the database from others. In the skeleton correction function, the user's skeleton data is linearly corrected and matched with the skeleton data of the database. By using this function, the user does not have to perform the database-creation

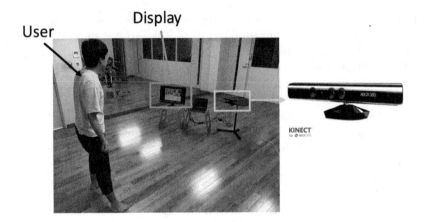

Fig. 7. Posing-training environment.

phase and is trained in posing by using a database prepared in advance from others. In addition, we implemented a posing correction feedback function that feeds back to the user the part of the body that is the cause of the posing that cannot be done. By using this function, the users can revise their posing to an appropriate posing. Figure 8 shows the application UI. The skeleton data from Kinect and that in the database are matched by using the nearest neighbor method and the appearance image of the stuffed suit that is the closest to the user's posing is visually presented. If the user performs posing that cannot be done with the stuffed suits or posing that is unmeasured during the database-creation phase, the appearance image of the stuffed suit is not displayed as shown in Fig. 9. Then, the parts of the body that are out of the motion range of the stuffed suit are displayed in red circles and fed back to the user. In addition, the

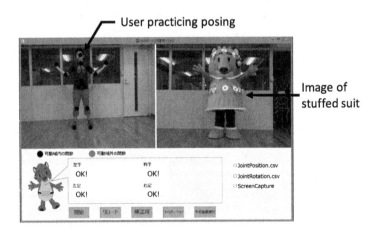

Fig. 8. Application UI.

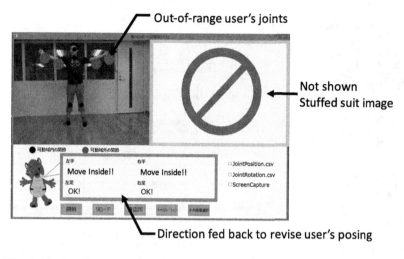

Fig. 9. Posing that cannot be done with a stuffed suit. (Color figure online)

parts shown by the red frame in the figure recognize which direction the body parts deviating from the motion range of the stuffed suit are deviated in the upward, downward, inward or outward directions. This application feeds back an instruction for pose correction to the user. Thus, users can learn the direction in which the pose should be corrected. By using this application, the users can be trained in posing while confirming the appearance image of the stuffed suits that is the closest to their posing in real time and can learn the motion range the stuffed suits allow.

6 Evaluation

6.1 Database Creation Phase

To use the system in the performed evaluation experiments, it was necessary to prepare the database in advance. In this experiment the principal author, whose height is about 175 cm, created the database that the subjects used to use the system. The procedure is shown below. First, the author wore the Xsens suit and the stuffed suit shown in Fig. 10 and performed the posing shown in Fig. 12. At this time, the author's skeleton data was measured by the motion capture system and the image of the stuffed suit was taken by a web camera. Data measurement was performed for 30 seconds, and a database of 300 data sets was created.

6.2 Experiment Environment

We conducted an experiment to evaluate whether the posing skill was improved by using our proposed system compared with the conventional method using

Stuffed suit B

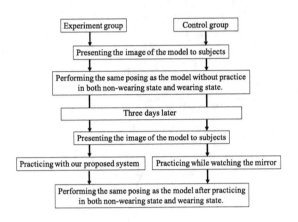

Fig. 10. The stuffed suit used in this experiment.

Fig. 11. Experimental procedure.

a mirror. In this experiment, the experiment group trained by using our proposed system and a control group were trained by watching a mirror. We evaluated whether the subjects' posing approached the models before and after the training.

The experimental procedure is shown in Fig. 11. Eight subjects who had had no experience with stuffed suits were randomly assigned to each of the experiment groups who received posing training by using our proposed system and the control group who received posing training with the conventional method by watching the mirror. The subjects' heights ranged from 165 to 180 cm. First, both groups were presented images for the three kinds of poses shown in Fig. 12. Second, the subjects who were not wearing a stuffed suit imagined the posing inside the stuffed suit and imitated the model posing. Then, the posing data of each subject was measured by using the motion capture system. Data measurements were performed at 17 joints of the body. Third, the subjects wore a stuffed suit and imitated the model posing. Finally, the posing data was measured by using the motion capture system and the appearance image was taken by using a camera.

Three days later, the experiment group received model posing training by using our proposed system and the control group was trained by watching the mirror. The control group trained in a comfortable environment to check their entire body because the mirror was positioned on a wall. We explained the function and usage of this application to the experiment group and they understood them and were trained in posing accordingly. Subjects performed various poses without wearing a stuffed suit so that images of the models could be displayed on the application. Posing training went on until the subject was satisfied. After practicing, subjects who were not wearing a stuffed suit performed the posing

Pose 1   Pose 2   Pose 3

Fig. 12. Models for the experiment.

that they were trained in and the posing data of each subject was measured by using the motion capture system. Then, the subjects wore the stuffed suit and performed the posing that they were trained in. Finally, the posing data was measured by using the motion capture system and the appearance image was taken by using a camera.

We used two ways to evaluate our method, one a non-wearing state (i.e., a state when a stuffed suit was not worn) and the other a wearing state in which a stuffed suit was worn. In the non-wearing state, we evaluated whether subjects can learn the range of motion the stuffed suits allow them by practicing the posing with our proposed system. To be specific, we quantitatively evaluated whether the subject's posing approached that of the model data before and after the training by comparing the posing data of subjects and that of the model. Finally, we compared the results in terms of the transition of their numerical values before and after the training.

In the wearing state, we evaluated whether or not the subject's posing skill improved by using our proposed system. In addition to the quantitative evaluation described above, we carried out a subjective evaluation of the evaluators. In this evaluation, we conducted a questionnaire survey with a seven-level Rickard scale about how closely a subject's posing approached that of the models by using our proposed system. We compared subjects' posing scores before and after the training on a scale from one to seven, where one meant "close agreement" and seven meant "agreement not totally consistent." Ten different evaluators from among the subjects answered the questionnaire.

6.3 Results

Table 1 shows the obtained quantitative evaluation results and also the subjective evaluation results obtained from the evaluators. The quantitative evaluation values are the total differences between the joint angle data of the subject's posing and that of the model posing. Small values mean that the subjects' posing performance was close to that of the model posing. The subjective evaluation

Table 1. Quantitative and subjective results.

| | | | Quantitative | | | | Subjective | | | | | | Quantitative | | | | Subjective | |
| | | | Non-wearing | | Wearing | | Wearing | | | | | | Non-wearing | | Wearing | | Wearing | |
		Sub	Before	After	Before	After	Before	After				Sub	Before	After	Before	After	Before	After
Exp[1]	Pose 1	A	305	187	214	204	3.9	5.4	Con[2]	Pose1	E	457	263	258	207	5.9	4.8
		B	376	270	345	226	2.1	3.6			F	375	372	263	252	5.1	4.4
		C	329	253	309	271	3.7	4.8			G	336	362	162	206	1.9	2.2
		D	306	251	289	281	3.0	4.1			H	339	389	419	369	3.2	3.1
	Pose 2	A	276	252	365	290	2.9	3.8		Pose 2	E	490	315	332	251	2.3	3.7
		B	387	313	502	435	2.9	4.1			F	399	331	383	328	4.1	4.0
		C	308	243	309	303	3.6	4.2			G	318	257	407	282	5.2	5.2
		D	403	323	481	410	3.3	3.3			H	175	228	285	223	2.4	4.3
	Pose 3	A	569	359	385	362	3.5	3.8		Pose 3	E	530	480	367	402	4.1	4.0
		B	554	376	464	367	4.3	5.4			F	768	583	522	611	2.6	2.7
		C	550	387	368	428	2.8	4.1			G	511	436	392	370	2.8	3.1
		D	678	457	440	459	3.8	4.1			H	553	581	570	484	2.5	3.3

values are the average of the score of subjects' posing before and after the training. Large values mean that the posing the subjects performed was close to the model posing.

Figure 13 shows the quantitative results obtained for the transition of the differences from the model data in the non-wearing state. The values represent the average of the differences from the model data before and after the training. ◎ is $p < 0.01$, ○ is $p < 0.05$ and △ is $p < 0.1$. The result with two-way ANOVA (analysis of variance) showed that the main effect of the training was significant ($F_{(1,22)} = 34.51, p < 0.01$) and interaction was significant ($F_{(1,22)} = 4.32, p < 0.05$). The simple main effect of interaction was as follows. The simple main effect of the method was significant only after the training ($F_{(1,22)} = 4.17, p < 0.1$). Therefore, the differences in the values from those of the model data for the experiment group were significantly smaller than those of the control group. Next, the simple main effect of the training was significant in the experiment

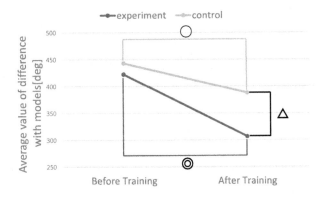

Fig. 13. Quantitative posing results obtained in non-wearing state.

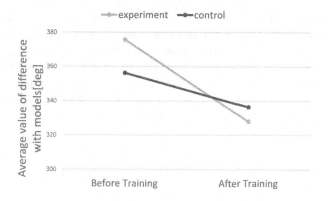

Fig. 14. Quantitative posing results obtained in wearing state.

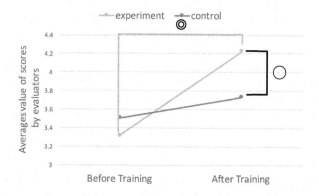

Fig. 15. Subjective posing results obtained in wearing state.

group ($F_{(1,22)} = 31.63, p < 0.01$). Therefore, the differences in values from the model data after the training were significantly smaller than those before the training. In addition, the simple main effect of the training was significant in the control group ($F_{(1,22)} = 7.20, p < 0.05$). Therefore, the differences in values from the model data after the training were significantly smaller than those before the training.

Figure 14 shows the quantitative results obtained for the transition of the differences from the model data in the wearing state. The values represent the average differences in the values from the model data before and after the training. The results obtained with two-way ANOVA showed that the main effect of the training was significant ($F_{(1,22)} = 11.70, p < 0.01$) but that interaction was not significant. Figure 15 shows the transition in the questionnaire scores before and after the training in the wearing state. The values represent the average difference in the questionnaire scores before and after the training. The results obtained with two-way ANOVA showed that the main effect of the training was significant ($F_{(1,6)} = 17.71, p < 0.01$) and that the interaction was also significant $(F_{(1,6)} = 7.17, p < 0.05)$. The only significant differences we observed between the methods were those found after the training $(F_{(1,22)} = 6.33, p < 0.05)$. The difference in values from the model data for the experiment group was significantly higher than that for the control group. In addition, the simple main effect of the training was significant only in the experiment group $(F_{(1,22)} = 23.71, p < 0.01)$. The scores obtained with the experiment group after the training were significantly higher than those obtained before the training.

6.4   Discussion

The results obtained for the quantitative evaluation in the non-wearing state and those obtained through a subjective evaluation made by a third party confirmed that our proposed system is useful for posing training without a stuffed suit.

The results obtained from the quantitative evaluation in the non-wearing state confirmed that using our proposed system enabled the experiment group to learn the range of motion that the stuffed suit allowed better than the control group. Figure 13 indicates that the differences between the experiment group's posing data and that of the control group were significantly reduced before and after the training. We consider that compared with the control group, the experiment group was able to perform posing closer to that of the models. The experiment group was able to do so by learning the range of motion the stuffed suit allows with our proposed system. This indicates that users wearing a stuffed suit can perform the posing with the same body sensations as they felt in practicing the posing. They can also grasp the rough structure of stuffed suits, thus enabling them to perform the posing in the suit in accordance with the image they wish to convey.

The subjective evaluation results we obtained confirmed that the experiment group improved their posing skill better than the control group. Although no significant differences were found in the quantitative evaluation results obtained in the wearing state (Fig. 14, we found that for the subjective evaluation results (Fig. 15 the experiment group increased their scores much more than the control group did before and after the training. This indicates that the experiment group, by using the proposed system and learning the range of motion the stuffed suit allows them, was better able than the control group to perform posing close to the sample posing. This indicates that the subjects who trained with our system can pose appropriately in performances while wearing stuffed suits. Although the quantitative evaluation results obtained for the groups showed no significant differences, we consider that subjective evaluations from evaluators are important because the performances people see are those presented by people wearing stuffed suits. This is why we feel that it was important to find that using our proposed system enabled users in the experiment group to improve posing skills more than the control group could. We also confirmed that subjects can train properly even with a database provided by others (i.e., the author).

7   Conclusion

In this paper, we described a system we propose that enables users not wearing a stuffed suit to train themselves in posing by visually presenting them with images of performers wearing stuffed suits posing in the same way as the users will. In a prototype application of the system, we implemented a function that allows users to learn whether they can perform the posing they intend whether or not they are wearing a stuffed suit. Using our system allows users to train themselves in how to pose while getting the same body sensations whether or not they are wearing stuffed suits. Experiments with the system confirmed that it was better able than the conventional method to help users to improve their posing skills.

We used only one type of stuffed suit in our work, but there are various types of stuffed suits having many different kinds of structures. The more the costume structure differs from the human structure, the more our proposed system can be expected to be useful because it is difficult to imagine how persons will pose when they are inside the costume. We need to investigate whether our proposed system is useful for costumes other than the one we used in our work. We also plan to demonstrate our proposed system to professional performers in stuffed suits and get opinions and impressions from them.

Acknowledgement. This research was supported in part by a Grant in aid for Precursory Research for Embryonic Science and Technology (PRESTO) and CREST from the Japan Science and Technology Agency.

References

1. Okazaki, T., Terada, T., Tsukamoto, M.: A system for supporting performers in stuffed suits. In: Nijholt, A., Romão, T., Reidsma, D. (eds.) ACE 2012. LNCS, vol. 7624, pp. 85–100. Springer, Heidelberg (2012). https://doi.org/10.1007/978-3-642-34292-9_7
2. Tei, Y., Terada, T., Tsukamoto, M.: A multi-modal information presentation method for performers in stuffed suits. In: Proceedings of the 12th International Conference on Advances in Mobile Computing and Multimedia (MoMM 2014), pp. 77–84, November 2014
3. Slyper, R., Lehman, J., Forlizzi, J., Hodgins, J.: A tongue input device for creating conversations. In: Proceedings of ACM Symposium on User Interface Software and Technology (UIST2011), pp. 117–126 (2011)
4. Microsoft Kinect. http://www.xbox.com/ja-JP/xbox-one/accessories/kinect
5. Kyan, M., Sun, G., Li, H., Zhong, L., Muneesawang, P., Dong, N., Elder, B., Guan, L.: An approach to ballet dance training through MS Kinect and visualization in a CAVE virtual reality environment. ACM Trans. Intell. Syst. Technol. (TIST) **6**(2), 23 (2015)
6. Alexiadis, D.S., Daras, P., Kelly, P., O'Connor, N.E., Boubekeur, T., Moussa, M.B.: Evaluating a dancer's performance using Kinect-based skeleton tracking. In: Proceedings of the 19th ACM International Conference on Multimedia (ACM 2011), pp. 659–662, November 2011

7. Saha, S., Ghosh, S., Konar, A., Nagar, A.K.: Gesture recognition from Indian classical dance using Kinect sensor. In: Proceedings of Computational Intelligence, Communication Systems and Networks (CICSYN 2013), pp. 3–8, June 2013
8. Chan, J.C.P., Leung, H., Tang, J.K.T., Komura, T.: A virtual reality dance training system using motion capture technology. IEEE Trans. Learn. Technol. 4(2), 187–195 (2011)
9. Tommi, H., Marc, R.T.: Learning and synchronising dance movements in South African songs: cross-cultural motion-capture study. Dance Res. 29(2), 303–326 (2011)
10. Van Der Linden, J., Schoonderwaldt, E., Bird, J., Johnson, R.: Musicjacket-combining motion capture and vibrotactile feedback to teach violin bowing. IEEE Trans. Instrum. Measur. 60, 104–113 (2011)
11. 3-Space Sensor. https://yostlabs.com/
12. Xsens motion capture system. https://www.xsens.com/
13. logicool HD PRO WEBCAM C920R. https://www.logicool.co.jp/
14. OpenCV. http://opencv.jp/

Demo Papers

An Eyeglass to Present Information to a User and Others Separately by LED Blinking

Takahiro Miki[2]([✉]), Tsutomu Terada[1], and Masahiko Tsukamoto[2]

[1] Graduate School of Engineering, Kobe University, JST PRESTO, Kobe, Japan
tsutomu@eedept.kobe-u.ac.jp
[2] Kobe University, Kobe, Japan
takahiro_miki0124@stu.kobe-u.ac.jp, tuka@kobe-u.ac.jp

Abstract. We propose an eyeglass to present information to a user and others. The proposed eyeglass is equipped with LED tapeson the outside and the inside of its edges. We also propose some applications that control LED blinking of the proposed eyeglass. In addition, we apply the proposed system in a variety of situation. We discuss about the effectiveness of the system in those situations.

Keywords: Wearable computing · Eyeware · LEDs
Information indications

1 Introduction

In recent years, wearable devices attract much attention with the miniaturization and the improvement of computers. They are used to present information to a user. There are many studies that present information with wearable devices. One is a person that is wearing a wearable device (referred to as user). The other is persons that are looking user's device (referred to as others). For example, FUN'IKI Glasses present the same information to a user and others. However, they are lacks of privacy protection. Because they present information that only user needs to others. Misawa and Rekimoto have proposed ChameleonMask as a system that presents information to a user and others separately [1]. This system presented information with the video to a user and others to aim at tele-presence. In this research, third parties present information to a user and others by remote control from another environment. However, a user presents information that the user wants himself/herself in the same environment as others. Moreover, he/she presents the intention of user and information of user to others. By presenting information to a user and others separately, the user can receive the notification, the navigation, and so on. The user can also communicate with others.

In this paper, we propose the system that presents information with an eyeglass to a user and others separately. The proposed system use the user's peripheral vision. Because the visual workloads is less. Also, although the user can look

© ICST Institute for Computer Sciences, Social Informatics and Telecommunications Engineering 2018
K. Murao et al. (Eds.): MobiCASE 2018, LNICST 240, pp. 203–209, 2018.
https://doi.org/10.1007/978-3-319-90740-6_12

at the inside of an eyeglass, he/she cannot look at the outside of it. In contrast, although others can look at the outside of an eyeglass, they cannot look at the inside of it. The proposed eyeglass is equipped with 20 LEDs on the outside and the inside edge of the eyeglass.

2   Application

We propose a various of applications to present information to a user and others. In this research, we propose more than 80 applications. Table 1 shows examples of those applications.

Table 1. Application examples

Situation	Function	
	A user	Others
Working	Reciving emails	Time signal
Time management	Timer	Timer
Reading	Bookmark	Concentration
Photo	Selfie angle	Light effect to face
Sleeping	Sleeping prevention	Sleep state
Interpersonal	Labeling others	User's color
Talking	Logging contents	Secret talking
Shopping	Coupons	Store introduction
Feeling	Mental care	False feeling
Impression	Control others's image	User's image
Moving places	Navigation	Traffic information
Wexting	Warning to user	Warning to others
Walking	Guiding user's behavior	User's winker
Labeling action	Controlling action	Start and end of action
Party	People with a taste	Unity sense of atmosphere
Game	Hit point	Signals for peers
Running	Time and distance	Fatigue
Music performance	Tempo	Communication
Muscle training	Count to do sit-up	Exercise amount
Sport	Score	Sign

3   System Design

In this study, we propose the device that can present information to a user and others separately. In this research, we aim to construct a system that presents information related to a variety of situations such as daily life and sports.

3.1   System Requirement

When the system present information to a user and others separately, each information is required to be different. In this research, the system is designed based on the following policy.

- Individualization of presenting information
- Presenting information with low visual workloads
- Visibility to others

First, we describe the individualization of presenting information. The proposed system presents different information to a user and others. On the proposed system, a user can get information that he/she needs. Also, others can get information that a user indicates. Next, we proposed the system that presents information so as not to make a user's eyes tired. Finally, it is necessary that the LED position is the place where others visually recognize easily in order to present information to others.

3.2   Proposed System

First, Fig. 1 shows the proposed device. We used JINS MEME, as eyeglass device. In addition, ten full color LED tapes were attached to the inside and the outside of the edges of it at intervals of 11 mm each. Moreover, in order to insulate the circuit part of the LED tape, edges of the eyeglass were coated with silicone rubber. We used Adafruit Feather 32u4 Bluefruit LE as a microcomputer board to control the LEDs. Also, the device was equipped with a 300mAh lithium ion battery. We use iPhone to control LED. They communicate by Bluetooth Low Energy. Next, Fig. 2 shows the application screen of Controller. In this study, we implement five functions to control LED in the proposed applications. They are winker, BPM controller and timer. Winker is that blinking LEDs indicating top, bottom, left and right. A user can switch the part presenting information to the inside and the outside. Timer is that blinking LEDs in a way to notify the remaining time in minutes. A user can set the time freely. BPM controller is that blinking LEDs at a tempo from 60 to 200 bpm inside of the device. A user can set BPM freely.

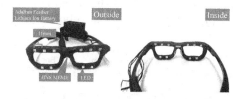

Fig. 1. Overview of the proposed method

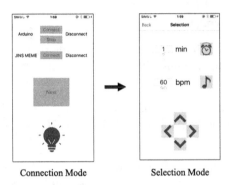

Fig. 2. Controller

4 Experiment

There are three targets presented information by the proposed device: a user, others, and both a user and others. We investigate to present information to a user and others separately. It is required to investigate whether presenting information to a user and others is possible in the assumed situation with the proposed device. Also, it is required to investigate whether the function of presenting information to a user and others is useful. Therefore, we asked subjects to use the proposed device in the four situations, game of scissors-paper-rock, presentation, musical instrument performance, typing in this experiment. Additionally, we asked subjects to answer the questionnaire after the experiment. From the results, we discussed the usefulness of the proposed device.

4.1 Procedure

In the game of scissors-paper-rock, we presented information to both a user and others. First, we told subjects (a user) wearing the proposed device to do the game of scissors-paper-rock against the experiment collaborator (others) in experiments targeting a user. Next, we told subjects (others) to do the game of scissors-paper-rock against the experiment collaborator wearing the proposed device (a user) in experiments targeting others. When we know the result of the scissors-paper-rock, we presented subjects the blinking pattern shown in Fig. 3. In the presentation, we presented information to both a user and others. A user

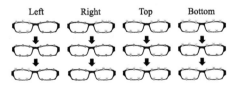

Fig. 3. Light pattern

Table 2. The average ratio of times subjects pointed their finger [%]

	Direction pointed the finger			
	Top	Bottom	Left	Right
Blinking top side	23.8	19.2	32.9	24.1
Blinking bottom side	21.7	23.3	37.5	17.5
Blinking left side	21.7	11.7	40.8	23.3
Blinking right side	28.3	16.7	25.8	31.7

Table 3. The average ratio of times subjects shook their head [%]

	Direction shook the head			
	Top	Bottom	Left	Right
Blinking top side	17.1	35.8	11.7	35.4
Blinking bottom side	26.7	25.0	23.3	25.0
Blinking left side	28.3	30.0	23.3	18.3
Blinking right side	24.2	23.3	22.1	30.4

wore the proposed device as a presenter. We presented the presenter the presentation tempo, notification that the presenter faces downward and timer function with blinking LEDs. Others listened to the user's presentation as the audience. Moreover, we presented the audience the noteworthy parts of the presentation, a user's tension state and timer function with blinking LEDs. In the musical instrument performance, we presented information to the user. The subjects played drums according to the metronome tempo. Moreover, they did it to the tempo blinking LEDs with the proposed device. Tempo presentation by proposed device blinks LED according to BPM. In the typing, we presented information to the user. The subject wearing the proposed device inputted 100 words of 2 to 10 characters displayed on the PC. In addition, the device would pay attention by LED blinking if we recognize their postures got worse by the sensor data from the device.

4.2   Result

In the experiment of the game of scissors-paper-rock targeting a user, there were many subjects who answered that they did not change their direction of movement by the blinking LED. Because the presentation of light was not visible because the position of the LED shifted depending on the weight of an eyeglass. In the experiment targeting the others, we focused on the average times that subjects point their finger after winning in the scissors-paper-rock when they saw the LED blinking in four directions (Table 2). Moreover, we focused on the ratio of the average times that subjects shook their head after losing in the scissors-paper-rock when they saw the LED blinking in four directions (Table 3). There was no particular change in their behavior by the blinking LED. They answered that they thought that the direction of the blinking LEDs was the same as the direction that the experiment collaborator moved. Thereby, when subjects won the scissors-paper-rock, they did an action to win the game to point their finger in the direction of the blinking LED. However, they answered that they ignored blinking LEDs in the remaining trials. Because they responded that the direction of blinking LEDs and the direction of movement of experiment collaborator actually differed. In the presentation, the presenter answered that he did not recognize the light much. In addition, he answered that it is because he was concentrating on the presentation. We assume this is because the light intensity of the LED was too weak The audience answered that they want to use the notification to the noteworthy parts of the presentation and the timer as a function. Moreover, they answered that they could not concentrate on the presentation because they were concerned about the blinking LED. In the musical instrument performance, more than half of the subjects answered that it was easy to perform tempo presentation by the blinking LED. Half of the people who said that blinking LED presentation is easy to perform answered that the blinking pattern was good. In the typing, from the questionnaire, when subjects received the notification by the blinking LED, they did not recognize that their posture were worse. Half of the subjects answered that the pattern of blinking was easy to understand.

5   Discussion

First, in the experiments targeting a user, there were subjects who said that they could not recognize the blinking LEDs. We consider that because the device case is heavy, the position of the eyeglass is shifted from usual. As the result, the LEDs blinked outside the peripheral vision of the subject. Moreover, based on experimental results of musical instrument performance, it is difficult to listen to tempo presentation by sound in a mixed environment of sound. However, it is intuitive and easy to match to present the tempo visually using the proposed device. We assume that presentation of information to the peripheral visual field is effective in the work environment that presenting information to the auditory sense is difficult. Next, in this experiment, the blinking pattern of LED was the one proposed by the author. Thereby, in the situations other than the game of scissors-paper-rock that we presenting information of "direction", which people can recognize intuitively, the interpretation of the blinking pattern of the LED differs for each subject. Therefore, it is necessary to present information with the blinking pattern of the LED that everyone recognizes easily.

6   Conclusion

In this study, we proposed a device that can present information to a user and others. Additionally, we proposed many applications that device is suitable for use. Therefore, we implemented an eyeglass that can present information to a user and others separately by LED blinking. We evaluated the proposed device under the four situations of the game of scissors-paper-rock, the presentation, the musical instrument performance, the typing. Based on the experimental results, we found that it is difficult to use only the proposed functions under the four situations. In the future works, we will improve the problems such as wearability of devices that we have known through experiments. In addition, we propose other functions in the environment we evaluated in this experiment. Furthermore, we need to investigate the usefulness of the proposed function using the proposed device under other situations.

Reference

1. Misawa, K., Rekimoto, J.: ChameleonMask: embodied physical and social telepresence using human surrogates. In: Proceedings of the 33rd Annual ACM Conference Extended Abstracts on Human Factors in Computing Systems (CHI EA 2015), pp. 401–411 (2015)

Energy Harvesting Sensor Node Toward Zero Energy In-Network Sensor Data Processing

Tatsuya Morita$^{(\boxtimes)}$, Masashi Fujiwara, Yutaka Arakawa, Hirohiko Suwa,
and Keiichi Yasumoto

Graduate School of Information Science, Nara Institute of Science and Technology,
Ikoma, Nara 630-0192, Japan
morita.tatsuya.mp3@is.naist.jp
http://ubi-lab.naist.jp/

Abstract. In this paper, we aiming to realize near-zero energy distributed IoT systems that do not need a battery, we design and implement a novel energy harvesting (EH) sensor node. The proposed EH sensor node consists of a solar panel, an energy charging/discharging circuit and a SenStick, an existing sensor node including 8 different types of sensors and BLE communication interface. We demonstrate that the proposed EH sensor node works in an indoor environment by harvesting power from indoor lights, periodically measuring sensor data (temperature, humidity, atmospheric pressure, UV, and illuminance) and by sending the data by BLE communication. The received information is visualized through a web application running on a PC.

Keywords: Internet of Things (IoT) · Wireless sensor networks
Distributed processing · Energy harvesting · PV system

1 Introduction

In recent years, thanks to the advancement of MEMS (Micro Electro Mechanical Systems) and wireless communication technologies, Internet of Things (IoT) has been attracting considerable attention. Cisco predicted that 50 billion things would be connected to the Internet by 2020 [1]. IoT devices will come into popular use in various environments such as homes, buildings, towns, and so on. On the other hand, new issues such as dramatic increase of data traffic and power consumption by those IoT devices arise. The left side of Fig. 1 shows the outline of the centralized architecture. At present, most of the IoT-based services are realized based on the centralized architecture at cloud servers. In the centralized architecture, however, each IoT device uploads data to the cloud server and data is processed on the cloud and finally, the result is delivered to the user. Accordingly, not only does the user suffer from large delays to get the service but also the data traffic to the cloud as well as the power consumption of the cloud is quickly growing.

© ICST Institute for Computer Sciences, Social Informatics and Telecommunications Engineering 2018
K. Murao et al. (Eds.): MobiCASE 2018, LNICST 240, pp. 210–215, 2018.
https://doi.org/10.1007/978-3-319-90740-6_13

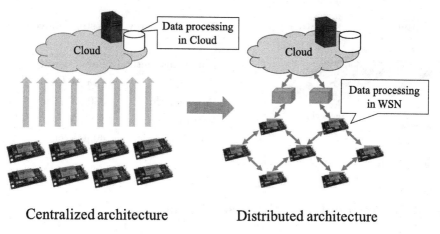

Fig. 1. Data processing architecture

To solve this problem, distributed edge/fog computing architectures have been proposed such as IFoT [2] and DIAT [3]. The right side of Fig. 1 shows the outline of the distributed edge/fog computing architecture. In the distributed architecture, since data is processed in the wireless sensor network (WSN), only the result of processing is uploaded to the cloud, leading to a reduction in bandwidth and power consumption to/at the cloud. On the other hand, the distributed edge/fog computing architecture needs processing at sensor/IoT nodes which are typically driven by a battery. How to reduce the power consumption at sensor nodes is an emerging issue to be solved.

Energy harvesting is an important technique to solve this issue. Sensor nodes that generate power by harvesting energy have been released [4], but many of them use CPUs with low processing performance to reduce power consumption. In the distributed architecture, the sensor node processes and learns data. Therefore, the sensor node is required to have high processing performance and wireless communication capability. As a result the power consumption increases. Also, we must assume both indoors and outdoors use.

In this paper, aiming to realize near-zero energy distributed IoT systems, we design and implement a novel energy harvesting (EH) sensor node. The proposed EH sensor node consists of a solar panel, an energy charging/discharging circuit and SenStick [5], an existing small sensor node that embeds 8 different types of sensors, a relatively high performance processor, and BLE communication interface. In the demonstration, we show that the proposed EH sensor node works in an indoor environment by harvesting power from indoor lights, periodically measuring sensor data (temperature, humidity, atmospheric pressure, UV, and illuminance) and by sending the data by BLE communication. The received information is visualized through the web application running on a PC.

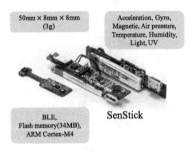

50mm × 8mm × 8mm
(3g)

Acceleration, Gyro,
Magnetic, Air pressure,
Temperature, Humidity,
Light, UV

BLE,
Flash memory(34MB),
ARM Cortex-M4

SenStick

Fig. 2. Overview of SenStick

Table 1. Energy harvesting sources

Harvesting method	Power density
Solar cells	15 mW/cm^3
Piezoelectric	330 μW/cm^3
Vibration	116 μW/cm^3
Thermoelectric	40 μW/cm^3

2   Development of EH Sensor Node

2.1   Survey of EH Technology and EH Sensor Node

Energy harvesting is a technology that converts natural energy sources such as light energy, mechanical energy, thermal energy, and environmental radio energy into electrical energy. The energy harvesting technology allows us to reduce the cost of charging and/or replacing rechargeable batteries used in the system. Therefore, energy harvesting technology has drawn attention in the field of sensor networks [6]. Table 1 shows some popular energy harvesting sources [7]. The solar cell has the highest power generation capacity compared to other methods. IoT devices need stable electric power supply both indoors and outdoors. Therefore, we use the solar cell as an energy source for the proposed EH sensor node.

Next, we describe the EH sensor node. Data processing and wireless communication capabilities are required in each node of our target distributed edge/fog computing architecture. It is also desirable to be compact and power-saving. Sensor nodes that generate electricity through energy harvesting are available [4], but many of them use CPUs with low processing performance to reduce power consumption.

Therefore, we use a comprehensive sensor node called SenStick [5]. Figure 2 shows the overview of SenStick. SenStick is an ultracompact and low power consumption node, which has BLE (Bluetooth low energy) connectivity and ARM Cortex-M4 as a micro control unit. Eight different sensors: accelerometer, gyrometer, magnetmeter, illuminance, pressure, temperature, humidity, and UV sensors are embedded in a tiny board with the size of 50 mm (W) × 10 mm (H) × 5 mm (D) and the total weight is around 3 g.

2.2   Design and Implementation of EH Sensor Node

In this demonstration setup, we use Intel Edison equipped with Intel Atom as a processing unit which processes the sensor data received from the EH sensor node. Since SenStick has ARM Cortex-M4 as CPU and it can perform simple data processing, our EH sensor nodes will be able to directly form a mesh network and process the sensed data by distributed processing among them in the future.

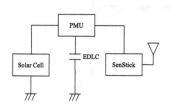

Front   Side

Fig. 3. Circuit diagram   **Fig. 4.** Overview of the EH sensor node

Table 2. Operatin result of EH sensor node

Illuminance (lux)	Operating interval (min)	Operating time (min)
450–560	100	1
850–980	30	1
4500–5500	5	1

It is difficult to continuously operate EH sensor nodes in an indoor environment even with solar cells [8]. Therefore, we developed a system to intermittently operate EH sensor nodes. Figure 3 shows the circuit diagram of the proposed sensor system. In the intermittent operation, first, the electric power converted by the solar cell is charged in the battery (capacitor). When electric power is charged enough to activate the sensor node (SenStick), the system discharges the power and activates the sensor node. When the electric power becomes insufficient to drive the sensor node, electricity is charged in the capacitor (rechargeable battery) again. These charging and discharging operations are repeated. Power control is performed by the PMU (Power Management Unit). EDLC (Electric Double-Layer Capacitor) is used for the battery because frequent charge and discharge operations have no influence on the electrode and its cycle life is long.

The EH sensor node developed based on the above design is shown in Fig. 4. We also have a video demonstrating, how EH sensor node works[1]. The size of the device is 90 mm (W) × 65 mm (H) × 28 mm (D). To easily change the battery capacity, three EDLCs of 1 F are connected in parallel as the storage battery. When the EDLC voltage exceeds 2.55 V, it is boosted to 3.6 V by the DC-to-DC converter, and the EH sensor node automatically starts sensing. The EH sensor node stops and recharging when the EDLC voltage drops to 1 V.

When the processing unit (Edison) detects BLE advertisement of the EH sensor node, it establishes a connection and receives data. It is possible to connect with multiple EH sensor nodes, process data and upload the result to the cloud according to the situation.

The operation result of the EH sensor node measured by preliminary experiment is shown in Table 2. The measurement was carried out with three luminance patterns of (a) 450–560 lux (dark indoor), (b) 850–980 lux (bright indoor), (c)

---

[1] Operation of the EH sensor node: https://youtu.be/_NsDvc8eiXE.

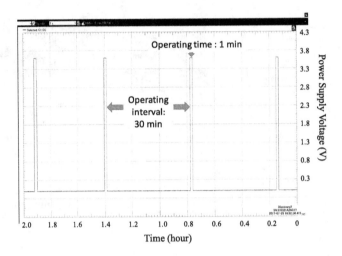

Fig. 5. Operation result of EH sensor node (850–980lux)

4500–5500 lux (near a window at the cloudy weather outside), and the shortest operation interval and operation time were confirmed. As a result of measurement, the operation intervals under each condition were (a) about 100 min, (b) about 30 min, (c) about five minutes. Also, the operation time was about one minute in all conditions.

The operation result at (a) is shown in Fig. 5. It was confirmed that about one minute operation can be repeated at an interval of 30 min. We also confirmed that the acquisition of sensor data by the processing unit was successfully done within the one minute operation time.

3   Demonstration Description

In the demonstration, we show that the proposed EH sensor node works in the indoor environment by harvesting power from indoor lights. Specifically, the EH sensor node periodically operates to acquire environmental information such as temperature, humidity, atmospheric pressure, UV, and illuminance. The acquired information is transmitted to the processing unit by BLE communication and uploaded to the cloud server. On the cloud side, the status of the current room is displayed by the web application. In addition, if an anomaly situation is detected, an alert is displayed.

4   Conclusion

In this paper, we designed and implemented a novel EH sensor node to realize near-zero energy distributed IoT systems that do not need a battery. In the demonstration, we showed that the proposed EH sensor node works in the indoor environment by harvesting power from indoor lights and periodically measures sensor data and sends the data by BLE communication. The received information is visualized through the web application running on a PC. In this demonstration setup, we used the Intel Edison as a data processing unit that receives the sensor data from our EH sensor node. For future work, we plan to implement mechanisms for a simple data processing and mesh-networking in the EH sensor node so as to realize in WSN processing with only EH nodes.

Acknowledgments. This work is supported by "Research and Development of Innovative Network Technologies to Create the Future," the Commissioned Research of National Institute of Information and Communications Technology (NICT), Japan.

References

1. Bradley, J., Barbier, J., Handler, D.: Embracing the Internet of Everything To Capture Your Share of $14.4 Trillion (White Paper). https://www.cisco.com/c/dam/en_us/about/ac79/docs/innov/IoE_Economy.pdf. Accessed 22 Nov 2017
2. Yasumoto, K., Yamaguchi, H., Shigeno, H.: Survey of real-time processing technologies of IoT data streams. J. Inf. Process. **24**(2), 195–202 (2016)
3. Sarkar, C., Nambi, A.U., Prasad, R.V., Rahim, A., Neisse, R., Baldini, G.: DIAT: a scalable distributed architecture for IoT. IEEE Internet Things J. **2**(3), 230–239 (2015)
4. Cypress: S6SAE101A00SA1002.   http://www.cypress.com/documentation/development-kitsboards/s6sae101a00sa1002-solar-powered-iot-device-kit
5. Nakamura, Y., Arakawa, Y., Kanehira, T., Fujiwara, M., Yasumoto, K.: SenStick: comprehensive sensing platform with an ultra tiny all-in-one sensor board for IoT research. J. Sens. **2017**, 16 (2017). https://doi.org/10.1155/2017/6308302. Article ID 6308302
6. Shaikh, F.K., Zeadally, S.: Energy harvesting in wireless sensor networks: a comprehensive review. Renew. Sustain. Energy Rev. **55**, 1041–1054 (2016)
7. Chalasani, S., Conrad, J.: A survey of energy harvesting sources for embedded systems. In: IEEE Southeastcon, pp. 442–447, April 2008
8. Wang, W.S., O'Donnell, T., Wang, N., Hayes, M., O'Flynn, B., O'Mathuna, C.: Design considerations of sub-mW indoor light energy harvesting for wireless sensor systems. J. Emerg. Technol. Comput. Syst. 6(2), 6:1–6:26 (2008)

Gamification for High-Quality Dataset in Mobile Activity Recognition

Nattaya Mairittha$^{(\boxtimes)}$ and Sozo Inoue

Kyushu Institute of Technology, 1-1 Sensui-cho, Tobata-ku,
Kitakyushu-shi, Fukuoka 804-8550, Japan
{fah,sozo}@sozolab.jp

Abstract. This paper presents a gamification concept for getting high-quality user-annotated datasets in the context of mobile activity recognition, as well as a cheating detection algorithm. The novel idea behind this concept is that users are motivated by getting feedback about the quality of their labeling activity as rewards or gamification element. For that, the collected sensor data and labels are used as training data for a machine learning algorithm for determining the dataset quality based on the resulting accuracy. By using the proposed method, the results show that the gamification elements increase the quantity (labels from the proposed method is higher than the naive by at least 305) and the quality (the accuracy of the proposed data outperformed the original data by at least 4.3%) of the labels. Besides, the cheating detection algorithm could detect cheating with the accuracy of more than 70% that is fascinating work.

Keywords: Mobile activity recognition · Quality of dataset
Gamification

1 Introduction

Mobile activity recognition is the technology of recognizing human activities with mobile sensors such as smartphones. It is widely researched [1], as in the preventive healthcare domain and process management and skill assessment of workers. To address the mobile activity recognition task [2], collecting high-quality training datasets with correct ground truth labels is very costly and non-trivial task. In many real-world situations, the number of training examples must be limited because obtaining samples in a form suitable for learning may be costly [3]. These costs include the cost of collecting the raw data, cleaning, storing and transforming the data into a representation suitable for learning, as well as the opportunity cost associated with suboptimal learning from large datasets due to limited computational resources [4].

To collect good quality of labels without tedious/costly tasks and limit disengagement., L'Heureux [5] proposed to motivate users to participate in various labeling or tasks. As such, increasing the stimulus of the labeling task itself

© ICST Institute for Computer Sciences, Social Informatics and Telecommunications Engineering 2018
K. Murao et al. (Eds.): MobiCASE 2018, LNICST 240, pp. 216–222, 2018.
https://doi.org/10.1007/978-3-319-90740-6_14

can address tedious tasks caused by user disengagement. Studies by Markey [6] revealed four effective strategies associated with heightened task engagement: offer performance feedback, provide social approval, increase challenge, and give incentives such as monetary rewards. Gamification, Which is commonly defined as *the use of game design elements in non-game contexts to improve user experience* [7], puts these strategies to advantage. Research on gamification has shown improvements in motivation and engagement [8]. Game elements such as progress and success feedback, goals, points, badges, levels, challenges, social feedback, and narrative, can all contribute to those engagement improvements, provided there is a good match between design and audience. Therefore, gamification offers a useful perspective from which to create and analyze engaging labeling experiences. Here, we can come up with the idea of if we synchronize the goal of gamification and the quality of the dataset. Then, we can expect that we could motivate people to provide high a quality dataset for activity recognition.

The contribution of our work is twofold. First is to get the high-quality datasets in the context of mobile activity recognition by exploiting gamification concept. We present an idea that users provide sensor data and activity labels as a training dataset, as well as obtaining gaming feedback as a gaming element. However, giving material rewards as motivators to drive specific user actions. One of the side effects of users getting too focused on the rewards because these motivators are tangible, visible and highly desirable [9]. For example, users who are more interested in rewards than in physical activity might cheat by labeling the data walk by without actually stepping it or labeling run by sitting still at their desk. Therefore as a second contribution, to prevent cheating, we propose to defeat the cheats by making algorithms detecting cheating, based on the assumption that cheating datasets are dissimilar to other (non-cheating) datasets.

As a result of evaluating our prototype system that provides an estimated labeling quality to users as notifications every 30 min with ten volunteers, the number of labels for the proposed method was greater than the naive by at least 305. Moreover, the quality of labels by the accuracy of the proposed data outperformed the original data by at least 4.3%. In addition, the proposed method detected cheating data with the accuracy of more than 70%.

2   Proposed Gamification System

2.1   Gamification Mechanism

The first goal of the integration is to synchronize the goal of gamification and the quality of the dataset by providing the 'point' (or a score) as a reward for each the user, which is the one that each user wants to maximize. On the other hand, the quality of the dataset can be represented by the accuracy of the activity dataset when they are trained with several machine learning algorithms. So, the first idea is *"to let the accuracy of the dataset of a user be the score of her/him."* The second idea is how gamification addresses the engagement. By giving feedback to the users periodically as notifications (Fig. 1).

Fig. 1. The overview of proposed method

2.2   Cheating Detection

To avoid cheating by the participants, we also propose a cheating detection algorithm based on supervised machine learning. By letting all users cheat intentionally, for example, labeling the data, such as running or by sitting still at their desk and pretending to be walking. Then, we train from the dataset with intentionally cheated, and with standard gamification which we assume they are not cheating. As a preprocessing, we use the data sample with activity labels, and as post-processing, we use voting to detect 'cheating' or 'non-cheating'.

In the following, we show the training and detection algorithms.

Training Algorithm:

– Input: sensor dataset X of size N, and the same size of labels

$$C = \{\text{'cheating', 'non-cheating'}\}^N$$

.
– Output: cheating estimation function f.

1. Remove samples with no activity labels from X and C.
2. Calculate feature vectors V from X.
3. Using supervised machine learning, train a model f with X and C to estimate cheating or non-cheating.
4. Output f.

Detection Algorithm:

– Input: sensor dataset X and function f.
– Output: 'cheating' or 'non-cheating'.

1. Remove samples with no activity labels from X.
2. Calculate feature vectors V from X.
3. Using f, estimate cheating or not by $f(v_i)$ for $\forall v_i \in V$.
4. Output the maximum voting results by

$$o = \arg_{y_i} \max_i f(y_i).$$

The output o is the detection results. If it is detected as 'cheating', we can consider fewer rewards or penalty to that user in the framework of gamification,

3   Evaluation Experiment

3.1   Evaluation Experiment

In this section, we evaluate the effectiveness of the proposed method by answering the following questions:

– Can the proposed method improve the data quality?
– Can the proposed method detect when users in the system are cheating?

Experiment Design

We split the subjects into two groups: one is the proposed or gamified group by getting feedback about the quality of their labeling activity as rewards or gamification element, and the other is non-gamified. By randomly assigned a participant into either of two groups in one day and switched them into other groups after on the second day of the experiment. To evaluate cheating detection, we asked the participants to intentionally cheat on the third day.

Labeled Data Collection

The experiment was carried out with a group of ten volunteers within an age bracket of 20–40 years, then dividing the candidates into two groups, with each group including five candidates. Each person performed wearing a smartphone with an armband. From them, we captured three-axial acceleration data.

Data Processing

In the data processing, we introduced the preprocessing stage to synchronize the times, remove artifacts, and prepare the acquired signals for feature extraction. Later, features that capture the activity characteristics are extracted from the signals within each segment. From the 3-axial acceleration data, we extracted feature vectors in the following way: At first, we divided the samples by every minute and calculated the median and standard deviation of each axis.

3.2   Evaluation Method

Data Quality

We evaluated the quality of the obtained data using supervised machine learning and by seeing several accuracy measures. For the machine learning algorithms, we used Random forests are an ensemble learning method for classification which is popular in achieving reasonable performance. Importantly, in evaluating accuracies, to take care of imbalances among activity classes, we adopt two countermeasures: first is to use one-class classification: to classify a specific activity class or not and repeat it for any activity class, and the second is to use also imbalance-robust metrics such as *Balanced Classification Rate (BCR)* [10]. The BCR is defined as follows:

$$BCR = \frac{TP\text{-rate} + TN\text{-rate}}{2}$$

Cheating Detection

To evaluate the cheating detection carefully, we exploited the cross-validation in a novel way. The details are described below:

1. From users U, take a pair of users (u_1, u_2) where $u_1 \neq u_2$,
2. take 'cheating' data from user u_1, and take 'non-cheating' data from user u_2, and let the merged data the test dataset D_E.
3. From the rest of the users $U - \{u_1, u_2\}$, take 'cheating' and 'non-cheating' data from D, and let them the training dataset D_T.
4. Train a with D_T by the cheating algorithm.
5. Estimate and take the maximum voting with D_E the cheating algorithm.
6. Repeat 1–5 to any pairs of users and sum up the results.

4   Results

4.1   Overview of the Obtained Data

Table 1 illustrates the number of labels per activity of the experiment.

Table 1. The number of labels per activity

No.	Activity class	#labels	No.	Activity class	#labels	No.	Activity class	#labels
1	Sleeping	22	8	Walking	112	15	Standing	39
2	Watching	10	9	Riding elevator	34	16	Carrying	20
3	Working on computer	54	10	Eating	26	17	Drinking	28
4	Reading	12	11	Cycling	18	18	Relaxing	20
5	Climbing stairs	25	12	Ridding escalator	12	19	Taking a bus	279
6	Taking a train	8	13	Sitting	50	20	Use the toilet	28
7	Washing	24	14	Dressing	6	21	Uses the phone	11
						22	Meeting	15

4.2   Improvement of Data Quality

Figure 2 shows the number of labels in each of the groups in our study, split per condition. As the results show that there are more labels in the gamified condition than other conditions. the number of labels for the proposed method from Group A is greater than the naive by 305, and the number of labels for the proposed method from Group B is greater than the naive by 109.

Figure 3 shows the results of accuracies for naive and proposed method. The BCR of the proposed method is greater than the naive by 4.32% the f-measure of the proposed method is greater than the naive by 27% the precision of the proposed method is greater than the naive by 26.6% the recall of the proposed method is greater than the naive by 8.02%

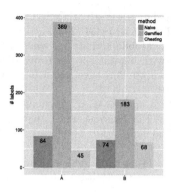

Fig. 2. Number of labels per condition

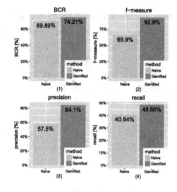

Fig. 3. Accuracies of methods

4.3 Cheating Detection

Table 2 is the confusion matrix of cheating detection after 1-pair-of-user-left-out cross-validation described in Sect. 3.2. From the table, we can calculate that the accuracy is 74.4%, the precision is 70.0%, the recall is 85.7%, the f-measure is 77.1%, and the BCR is 74.4%.

Table 2. Confusion matrix of cheating detection.

Truth\estimate	Non-cheating	Cheating
Non-cheating	31	18
Cheating	7	42

5 Conclusion

This paper aims to get high-quality user-annotated datasets in the context of mobile activity recognition by exploiting gamification concept. The results show that the gamification elements increase the quantity and 'quality' of the labels. Besides, the cheating detecting algorithm is fascinating work; we could detect cheating with the accuracy of more than 70%. Future research includes analyzing differences between users, groups, classes, as well as future research, should target a large in-field study such as applying crowdsourcing.

References

1. Kwapisz, J.R., Weiss, G.M., Moore, S.A.: Activity recognition using cell phone accelerometers. ACM SigKDD Explor. Newsl. **12**(2), 74–82 (2011)
2. Bao, L., Intille, S.S.: Activity recognition from user-annotated acceleration data. In: Ferscha, A., Mattern, F. (eds.) Pervasive 2004. LNCS, vol. 3001, pp. 1–17. Springer, Heidelberg (2004). https://doi.org/10.1007/978-3-540-24646-6_1

3. Weiss, G.M., Provost, F.: Learning when training data are costly: the effect of class distribution on tree induction. J. Artif. Intell. Res. **19**, 315–354 (2003)

4. Inoue, S., Ueda, N., Nohara, Y., Nakashima, N.: Mobile activity recognition for a whole day: recognizing real nursing activities with big dataset. In: Proceedings of the 2015 ACM International Joint Conference on Pervasive and Ubiquitous Computing, pp. 1269–1280. ACM, September 2015

5. L'Heureux, A., Grolinger, K., Higashino, W.A., Capretz, M.A.: A gamification framework for sensor data analytics. In: 2017 IEEE International Congress on Internet of Things (ICIOT), pp. 74–81. IEEE, June 2017

6. Markey, A.R.: Three essays on boredom (2014)

7. Deterding, S., Dixon, D., Khaled, R., Nacke, L.: From game design elements to gamefulness: defining gamification. In: Proceedings of the 15th International Academic MindTrek Conference: Envisioning Future Media Environments, pp. 9–15. ACM, September 2011

8. Hamari, J., Koivisto, J., Sarsa, H.: Does gamification work?-a literature review of empirical studies on gamification. In: 2014 47th Hawaii International Conference on System Sciences (HICSS), pp. 3025–3034. IEEE, January 2014

9. Glas, R.: Breaking reality: exploring pervasive cheating in Foursquare (2015)

10. Fawcett, T.: An introduction to ROC analysis. Pattern Recogn. Lett. **27**(8), 861–874 (2006)

Improving Ultrasound-Based Gesture Recognition by Partially Shielded Microphone

Hiroki Watanabe[1]([✉]) and Tsutomu Terada[2]

[1] Hokkaido University, Kita 14, Nishi 9, Kita Sapporo 060-0814, Japan
hiroki.watanabe@ist.hokudai.ac.jp
[2] Kobe University, 1-1 Rokkodai, Nada Kobe 657-8501, Japan
tsutomu@eedept.kobe-u.ac.jp

Abstract. We propose a method to improve ultrasound-based in-air gesture recognition. Doppler effect is often used to recognize ultrasound-based gesture. However, increasing the number of gesture is difficult because of limited information obtained from that. In this study, we partially shield the microphone by a 3D printed cover. Acoustic characteristics of the microphone is changed by the cover, and it increases the obtained information. Since the proposed method utilizes a 3D printed cover and a pair of embedded speaker and microphone of a device, it does not require additional electrical device to improve gesture recognition. We implemented five microphone covers and investigated the performance of the proposed method in six gestures with four participants. Evaluation results confirmed that the recognition accuracy increased 12% in the most effective device by using the proposed method.

Keywords: Gesture recognition · Ultrasound · Mobile computing
Wearable computing

1 Introduction

Mobile/wearable computers are commonly available in these days, such as smartphone and smartwatch. We can intuitively control these devices by using touch screen. However, one of the major problem of a touch screen is an occlusion. When user interacts with the device by his/her finger, it hides the screen. Moreover, touch screen is needed to be directly touched. There are some situations that user does not want to/cannot touch the screen, for example, when user's hands are wet or dirty and when user wears gloves. Therefore, in-air gesture is useful for interaction with mobile/wearable devices. There are several methods to recognize in-air gesture. Additional device, such as infrared sensor [1], enables to recognize in-air gesture. However, this method needs additional electrical devices that require power supply. Although built-in camera can recognize in-air gesture [5], camera-based method is regarded as privacy-invasive. It also

© ICST Institute for Computer Sciences, Social Informatics and Telecommunications Engineering 2018
K. Murao et al. (Eds.): MobiCASE 2018, LNICST 240, pp. 223–229, 2018.
https://doi.org/10.1007/978-3-319-90740-6_15

requires the user is within line of sight of cameras and high computational cost. Moreover, most smartwatches do not have built-in camera. Built-in speaker and microphone also can recognize in-air gesture [3,4]. The speaker transmits ultrasound, and the microphone receives the reflected ultrasound. These studies utilize Doppler effect or the time difference of arrival to the stereo microphone. However, Doppler effect can detect only whether the target is approaching or away and its velocity. Thus, recognizing the gesture direction is difficult. Moreover, smartwatch generally does not have multiple microphones.

In this study, we focus on the method that physically changes the characteristic of a sensor [2]. We apply this method to a microphone. Specifically, we attach a cover that changes the acoustic characteristics to the built-in microphone of the device. This method increases the features obtained from microphone and improves the gesture recognition. We proposed three types of microphone covers, and evaluation results confirmed that the recognition accuracy improved by 12% in the most effective device. The contributions of this paper are as follows: (1) We proposed a method to improve ultrasound-based gesture by using the microphone cover. (2) We designed three types of microphone covers and investigated that which is suitable for the proposed method. (3) Evaluation results confirmed that the microphone cover can improve ultrasound-based gesture recognition.

2   Proposed Method

2.1   Assumed Environment

In this study, the device transmits ultrasound from the speaker, and receives the reflected ultrasound by the microphone, as shown in Fig. 1. The system recognizes in-air gesture by computing the frequency shift caused by Doppler effect. As a characteristic of Doppler effect, received frequency becomes high during the sound source is approaching to the receiver and becomes low during the sound source is moving away from the receiver. In the assumed environment, a transmitter is the built-in speaker and a receiver is the built-in microphone. We set 20 kHz as the frequency of the transmitted ultrasound because most of human cannot hear around 20 kHz and existing smartphone/smartwatch can transmit it. Ultrasound is not adversely affected by the environmental sound and it is easy to separate from the environmental sound.

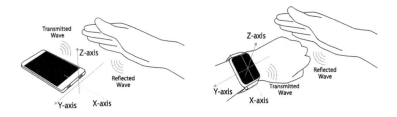

Fig. 1. Assumed environment

2.2   Cover Design

As reported in literature [4], the number of gesture is limited when we utilize Doppler effect with a pair of microphone and speaker. The left of Fig. 2 shows the gesture and correspond spectrogram. When the hand approaches to the microphone, frequency shift occurs in the high frequency side and when the hand moves away from the microphone, frequency shift occurs in the low frequency side. As this figure shows, it is difficult to classify left swipe and right swipe because spectrograms of both gestures are similar in this speaker-microphone configuration. The basic idea of the proposed method is changing acoustic characteristic of the microphone by just attaching microphone cover. As shown in the right of Fig. 2, we shield one side of the microphone, and change the sensitivity of the microphone between the left side and the right side. As the spectrogram of the right of Fig. 2 shows, the cover weaken frequency shift of the left side of the microphone and the difference between left swipe and right swipe is emphasized. Therefore, we consider that the system can classify these two gestures by the proposed method.

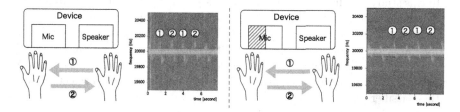

Fig. 2. Gestures and spectrograms of conventional method (left) and proposed method (right)

We consider three types of covers to partially shield the microphone as follows: opening multiple holes of 1 mm in diameter (Fig. 3A), closing with sponge that absorbs the ultrasound (Fig. 3B), and changing the directivity of the microphone (Fig. 3C). We preliminarily investigate which types of the shield is suitable for the proposed method. The used device was iPhone 5, and the target gestures are left swipe and right swipe. The participants are three. They performed each gesture 10 times. For simplicity, we just utilize the magnitude caused by the Doppler effect to classify gestures. When the high frequency magnitude caused by the Doppler effect is bigger than the lower one, we recognize the gesture is left swipe, and the gesture is recognized as right swipe in the opposite case. The result of preliminarily investigation is shown in the bottom of Fig. 3. As this figure shows, cover A and cover B had little effect. On the other hand, cover C could distinguish the left swipe and right swipe with high accuracy. Therefore, in this study, we adopt the design of cover C. Cover C has an angle of 45° to Y axis and Z axis to capture the gestures along Y/Z axis.

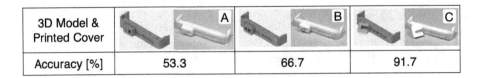

3D Model & Printed Cover	A	B	C
Accuracy [%]	53.3	66.7	91.7

Fig. 3. Cover design candidates

2.3 Recognition Method

The recognition method is based on the method described in literature [4]. It includes the following step: (1) We compute the fast Fourier transform (FFT) to the input of the microphone, and since the input signal fluctuates, we normalize the FFT result of each frame. (2) To emphasize the magnitude change of frequency bins, we subtract the normalized spectrum of current frame by previous frame and then square the magnitudes of frequency bins. (3) To extract the reacted area, we utilize Gaussian smoothing to smooth, and binarize the smoothed data with a certain value.

In this study, we divide the area into two sections by the line of the frequency of the transmitted signal (20 kHz), as shown in Fig. 4. We compute 12 features from these two sections; width of upper/lower section, height of upper/lower section, area of upper/lower section, width ratio of upper section and lower section, height ratio of upper section and lower section, and area ratio of upper section and lower section. We utilize WEKA for classification and selected SVM for the classifier with default parameters.

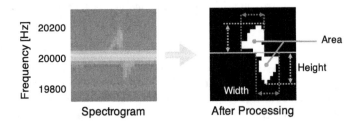

Fig. 4. Feature extraction

3   Implementation

We implemented the microphone covers based on the cover design discussed in Sect. 2.2. The implemented covers are shown in Fig. 5. The thickness of the cover was 1.5 mm. However, only the microphone part was 3 mm to enough shield ultrasound. The used devices were four smartphones (Apple iPhone 5, Apple iPhone 6s, Huawei P9 Lite, and Asus ZenFone 3 Laser) and one smartwatch (Asus ZenWatch 2). These all smartphones have a speaker at the bottom right side of the device and a microphone at the bottom left side of the device. Smartwatch has a speaker at the top of the left side and a microphone at the bottom of the left side. The used 3D printer was PP3DP UP Plus 2 and we used ABS filament to make the covers. We used Autodesk Fusion 360 to make 3D models.

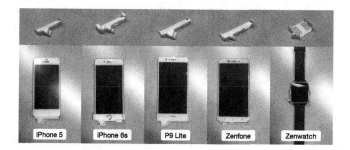

Fig. 5. Implemented cover

4   Evaluation

We evaluate the proposed method. In this study, we assume a situation that although the users want to browse recipe and manual during cooking and maintenance of the machine, they cannot touch the screen because their hand is wet or dirty. In this situation, we assume six gestures along three axes that is shown in Fig. 1. We assume that the gestures along X axis are scroll up/down, Y axis are go/back to the next/previous page, and Z axis are enter/cancel. The used devices are four smartphones and one smartwatch described in Sect. 3. The four participants are 22 to 27-year-old males and all of them use right hand to perform gesture. They conducted each six gestures 10 times. We evaluated the acquired data by 10-fold cross validation. When conducting the evaluation, the smartphones are put on the table and the smartwatch was worn on participants' left wrist, as shown in Fig. 1.

Table 1 shows the result of the evaluation. As this table shows, in most devices, the recognition accuracy improved when the device wears the microphone cover. Figure 6 shows the confusion matrix of iPhone 5 with/without cover. As this figure shows, the variation of the recognition result decreased in the whole. The effect of the cover differed depending on the devices. The most improvement was 12% at iPhone 5. On the other hand, the recognition accuracy of smartwatch decreased by attaching cover. This is because the detected volume of the reflected ultrasound was small even if the cover was not attached. Thus, the acquired volume became smaller when the cover attached, and we could not extract features effectively.

In this study, the gestures were performed with the devices placed in the center. However, if the device is not centered, the proposed method cannot recognize the gestures accurately because the characteristics of the gestures change in such situation.

Table 1. Recognition accuracy of evaluation with/without cover [%]

Participants	iPhone 5		iPhone 6s		P9 Lite		ZenFone		ZenWatch	
	w/o	w/	w/o	w/	w/o	w/	w/o	w/	w/o	w/
A	73.3	88.3	75	60	71.7	73.3	60	66.7	43.3	40
B	80	80	46.7	55	56.7	60	50	66.7	48.3	20
C	55	78.3	76.7	80	46.7	65	63.3	71.7	51.7	41.7
D	76.7	86.7	73.3	78.3	73.3	66.7	66.7	65	50	55
Average	71.3	83.3	67.9	68.3	62.1	66.3	60	67.5	48.3	39.2

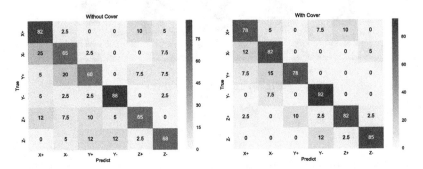

Fig. 6. Comparison of confusion matrix with/without cover [%]

5 Conclusion

We proposed a method to improve ultrasound-based gesture recognition by attaching cover to the microphone. Since the proposed method utilizes a 3D printed cover and a pair of a speaker and microphone that is embedded to the device, electrical additional devices are not needed to improve gesture recognition. We proposed and compared designs of microphone cover. Evaluation results confirmed that recognition accuracy increased 12% by using the proposed method.

References

1. Kratz, S., Rohas, M.: HoverFlow: expanding the design space of around-device interaction. In: Proceedings of the 11th International Conference on Human-Computer Interaction with Mobile Devices and Services (MobileHCI 2009), no. 4, pp. 1–8 (2009)
2. Manabe, H.: Multi-touch gesture recognition by single photoreflector. In: Proceedings of the 26th ACM Symposium on User Interface Software and Technology (UIST 2013), pp. 15–16 (2013)
3. Nandakumar, R., Iyer, V., Tan, D., Gollakota, S.: FingerIO: using active sonar for fine-grained finger tracking. In: Proceedings of the SIGCHI Conference on Human Factors in Computing Systems (CHI 2016), pp. 1515–1525 (2016)

4. Ruan, W., Sheng, Q.Z., Yang, L., Gu, T., Xu, P., Shangguan, L.: AudioGest: enabling fine-grained hand gesture detection by decoding echo signal. In: Proceedings of the 2016 ACM International Joint Conference on Pervasive and Ubiquitous Computing (UbiComp 2016), pp. 474–485 (2016)
5. Song, J., Sörös, G., Pece, F., Fanello, S.R., Izadi, S., Keskin, C., Hilliges, O.: In-air gestures around unmodified mobile devices. In: Proceedings of the 27th ACM Symposium on User Interface Software and Technology (UIST 2014), pp. 319–329 (2014)

Poster Papers

A Comparison Result Between Garment-Type and Bed-Sheet-Type Pressure Sensor for Pressure Ulcer Prevention

Ryosuke Onose[1(✉)], Yu Enokibori[2], and Kenji Mase[2]

[1] Graduate School of Information Science, Nagoya University,
Furo-cho, Chikusa-ku, Nagoya, Aichi, Japan
onose@cmc.ss.is.nagoya-u.ac.jp
[2] Graduate School of Informatics, Nagoya University,
Furo-cho, Chikusa-ku, Nagoya, Aichi, Japan
enokibori@i.nagoya-u.ac.jp, mase@nagoya-u.jp

Abstract. Preventing pressure ulcer is one of important aims in nursing. Our project has tried to estimate and reduce the risk of pressure ulcer using the sheet-type pressure sensor. However, we found a problem that body-pressure dispersion cushions interfere with accurate sensing when the previous experiment in nursing institute. A garment-type pressure sensor proposed in this paper successfully detected body-pressure changes regardless cushion replacement as the sensor could classify more accurate score in the classification task of postures using both of sensors.

Keywords: e-garment · e-textile pressure sensor · Sleeping posture
Pressure ulcer prevention

1 Introduction

Pressure ulcer prevention is one of important achievements in the field of elderly care. One cause of pressure ulcer is high continuous pressure that is put on the same skin position. Some seniors and patients, e.g. bed-ridden seniors and spinal cord patients, cannot sufficiently move their bodies to prevent such cause. Therefore, care givers make sleeping-posture of patients change every 2 h to avoid pressure ulcer developing, even at midnight. It causes heavy workload of care givers. On the other hand, actual pressure ulcer developing threshold is depending on individuals' characteristics, such as micro existence of slight movement. Thus, there is a possibility of workload reducing by interval optimization of the care depending on the actual risk level changes estimated by sensors.

In order to establish that workload reducing, our project has been implementing a bed-sheet-type pressure sensor [3]. However, such bed-sheet-type sensor sometime cannot measure suitable values to estimate pressure ulcer development risks in unusual contact situations, such as body-pressure-dispersion cushion use

© ICST Institute for Computer Sciences, Social Informatics and Telecommunications Engineering 2018
K. Murao et al. (Eds.): MobiCASE 2018, LNICST 240, pp. 233–238, 2018.
https://doi.org/10.1007/978-3-319-90740-6_16

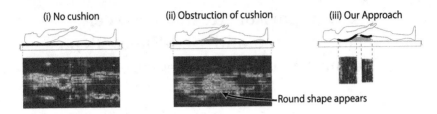

Fig. 1. Overview of approach difference and cushion's obstruction

and severe joint structure developing. An example is shown as Fig. 1(ii). There-fore, now we have been trying to implement a garment-type pressure sensor that can measure pressures put on patients' skin directory in most of situations [2]. An overview of our approach is shown as Fig. 1(iii).

In this paper, we introduce a result of comparison between the bed-sheet-type and garment-type pressure sensors. We collected the pressure-distribution data using bed-sheet-type and garment-type sensors and evaluated their perfor-mance to detect pressures on human body surfaces. Such evaluation was dis-cussed through sleeping posture classification as described in Sect. 6. As the result, we found that the proposed garment-type pressure sensor could detect the pressure changes on the skin rather than a bed-sheet-type since the proposed garment-type sensor could classify postures more accurately.

2   Related Work

Sleeping-posture detection studies are used for pressure ulcer prevention because they can identify how long patients have remained in the same posture. Weimin et al. classified sleeping posture by a multi-modal approach using video and a 60-points pressure sensor [4]. However, use of video introduces privacy and refusal issues. Mineharu et al. [6] estimated sleeping postures only using the pressure distribution that is exerted on the bed. However, this study suffers from the same issues causes by body-pressure dispersion cushions described in Introduction.

The following are typical studies related to garment-type sensors. Paradiso et al. proposed a knit-type garment sensor that measures heart-rate, respiratory functions, and monitors body temperature [7]. Leong et al. implemented a sock-type pressure sensor to estimate the fitting of artificial legs [5]. However, no current device can measure the whole body-pressure, and no study uses such a device for pressure ulcer prevention.

3   Overview of Compared Sensors

In this section, we introduce an overview of our e-textile sensor and the compared two types of sensors.

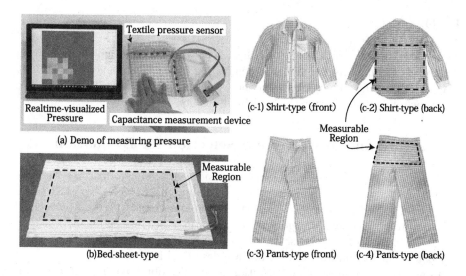

Fig. 2. Pressure sensor devices

3.1   Pressure Sensor Textile

An example of our textile pressure sensor is shown in (a) of Fig. 2. Our textile sensor has multiple capacitance sensors between the weft and the warp in the cross points of the gray conductive yarn lines. The capacitance value changes depending on the distance between the weft and the warp that is altered if additional load is added to the textile surface. Thus, we can measure the size of the load that is placed on the textile through capacitance value change measurements using a capacitance measuring device. The sensing point is 7.5 mm by 7.5 mm square, and the distance between neighboring sensing points is 10.0 mm.

3.2   Bed-Sheet-Type Pressure Sensor

An overview of our bed-sheet-type pressure sensor is shown in (b) of Fig. 2. The dashed region is the measurable area. Although the e-textile has 158×78 sensor points in the area of 158 by 78 cm, we combined four adjacent sensor points, 2×2, as one sensor point. Thus, there are 79×39 sensor points in the area. It is depending on a limitation of the capacitance measurement device.

3.3   Garment-Type Pressure Sensor

An overview of our garment-type sensors are shown in Fig. 2 (c-1)–(c-4). They are composed of the pressure sensor textile, except for the collar, sleeves, pockets, and front placket. They can measure the pressure wherever we set up electrodes and wires. Figure 2 shows the measurable region as a dashed region that covers the areas at risk for pressure ulcers. The shirt-type sensor has 18×31 sensor points. The pants-type sensor has 12×23 sensor points.

4   Dataset

We acquired matrix data using bed-sheet-type and garment-type sensors from 20 subjects (4 males and 16 females, height: 162.95 ± 6.57 cm, age: 34.65 ± 7.18, BMI: 20.06 ± 1.90). They alternated between supine and lateral positions five times each in 2 situations: with or without cushion.

5   Feature and Test Method Selection for Evaluation

Since pressure-distribution data can be considered as image, features that are suitable for image processing, such as HOG and SIFT, were expected to be suitable for in-bed posture classification. On the other hand, our data set seemed too small to applied such image processing features because the bed-sheet-type sensor has only 79×39 pixels. Therefore, we investigated which feature works well before the evaluation. The details are described in Sect. 5.1.

In addition, the most of classification accuracies obtained through the evaluation were higher than 0.9. It means that those distribution did not have normality and homoscedasticity. Therefore, we considered the use of a test method that do not require normality and homoscedasticity. The details are described in Sect. 5.2.

5.1   Selection of Features

Before the sensor comparison, we investigated the best feature vector from basic method in image classification. Candidate feature vectors are (1) F_a for measured value as they are, (2) F_b for HOG mainly used for human body detection, (3) F_c for SIFT used for key point detection in images. SVM with RBF kernel was used for classification. Parameters are set as: gamma-value is set from $1 \times 10^{-3}, 1 \times 10^{-4}$, automatic (reciprocal number of dimensions' amount), and C-value is set from 1, 10, 100, 1000. These were optimized with Grid Search. In addition, the accuracies were derived by leave-one-subject-out cross validation.

The results of taking the average values of accuracies were $\bar{F}_a = 0.93$, $\bar{F}_b = 0.73$, $\bar{F}_c = 0.72$. Therefore, we used measured value as they are in consequent experiments.

5.2   Selection of Test Method

The distribution of accuracies when the pressure-distributions were classified lateral and supine postures is tend to come one side. In addition, homoscedasticity cannot be expected because there is no value of 1.0 or more and the mode value is close to 1.0. Therefore, we used Brunner-Munzel's test that does not assume normality and homoscedasticity [1]. Brunner-Munzel's test shows the almost same performance as Welch's test even in the case that samples have normality or homoscedasticity.

6   Comparison of Detecting Performance of Two Types

We investigated the detecting performance with both of bed-sheet-type and garment-type sensors. We used the data acquired by both of sensors.

6.1   Investigation

We assumed that classifier can provide the almost same performance for cushion use situation if sensors can detect correct pressure-value. Therefore, we evaluated accuracies for classification with cushion placement using the classification-model that is learnt from pressure-distribution without cushions. SVM with RBF kernel was used for the identification. The parameters were optimized by Grid Search for every trial. As the result in Sect. 5.1, we used one-dimensional vector reshaped from raw pressure-value matrix as the feature vector. In addition, the accuracy were derived by leave one subject out cross validation.

6.2   Result

Figure 3 shows the box-plotted accuracy derived from posture classification using the data acquired with bed-sheet-type and garment-type sensors. The garment-type pressure sensor showed higher intermediate value then the bed-sheet-type pressure sensor, with 15% type I error according to the Brunner-Munzel's test. It means that there would be a tendency that the garment-type pressure sensor can classify at more accurate than bed-sheet-type. From this result, garment-type pressure sensor caught the pressure-value change more sensitively regardless cushion replacement.

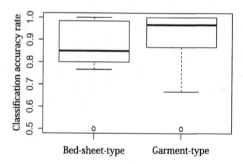

Fig. 3. Box-plotted accuracies of binary classification (supine and lateral postures)

7   Conclusion

We investigated the performance of detecting pressure-value changes with garment-type and bed-sheet-type pressure sensors aiming to detect the risk of pressure ulcer. We acquired the pressure-distribution data using both of sensors with 20 users and evaluated with posture classification with cushion placement. As the result, although type I error will occur at 15% according to Brunner-Munzel's test, there was tendency that the garment-type pressure sensor could classify more accurately. It leads the conclusion that is the garment-type pressure sensor has higher performance to detect high pressure than bed-sheet-type pressure sensor.

Acknowledgements. This work was supported by JSPS KAKENHI Grant Number 15H02736.

References

1. Brunner, E., Munzel, U.: The nonparametric Behrens-Fisher problem: asymptotic theory and a small-sample approximation. Biom. J. **42**(1), 17–25 (2000)
2. Enokibori, Y., Mase, K.: Are they effective in actual workspace? - case of pressure ulcer prevention features. In: Internal Workshop on Informatics 2016 (IWIN 2016), Riga, Latvia, pp. 13–18 (2016)
3. Enokibori, Y., Suzuki, A., Mizuno, H., Shimakami, Y., Mase, K.: E-textile pressure sensor based on conductive fiber and its structure. In: Proceedings of the 2013 ACM Conference on Pervasive and Ubiquitous Computing Adjunct Publication, UbiComp 2013 Adjunct, pp. 207–210. ACM, New York (2013). https://doi.org/10. 1145/2494091.2494158
4. Huang, W., Wai, A.A.P., Foo, S.F., Biswas, J., Hsia, C.C., Liou, K.: Multimodal sleeping posture classification. In: 2010 20th International Conference on Pattern Recognition (ICPR), pp. 4336–4339. IEEE (2010)
5. Leong, J., Parzer, P., Perteneder, F., Babic, T., Rendl, C., Vogl, A., Egger, H., Olwal, A., Haller, M.: proCover: sensory augmentation of prosthetic limbs using smart textile covers. In: Proceedings of the 29th Annual Symposium on User Interface Software and Technology, pp. 335–346. ACM (2016)
6. Mineharu, A., Kuwahara, N., Morimoto, K.: A study of automatic classification of sleeping position by a pressure-sensitive sensor. In: 2015 International Conference on Informatics, Electronics & Vision (ICIEV), pp. 1–5. IEEE (2015)
7. Paradiso, R., Loriga, G., Taccini, N.: A wearable health care system based on knitted integrated sensors. IEEE Trans. Inf. Technol. Biomed. **9**(3), 337–344 (2005). http:// dblp.uni-trier.de/db/journals/titb/titb9.html#ParadisoLT05

Automatic Classification of Traffic Accident Using Velocity and Acceleration Data of Drive Recorder

Moe Miyata[⊠], Kojiro Matsuo, and Ren Omura

1-1, Hibari-ga-oka, Tnepaku-cho, Toyohashi, Aichi 441-8580, Japan
miyata@usl.tut.ac.jp, k-matsuo@ace.tut.ac.jp,
ren@tut.jp

Abstract. In recent years, a drive recorder becomes common and is installed in a car to record sensor data, such as images, acceleration, and speed, about driving. The recorded data is useful to confirm and analyze a dangerous driving scene of a traffic accident and an incident. However, analyzing such data takes long time because it is done by a person who checks data one by one. Therefore, a method of automatic classification of drive recorder data is explored in this study. First, we labeled three types of incidents on the recorded data. Then, after extracting features from the acceleration and velocity, machine learning techniques are applied for the classification. Our preliminary evaluation showed that the classification result achieved about 0.55 of f-measure value.

Keywords: Acceleration · Classification · Machine learning · Drive recorder

1 Introduction

In recent year, a drive recorder [1] becomes common, and are installed in many cars. It records driving conditions, such as acceleration, braking, and turn signal, and video data, before and after getting an impact by some reasons. The recorded data are useful to confirm a dangerous driving scene of a traffic accident and an incident where a car accident almost happens. However, in many cases, analyzing data takes long time because it requires a person to check it one by one.

Some existing studies addressed a method to analyze and classify recorded data automatically. Kubo and Midori proposed a method to automatically classify the data using acceleration waveform [2]. In their study, videos of driving recorder obtained from taxis are confirmed by authors and labeled by ten types of incidents. Then, classification rules that classify the data into 7 types was manually constructed based on observed characteristics of acceleration waveform and was implemented as a software. As a result, Kappa coefficient between automatic classification result and visual confirmation result showed 0.73.

In recent years, sophisticated machine learning technique is available and is expected to show better classification performance. Takenaka *et al.* proposed a method to pick up a certain event in a video recorded by a drive recorder using sensor data [3]. This study classified some situations of driving, such as acceleration, deceleration, and

© ICST Institute for Computer Sciences, Social Informatics and Telecommunications Engineering 2018
K. Murao et al. (Eds.): MobiCASE 2018, LNICST 240, pp. 239–244, 2018.
https://doi.org/10.1007/978-3-319-90740-6_17

curve, with sensor data as semantic information of driving. By summarizing these semantic information, the data was labeled with more abstracted driving situation, such as normal progress, downhill, and change lanes. For detecting an event, several frames of the video before and after the point where label changes were automatically picked up and displayed in an analyzing software. However, the event type of picked up data had to be confirmed manually. Also, since the method is based on video analysis, it requires high calculation load when analyzing data of whole day.

NTT Communications proposed a method to automatically identify an incident of "crossing collision" using deep learning algorithm with the combination of image and acceleration data recorded by a drive recorder [4]. They used 9000 drive recorder's data of collaborative research company, and the result showed 85% of precision [5]. In addition, another study of them also confirmed the same method can automatically identify "stop sign violation" with 89% of true positive rate [6]. These studies can be expected to be useful for an analysis to prevent accidents. However, these studies have identified only one type of incident and do not identify multiple accident simultaneously.

Therefore, we study a method to automatically classify multiple types of driving incident using machine learning technique with simple sensor data of acceleration and speed recorded as a small amount of data around an event. In our study, more than 12376 drive recorder data are checked and labeled into three types of incidents, and we obtained 396 data in each incident type (1188 data in total). Multiple ranges of sensor data for extracting 41 dimensional feature values were explored to obtain better performance of classification. Moreover, several types of classification algorithm of supervised learning were evaluated and compared.

In the next section and Sect. 3, the recorded data and labeled data used in this study are explained. Sections 4 and 5 describes extracted feature values and machine learning algorithm. Section 6 shows the results of evaluation. Section 7 conclude this study.

2 Recorded Data

The sensor data used in this study was recorded by driving recorders installed in 224 taxis of a taxi company in Toyohashi city, Aichi prefecture, Japan. All recorded data was recorded from August 26, 2006 to December 14, 2011. The driving recorder records data 12 s before and 8 s after an event happens on the two-dimensional acceleration sensor (20 s in total before and after the event). The event is defined as a timing where the acceleration sensor observes more than 0.4 G on either the x or the y axis. The driving recorder records video, two-dimensional acceleration (vertical and horizontal), date and time, and the number of rotation of the tire of the car as its speed, on each frame at about 7 fps. As a result, one recorded data consists of 20 s of video and 135 frames of sensor data. In addition, the sizes of the tire of the cars are stored separately in another table.

Each recorded data is labeled into three types, "collision", "in passing another", and "others". "Collision" is a case that a rear vehicle collided with a front vehicle during vehicles traveling in the same direction [7]. "In passing another" is a case that vehicles going opposite direction collides. "Others" includes the cases where no accident happens but an event occurs, such as car bounds and sharp curves, as well as an accident other than "collision" and "in passing another".

We obtained 12376 recorded data in total. First, all the recorded data were roughly labeled as 462 data of "Collision", 1577 data of "in passing another", and 10337 data of "Other". Then, the videos are confirmed, and unobvious cases are eliminated.

3 Learning Data

We visually checked the video, recorded sensor data (frame number, number of rotations of the tire, horizontal and vertical acceleration value), and car information.

First, we confirmed the record data labeled "collision" of all recorded data. Since "collision" has the smallest number of recorded data in three types, the number of it was considered as the base line for the total number of learning data on each label. When the video was ambiguous with the definition of the label, the data was excluded from the learning data, which is named "pending data". When the recorded data corresponded to the conditions in Table 1, the data was also excluded from learning data, which is named "exclusion data". As the result, 396 learning data labeled "Collision" were obtained. By spending similar process, 396 cases of learning data labeled "in passing another" and learning data labeled "others" are obtained.

Table 1. Definition of exclusion data

Condition name	Explanation
Traffic accident	There is a contact accident of two or more cars
Incomplete frame	Number of frames is less than 135
No car information	There is no car number, or the size of the tire of the car is unknown
Incomplete hertz	Although the car equipped with the event data recorder is in progress, the rotation speed of the recorded tire is 0.0 [km/h]

Table 2 shows the confirmation results of recorded data. "Total" indicates the initial number of number of each data. "Pending" indicates the number of recorded data classified as pending data, "exclusion" indicates the number of recorded data classified as exclusion data. Learning data indicates the number of recorded data classified as learning data. Finally, 396 labeled data of each incident type are exploited for machine learning.

Table 2. Result of recorded data

Label name	Total	Pending	Exclusion	Learning data
Collision	462	50	16	396
In passing another	623	208	19	396
Others	530	109	25	396

4   Extracting Feature Value

Feature values used in machine learning were extracted from learning data selected in Sect. 3. First, velocity was calculated from the number of rotations of the tire and the size of the tire for each car using the Eq. (1) [8]. In this equation, V is the velocity of the car between two frames, H is the number of tire rotations per frame, n_1 is a constant determined by the size of the tire of the car, and N_2 is a constant of 637 [rpm].

$$V = \{H * 60\,[s] * 60\,[Km/s]\}/\{n_1 * N_2\} \tag{1}$$

Next, each feature values were calculated from the speed, vertical acceleration, horizontal acceleration, and combined acceleration in certain ranges of sensor data. For investigating the useful range of sensor data, the ranges for extracting feature values ware varied as shown in Table 3. 10 kinds of feature values are calculated; maximum value, minimum value, average value, standard deviation, zero cross rate, peak frequency, frequency entropy, kurtosis, skewness, spire degree [2]. Discrete Fourier transform (DFT) was used to calculate the peak frequency and frequency entropy. As the result, 40 features are exploited for machine learning.

Table 3. Feature values extraction range of acquisition

Range of acquisition [s]	Explanation	Number of total frame
0–20	From start recording to end	135
0–12	From start recording to the sensor reacts	81
12–20	The sensor reacts to end of recording	54
11–13	Before and after sensor reaction 1 s	14
9–15	Before and after sensor reaction 3 s	40
7–17	Before and after sensor reaction 5 s	68

5   Machine Learning

For the evaluation, a free machine learning software, "Weka" [9], was used. We converted feature values to ARFF files, which is data format for Weka. As the classification algorithm of machine learning, nearest neighbor algorithm (kNN, k = 1), random forest (RF), and support vector machine (SVM) were tested. The reason for choosing RF and SVM is that they are not affected by the curse of dimensionality very well. The evaluation is done by 10-fold cross validations using 396 training data (instances) for each class, 1188 instances in total. As the criteria of the classification performance, averaged accuracy, averaged F-measure values, and Kappa coefficient ware reviewed.

6   Result

The results are shown by Fig. 1 (a) to (c). From these results, the best performance for each evaluation is: (a) 0.70 of accuracy with the acquisition range of 7–17 using RF, (b) 0.55 of F-measure in the acquisition range of 7–17 using RF, (c) 0.33 of the Kappa coefficient in the acquisition range of 7–17 using RF. All results showed that the best performance gives with the acquisition range of 7–17 using RF.

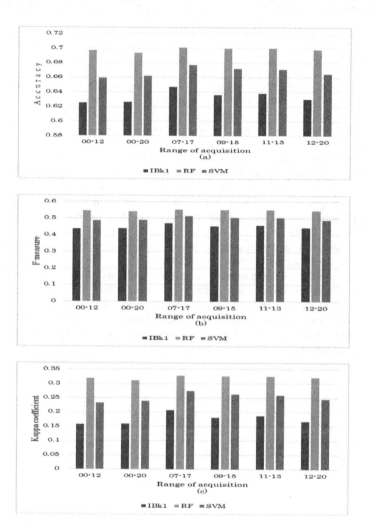

Fig. 1. Result with 396 learning data (10-folds cross validation). The horizontal axis represents the acquisition range, and the vertical axis represents the value of each criteria; (a) averaged accuracy, (b) averaged F-measure, (c) Kappa coefficient.

7   Conclusion

We studied a method to automatically classify driving incidents using acceleration and speed data recorded by a driving recorder with machine learning techniques. Using the 41 feature values, we compared the several ranges of sensor data used for feature extraction, 0–20, 0–12, 12–20, 11–13, 9–15, and 7–17, and three types of classification algorithms, nearest neighbour algorithm, SVM and random forest. The evaluation showed that the classification result achieved the best performance, 0.70 of accuracy, 0.55 of F-measure, 0.33 of Kappa coefficient, with the range of 7–17 using RF.

References

1. Safety measures for business vehicles: vehicle comprehensive safety information (in Japanese). http://www.mlit.go.jp/jidosha/anzen/03driverec/dorareco.html
2. Kubo, N., Midori, M.: Efficient automatic classification method of drive recorder. Trans. Jpn. Soc. Mech. Eng. Ser. (C) **77**(778), 338–353 (2011). (in Japanese)
3. Takenaka, K., Bando, T., Nagasaka, S., Taniguchi, T.: Drive video summarization based on double articulation structure of driving behavior. In: MM 2012 Proceedings of the 20th ACM International Conference on Multimedia, pp. 1169–1172 (2012)
4. News September 26, 2016: Succeeded in automatic detection of dangerous driving using artificial intelligence (AI) – NTT Com Corporate Information, NTT Communications Company Information (in Japanese). http://www.ntt.com/about-us/press-releases/news/article/2016/20160926_2.html
5. NTT Com: Successful automatic detection of dangerous driving using AI (in Japanese). http://www.atmarkit.co.jp/ait/articles/1609/27/news117.html
6. NTT Com and NCS: 96% probability to detect a temporary stop violation from video of drive recorder (in Japanese). https://it.impressbm.co.jp/articles/-/15087
7. Traffic Accident Statistics Glossary (in Japanese). https://www.itarda.or.jp/service/term.php
8. Japanee Industrial Standards JIS D 5601 – 1992 Automobiles speedometer (in Japanese)
9. Weka 3 - Data Mining with Open Source Machine Learning Software in Java. https://www.cs.waikato.ac.nz/ml/weka/

Dialogue Breakdown Detection with Long Short Term Memory

Tittaya Mairittha$^{(\boxtimes)}$, Tsuyoshi Okita, and Sozo Inoue

Kyushu Institute of Technology, 1-1 Sensui-cho, Tobata-ku, Kitakyushu-shi,
Fukuoka 804-8550, Japan
{fon,okita,sozo}@sozolab.jp

Abstract. This paper aims to detect the utterance which can be categorized as the breakdown of the dialogue flow. We propose a logistic regression-based and a Long Short-Term Memory (LSTM)-based methods. Using the input with utterance-response pairs, the performance of the LSTM-based method is superior to that of the logistic regression-based method in 36% measured with F-measure. We also measured the performance using the performance with utterance-response pairs: the performance with the input only with responses is unexpectedly inferior to those with responses in 6% to 23% measured with F-measure.

Keywords: Dialogue breakdown · Dialogue systems
Text classification

1 Introduction

Among dialogue services, the voice agent service provides critical functionalities in daily life. This agent gives a series of answers to the questions by the caller, continuing the conversation for a minute. Ideally, this agent should respond appropriate answers as if a human being is behind the line. This goal is far from being attained. One reason for this lies in our lack of understanding what is the natural way we humans talk and produce a response, leading to dialogue breakdowns in conversation. Here, *dialogue breakdowns* refer to a situation in which users cannot proceed with the conversation [1]. The dialogue breakdown detection will be useful for continuing the conversation in dialogue systems and may improve the conversation with the agent. Dialogue breakdown detection could be seen as the same problem of classification, where the input to the classification model is a sequence of words and the output is a predicted class. More structured neural network approaches for utterance classification include using recursive neural network [2].

In this paper, we aim to detect inappropriate utterances that cause dialogue breakdown. Our first method used logistic regression to model the task. The second method used embeddings to represent the utterances and neural network called LSTM [3] to model the task. We compared two methods with two baselines. One is the input only with responses. The other one is utterance-response

© ICST Institute for Computer Sciences, Social Informatics and Telecommunications Engineering 2018
K. Murao et al. (Eds.): MobiCASE 2018, LNICST 240, pp. 245–250, 2018.
https://doi.org/10.1007/978-3-319-90740-6_18

pairs which the features used are words in the target utterance and its previous utterances. The results of these experiments show that LSTM-based method can successfully handle dialogue breakdown detection.

2   Background and Related Work

There have been a few papers published that have presented dialogue breakdowns in the conversation. One is a report from dialogue breakdown detection challenge [4] where the task is to detect a system's inappropriate utterances that lead to dialogue breakdowns in chat systems. Several of the methods submitted to the challenge use neural networks to model the task or advances in natural language processing. The results show very similar performances across the different feature sets. Apparently, the recent advances in both approaches, however the research was conducted only in Japanese.

3   Methods

3.1   Logistic Regression-Based Method

We will start by considering logistic regression. The logistic regression refers to a classifier that classifies an observation into one of two classes, and multinomial logistic regression is used when classifying into more than two classes. We considered these tasks as multi-label classification tasks which our targets there are three types of labels: O (not a breakdown), T (possible breakdown), and X (breakdown).

The inputs to the multinomial logistic regression are the features we have in the dataset, the utterances we converted them into numerical values by sum all of the vectors for each in the in the utterance, concatenate the two together, and then use this as the input to the linear model. We then use the softmax function which calculates the probabilities for the given score and return a probability distribution on the output breakdowns. And the last stage of multinomial logistic regression uses the cross-entropy function to find the similarity distance between the probabilities calculated using the softmax function.

3.2   LSTM-Based Method

We turn now to a second algorithm for classification called LSTM to classify the breakdowns. The first layer is the embedded layer that uses 32 length vectors to represent each word. The next layer is the LSTM-based layer with 100 memory unit, in and the output layer we used a softmax activation function. Finally, the network uses the efficient Adam gradient descent optimization algorithm [6] with a logarithmic loss function. The hyperparameters of the neural network model are as follows: the model parameters are a learning rate of 0.01, a dropout rate of 0.2 for both LSTM and softmax layer outputs and a batch size of 64 to use when training the model, we trained with 5 epochs with early stopping. As discussed above, there are many factors that can influence the model and effect of training. To achieve the best performances, we may fine-tune hyperparameters.

4   Breakdown Detection Task

For training and development data sets, annotations were provided by the dialog system technology challenges (DSTC6) [7]. The original dialogue datasets were collected by the WOCHAT dataset and the Conversational Intelligence Challenge (CIC). A total of four data sets, resulting in 4,150 dialogues. Each dialogue was controlled to be 20–21 utterance sequences from the user and the system. All utterances are annotated by 30 annotators (only for system utterances), each element of the annotation fields is one the followings: (NB) Not a breakdown, (PB) Possible breakdown, and (B) Breakdown. Example dialogue is shown in Fig. 1.

	Speaker	Utterance	NB	PB	B
0	U	Hi Alex	0	0	0
1	S	Hi.	28	1	1
2	U	can you say something different?	0	0	0
3	S	How different?	20	10	0
4	U	very different please	0	0	0
5	S	What you reading?	17	7	6
6	U	harry potter	0	0	0
7	S	'Mr. Potter...	11	16	3
8	U	yes, have you read it?	0	0	0
9	S	No. Not yet. Soon.	22	2	6

Fig. 1. An example of a dialogue with the number of breakdown labels for each system utterance (S means the system and U means the user)

5   Experimental Setup

5.1   Data Preprocessing

The data cannot be used directly for performing analysis process. Therefore, certain steps are executed to solve this problem to convert the raw data into a clean data set. We also generated output predictions from a baseline detector that the DSTC6 prepared. The baseline program uses words included in each utterance as features (Bag-of-Words) and detects dialogue breakdowns by using Conditional Random Fields (CRFs). This program outputs three kinds of labels with probability distributions. The correct label for each instance is the majority of the labels given to the instance. We also split randomly the dataset into the train (90%) and test (10%) sets.

5.2   Models

Our proposed model encodes utterances in context into fixed-length vectors, then processes these encoded vectors in the model. Our first step is to encode raw text inputs from the utterances into distributed vector representations; each utterance is represented by a sequence word index, the index is ordered by the most frequent words. For each sequence, we truncated words to make the consistent length. Then, looked up the embedding for each index, we also initialized the embedding with GloVe [8] embeddings on 50-dimensional vectors of Wikipedia 2014 and returned a matrix of d-dimensional vectors for passing them to the model. The second step is to create the models that detect dialogue breakdowns as implemented in the Keras framework.

5.3 Analyzing

We used a type of evaluation metrics to evaluate the classification of the breakdown labels.

- Accuracy: The number of correctly classified labels divided by the total number of labels to be classified.
- Precision, recall, F-measure for the classification of the B labels.
- Precision, recall, F-measure for the classification of PB + B labels; that is, PB and B labels are treated as a single label.

6 Results

Table 1 reports the best results we obtained from the methods. As can be seen from the table, deep learning LSTM, achieved good precision, also seem to be reasonable from the input only with responses and utterance-response pairs. However, the B label is still more difficult to classify compared to PB+B labels. This indicates that it is difficult to discriminate between possible breakdowns and breakdowns, but it is possible to discriminate breakdowns from non-breakdowns.

Table 1. The precision, recall, and F-measure for the classification of (B) labels. and (B + PB) labels

Model	Accuracy	Breakdown			Possible breakdown + breakdown		
		Precision	Recall	F-measure	Precision	Recall	F-measure
LSTM pair	0.636	0.58	0.59	0.59	0.78	0.67	0.71
LSTM single	0.598	0.52	0.48	0.5	0.85	0.52	0.57
Logistic pair	0.609	0.13	0.43	0.2	0.13	0.43	0.2
Logistic single	0.562	0.1	0.33	0.14	0.5	0.35	0.2

Table 2 shown in patterns of errors of in dialogue breakdown detection, presenting a confusion matrix.

Table 2. An example results for a three class classifier.

Actual	Prediction outcome		
	NB	PB	B
NB	U: How are you today? S: Good. How are you?	U: So, what else? S: Okay, okay. What else you got?	U: What? S: We're skinny dipping, Danny
PB	U: Just like dogs. S: What kind of dog	U: Lock him up! S: Okay! Who else should we lock up?	U: well, I can do many things S: Ten
B	U: Oh, my god! S: 1 plus 1?	U: Amoroso renato S: where are you from?	U: Who's Mr. Vitti? S: Where's Vitti? I don't see Vitti

Figure 2 shows example dialogue between our dialogue system and a user where the annotated breakdown.

	Speaker	Utterances
0	U	what did happen to juliet?
1	S	So was Juliet – at fifteen.
2	U	Why?
3	S	It's not right. I feel horrible. Besides...
4	U	Still incorrect :(I think that correct answer is: first:)
5	S	I don't know. what do you think
6	U	You sure like to not talk about thing
7	S	I don't know. That's interesting.
8	U	I don't hate anything about it
9	S	So you're less intelligent than a computer?!

Fig. 2. An example of a dialogue breakdown

When we looked at the incorrect predictions cases in Fig. 3, we found that those utterances may breakdown from a proper noun or a named entity. So future studies will include identifying and extracting entities (people, places, companies, etc.) to improve the performance of classification efficiency.

	Speaker	Utterances
0	U	goodYou are rigth!How can I reward you?
1	S	... not for you and this post.
2	U	Grover Cleveland Golf Course
3	S	Who is Aung San Suu Kyi?
4	U	Nope. I don't know that she's anything like Christmas.
5	S	Do you like my girlfriend?
6	U	What?
7	S	We're skinny dipping, Danny.
8	U	Still incorrect. I think that true answer is: jesus.
9	S	jesus

Fig. 3. An example dialogues which incorrect predictions

7   Conclusion

In this paper, we verified the implementation of our models by achieving results very similar to those achieved by previously published works within the challenge, the accuracy for the former is 0.643 while that of the latter is 0.636. When we look at the details, we can see the performing of utterance-response pairs, rather than the input only with responses. However, the accuracies are low; it is still difficult to detect breakdowns. Future research should aim to improve the systems with the sentence-based classification.

References

1. Martinovsky, B., Traum, D.: The error is the cue: breakdown in human-machine interaction. In: Proceedings of Error Handling in Spoken Dialogue Systems, pp. 11–16 (2003)
2. Ravuri, S.V., Stolcke, A.: Recurrent neural network and LSTM models for lexical utterance classification. In: INTERSPEECH (2015)
3. Hochreiter, S., Schmidhuber, J.: Long short-term memory. Neural Comput. **9**(8), 1735–1780 (1997)
4. Higashinaka, R., et al.: The dialogue breakdown detection challenge: task description, datasets, and evaluation metrics. In: LREC (2016)
5. Socher, R., Perelygin, A., Wu, J., Chuang, J., Manning, C., Ng, A., Potts, C.: Recursive deep models for semantic compositionality over a sentiment treebank. In: EMNLP (2013)
6. Kingma, D., Ba, J.: Adam: a method for stochastic optimization. arXiv preprint arXiv:1412.6980 (2014)
7. Dialogue System Technology Challenge 6 (DSTC6). http://workshop.colips.org/dstc6/call.html
8. Pennington, J., Richard, S., Manning, C.: Glove: global vectors for word representation. In: Proceedings of the 2014 Conference on Empirical Methods in Natural Language Processing (EMNLP) (2014)

Estimation of Person Existence in Room Using BLE Beacon and Its Platform

Fumitaka Naruse$^{(\boxtimes)}$ and Katsuhiko Kaji

Faculty of Information Science, Aichi Institute of Technology, Toyota, Japan
{k14092kk,kaji}@aitech.ac.jp

Abstract. In this research, estimation of person existence in room using BLE beacon and that propose application method. Create a platform for that. For estimating of person existence, BLE beacons are used as individual identifiers. Install a receiver in the room. By doing this, we can estimation with high degrees of freedom not dependent on Devices. Acquire Information on estimation of person from the platform we created. Based on this information, we disclose real-time person's stay information and person's stay information history. We also propose applications such as notification systems and visit promotion systems.

Keywords: BLE beacon · Room estimation · Platform

1 Introduction

Various uses can be considered for person staying information. Approach becomes easier if person know whereabouts. Also, if you know the number of users in the room and the time zone to be used, it will be an index of the improvement of the environment including the temperature adjustment of the room.

There are several ways to estimate a person staying in the room. It is a method using an IC card or a live camera. The former method is to use IC card and card reader. It is a detection method based on the voluntary action of the user [1]. Therefore, it is labor when entering or leaving the room. In the latter case, the user need not act voluntarily However, taking permanent indoor photography requires privacy consideration for users [2]. In this research, We estimate with a device that do not require user's voluntary actions and do not inspect precise behavior, so focus on BLE beacon.

In recent years, tracking of people using BLE and BLE beacons has been done [3,4]. Among them, there are many attendance management systems using smartphones and BLE beacons [5]. These are methods of installing a BLE beacon in a room using an individual's smartphone as a device. From the viewpoint that many users have smartphones, it is an advantage that operation costs are reduced. However, person's who do not have a smartphone can not use it. In addition, there are problems such as requiring user's voluntary operation for

© ICST Institute for Computer Sciences, Social Informatics and Telecommunications Engineering 2018
K. Murao et al. (Eds.): MobiCASE 2018, LNICST 240, pp. 251–257, 2018.
https://doi.org/10.1007/978-3-319-90740-6_19

application operation. In this research, priority is given to a method need not voluntary action without limiting users. As a method, the user owns the BLE beacon and Install a receiver in the room.

With this approach, The user only has to hold a small beacon. For example, put it in a wallet or Attach to the key holder. It is possible to estimate people simply by attaching BLE beacon to items that are always carried around. There is no need for the user to pay attention. There is no worry that the user will make an operation mistake.

We think person's stay information can used in various places such as university lecture room and office. In this research, we aim to promote smooth communication and promote visit to university laboratories.

We create a platform so that person's stay information can be obtained from various applications. Applications can refer to the person's stay information from the API created by us. We think that referencing information of person's in the room from various programs leads to improvement of accessibility of users.

The rest of this paper is structured as follows. In Sect. 2, we explain related research. Section 3 we explain about the stay management system. Section 4 make a simple visualization system using API and propose methods for promoting visits. Section 5 Consider improvement of user's accessibility by concrete application development. Section 6 summarizes and discusses future issues.

2   Related Research

Information on occupants is very useful. There are several studies to investigate occupancy situation of buildings [6–8]. For example, if you know the building's occupancy situation, you can effectively use vacant conference rooms [7] and conserving energy in buildings [8]. It is important to create an estimated platform for passengers to use for such applications. In this research, we will create a platform that can be applied in various situations.

In recent years attendance management using BLE beacon is flourishing. For example, attendance management method in lecture room of university [9] and Smart Building Management [10]. This research, a beacon is installed in the room and the corresponding application is downloaded to the smartphone owned by the individual. Attendance management is possible with reduced cost because beacon detection is carried out using smartphones owned by individuals. Applications are required to perform actions such as voluntary startup, so in some cases it is possible to forget to launch applications. Also, person's who do not have smartphones can not use the system, they will need separate teacher's cope. We think that the method that the user possesses BLE beacon can solve such a problem.

There is an estimation method that places no burden on users. It is a method of using environmental sensors [11]. It measures human occupancy by environmental indicators such as CO_2 concentration. The drawback of this problem is that we can not identify individuals. There is no problem if you want to know only whether there are people or not. However, in this research, we use information on people in the room to promote communication. Therefore, it must be a method that can identify individuals. A BLE beacon has a unique identifier. We can identify individuals by using this.

3   Stay Management System

An overview of the entire system is shown in Fig. 1. Users carry small beacons. Beacon used MAMORIO sold by MAMORIO Corporation[1]. Install raspberry pie in the room as a receiver for BLE reception. The device constantly monitors the radio waves of BLE, makes a determination on entry and exit, and sends it to the server if there is a change. Refer to the data on the server using the API created independently. You can refer to personal or multiple current stay information, past stay information history, etc.

3.1   Linking Beacons and Individuals

Beacons have UUID, major, minor identifiers. Save this beacon specific identifier and personal name in the database. We are also considering adding attributes in addition to individual names when linking beacons and individuals. For example, it is the name of the laboratory to which you belong, the team that belongs to it, the grade, etc. These information facilitate identification of individuals in the visualization system. Also in the visit promotion system, we think that grouping such as laboratory or grade can stimulate solidarity and competitiveness.

3.2   Method for Estimation of Person

Refers to the beacon information of the corresponding room periodically detected by the device and the registrant information stored in the database to determine the person's stay. If the information of the corresponding beacon is not included in the periodically detected, it is assumed that it does not already exist in the room. With this, it is possible for a user to detect a person in the room without carrying out voluntary action just by having the beacon by the user. Record the name of the room in which the device is installed in the device. As a result, it is possible to estimate the person in multiple rooms.

3.3   Stay Information Management Server

The stay information estimated by the device is sent to the server. It is recorded in the database together with the date and the room name in which person is present. The stay information can also be used from other programs through the API. For example, we are thinking about systems such as visualization of stay information, visitors notice, promotion of visitors to the laboratory.

---

[1] http://company.mamorio.jp.

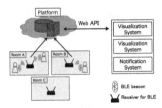

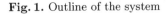

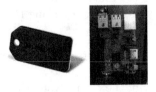

Fig. 1. Outline of the system

Fig. 2. MAMORIO (BLE beacon) and Raspberry Pi (Receive for BLE)

4   Smooth Communication and Promotion of Visit

The stay information of the person in the room is useful information for both the user and the administrator. It is important to know where that person is in order to communicate directly with other person's. Also, for administrators too, such information is important for improving the indoor environment. In this research, we focus on improving the convenience of users by using the information of person's in the room. The stay information of the person in the room is divided into the present stay situation and the past stay situation. The display of the person staying present serves as an aid for smooth communication at the present time. In the display of the past stay status, future prediction can be made from the tendency of the visiting place.

It is important that users increase in public rooms such as laboratories. It leads to an increase in information exchange and communication opportunities. In addition to the name of the information of the person in the room, attribute such as grade or team is given. We think that segmentation of user information strengthens individual recognition and increases sense of solidarity. In addition to that, We think that we can measure the total staying time and increase the competitiveness by ranking overall, every grade or team.

4.1   Visibility of Stay History Information

Examples of visualization of stay information history information is as follows. Information is displayed as shown in Left of Fig. 3. If you know the current person's location, it will be easier to contact with the target person. The figure to the right of Fig. 3 shows information on stay information history. If you can grasp the past stay information, you can grasp the trend and usage situation of the visiting place. We think this will lead to smooth promotion of communication as above. Also, we can know the time zone when users use the room. Therefore, we believe that it will be able to assist the maintenance of the environment such as the temperature adjustment of the room.

4.2   Total Staying Time and Grouping

Examples of display of total staying time and an grouping are shown below. Display the total staying time as shown in Left of Fig. 4. We think that the promotion of visit can be aimed at by setting compensation based on cumulative points and competition by ranking. Also, compare this total staying time even within the group as shown in to the right of Fig. 4. We think this will stimulate the competition by competition among groups like all laboratories and grade and will lead to promotion of visit.

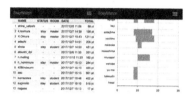

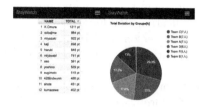

Fig. 3. Stay history information   **Fig. 4.** Total stay time and grouping

5   Application Deployment

Use stay information by other program through API. We think this will lead to an increase in the opportunity for users to browse information. For example, as shown in Left of Fig. 5, a display is set at an eye-catching place and the stay status of a specific person is always displayed. Displaying information on stays on SNS as shown in to the right of Fig. 5. Collaboration with other applications frequently used and encouraging surrounding environment will improve accessibility of users to this system.

Fig. 5. Teacher's stay status display monitor

6   Conclusion

In this research, the user possessed the BLE beacon and installed the receiver in the room. As a result, we can only the stay information was detected without restriction of the user, voluntary action. Also, in order to increase the opportunity to view the information of persons stay in the room, we also made it possible to reference from an external program through the API.

We classified information on stays into two occupancy situations. One is the indication of real-time staying information. The other is a display of the stay histories. Regarding the visit promotion system, we set compensation and ranking about stay time and proposed as one method for promoting visit. Also, as application development, we constantly displayed the stay information of a specific person, and proposed proposals to increase the number of browsing opportunities through cooperation with LINE.

In the future we will evaluate the proposed visit promotion. Also, consider other approaches to promoting visits. On that basis, we will consider visualization of information on stay history more effective than now.

References

1. Redetzke, S., Vanner, A., Otieno, R.: Smart room attendance monitoring and location tracking with iBeacon technology. Worcester Polytechnic Institute, Electrical and Computer Engineering Department as a Major Qualifying Project (MQP) (2017)
2. Sohn, H., Neve, W., Ro, Y.: Privacy protection in video surveillance systems: analysis of subband-adaptive scrambling in JPEG XR. IEEE Trans. Circuits Syst. **21**(2), 170–177 (2011)
3. Mahendraker, V., Savitha, D.: Student tracking system with bluetooth low energy. IJETSR **4**, 2394–3386 (2017)
4. Doug, D.: Using beacons for attendance tracking, frontiers in education: CS and CE. In: FECS, pp. 155–161 (2016)
5. Bae, Y., Cho, J.: Design and implementation of automatic attendance check system using BLE Beacon. Int. J. Multimed. Ubiquit. Eng. 10, 177–186 (2015)
6. Conte, G., Marchi, M., Nacci, A., Rana, V., Sciuto, D.: BlueSentinel: a first approach using iBeacon for an energy efficient occupancy detection system. In: BuildSys@ SenSys, pp. 11–19 (2014)
7. Conner, W.S., Krishnamurthy, L., Want, R.: Making everyday life easier using dense sensor networks. In: Abowd, G.D., Brumitt, B., Shafer, S. (eds.) UbiComp 2001. LNCS, vol. 2201, pp. 49–55. Springer, Heidelberg (2001). https://doi.org/10.1007/3-540-45427-6_6
8. Kwak, J., Varakantham, P., Maheswaran, R., Tambe, M., Jazizadeh, F., Kavulya, G., Klein, L., Becerik-Gerber, B., Hayes, T., Wood, W.: SAVES: a sustainable multiagent application to conserve building energy considering occupants. In: Proceedings of the 11th International Conference on Autonomous Agents and Multiagent Systems, International Foundation for Autonomous Agents and Multiagent Systems, vol. 1, pp. 21–28 (2012)

9. Pack, J., Ko, J., Shin, H.: A measurement study of BLE iBeacon and geometric adjustment scheme for indoor location-based mobile applications. Hindawi Publ. Corp. Mob. Inf. Syst, Article ID 8367638 (2016)
10. Corna, A., Fontana, L., Nacci, A., Sciuto, D.: Occupancy detection via iBeacon on Android devices for smart building management. In: Proceedings of the 2015 Design, Automation and Test in Europe Conference and Exhibition, EDA Consortium, pp. 629–632 (2015)
11. Meyn, S., Surana, A., Lin, Y., Oggianu, S., Narayanan, S., Frewen, T.: A sensor-utility-network method for estimation of occupancy in buildings. In: 48h IEEE Conference on Decision and Control, pp. 1494–1500 (2009)

Evaluation of Priority Control Mechanism for Remote Monitoring IoT System in Greenhouses

Takuma Tachibana[1](✉), Eisuke Kasahara[2], Takamasa Yoshida[2],
and Hiroshi Mineno[3]

[1] Graduate School of Integrated Science and Technology, Shizuoka University,
3-5-1 Johoku, Naka-ku, Hamamatsu, Shizuoka 432-8011, Japan
tachibana@minelab.jp
[2] Central Research Laboratory Technology Group, Hamamatsu Photonics K.K.,
5000 Hirakuchi, Hamakita-ku, Hamamatsu, Shizuoka 434-8601, Japan
{eisuke.kasahara, takamasa.yoshida}@crl.hpk.co.jp
[3] College of Informatics, Shizuoka University/JST PRESTO, 3-5-1 Johoku,
Naka-ku, Hamamatsu, Shizuoka 432-8011, Japan
mineno@inf.shizuoka.ac.jp

Abstract. The Internet of Things (IoT) has expanded rapidly in recent years. Therefore, there are various types of data available from IoT devices, such as texts, images, and sound. It will become possible to construct a heterogeneous remote monitoring IoT system using a variety of IoT devices. However, a heterogeneous remote monitoring IoT system cannot send complete data because most mobile network services for the IoT system do not guarantee bandwidth. Therefore, we proposed a priority control mechanism for a heterogeneous remote monitoring IoT system that controls the amount of data, and the time it takes to send it for IoT devices, which is decided in accordance with the quality of service. In this paper, we show how we improved the applicability of the operations of a priority control system and evaluated the effectiveness of an actual remote monitoring IoT system by using a greenhouse data-collection system.

Keywords: Internet of Things · Priority control · Mobile networks
Data collection

1 Introduction

All people expect the Internet of Things (IoT) to grow because of downsized sensors and the appearance of various mobile networks [1–3]. The extremely wide variety of IoT devices generate various types of data, such as texts, images, and sounds. Therefore, it has been indicated that the number of devices connected to the IoT and network traffic per device will grow in the next five years [4]. In addition, mobile network service providers have deployed handle services for the IoT system in recent years. However, there is a problem regarding remote monitoring IoT systems [3] that collect multifarious data from remote locations (referred to as heterogeneous remote monitoring IoT systems). The problem is that mobile network services for the IoT

© ICST Institute for Computer Sciences, Social Informatics and Telecommunications Engineering 2018
K. Murao et al. (Eds.): MobiCASE 2018, LNICST 240, pp. 258–264, 2018.
https://doi.org/10.1007/978-3-319-90740-6_20

cannot completely sustain the required traffic from a heterogeneous remote monitoring IoT system because almost all mobile network services for the IoT system do not guarantee throughput. To solve this problem, we proposed a priority control mechanism for a heterogeneous remote monitoring IoT system [5]. We proved its effectiveness in enabling a IoT system that guarantees telecommunications at the lowest limit. In this paper, we evaluate the effectiveness of an actual remote monitoring IoT system. In accordance with the availability in actual system operations, we improved the proposed mechanism. The evaluation target in this paper is a greenhouse data-collection system. Through this evaluation, we show the effectiveness of the proposed mechanism for various mobile networks and systems.

The remainder of this paper is organized as follows: Sect. 2 shows related work in terms of methods and protocols for IoT telecommunications. The improved priority mechanism and implementation in the actual system is described in Sect. 3. The experimental results and discussion are shown in Sect. 4, and following that is the conclusion.

2 Related Work

Various methods and protocols for IoT telecommunications have been proposed [6–8]. One protocol for the IoT, MQ Telemetry Transport (MQTT) [9], targets IoT traffic from many devices that send and receive small amounts of data at high frequency. MQTT is a very effective protocol for IoT devices regarding sending lightweight data. In contrast, header size reduction does not affect IoT devices, for example cameras, when they send a large amount of data. In addition, MQTT has a quality of service (QoS) control mechanism for unstable mobile networks. However, this mechanism does not consider data characteristics and does not screen the data to be sent.

Probabilistic prediction-based scheduling [10] is a scheduling model for IoT system traffic. The objective of probabilistic prediction-based scheduling is to reduce the waiting time of high priority packets and keep the waiting time of other priority packet services within tolerable limits. However, probabilistic prediction-based scheduling is unable to meet the IoT application requirements because it does not consider how to determine data that has high priority.

Most existing methods cannot solve the problems in IoT telecommunications in regard to data amount, frequency, and number of devices. Additionally, IoT telecommunications must consider the QoS required by applications. Therefore, it is important to implement a telecommunication mechanism for IoT that considers multiple data characteristics, mobile networks, and QoS required by applications.

3 Priority Control Mechanism

In this section, we explain our mechanism [5]. The mechanism focuses on the priority and characteristics of data to control the data-sending order and data amount by setting the application configuration as a requirement. Therefore, it enables a level of control that satisfies the requirements from the application's QoS.

Figure 1 shows the architecture of the proposed mechanism. The proposed mechanism consists of three elements: IoT devices, a broker server, and an application server. The IoT devices are endpoint devices that are connected to mobile networks.

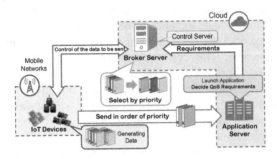

Fig. 1. Architecture of priority control mechanism

The application server is an IoT system server that processes the data from the IoT devices, and the broker server is a priority control server in the mechanism. The application server and broker server are split by function; therefore, they can run on the same physical server. Because of this split, the elements' roles can be clearly defined.

Figure 2 shows the flow of the proposed mechanism. The proposed mechanism consists of three phases; a register phase, a priority telecommunication phase, and a release phase. In the register phase, the application server registers the QoS requirements of its own application. The broker server creates a "priority decision table" and tells the IoT devices the application server address. After that, all the elements establish a TCP connection with each other. In the priority telecommunication phase, the broker server gives priority to the data, which is generated by the IoT devices (referred to as 'content data'), and manages it. Additionally, the broker server permits the content data that has the highest priority to be sent.

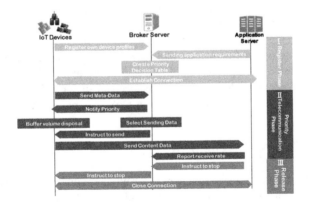

Fig. 2. Flow of priority control mechanism

We improved the priority control mechanism to operate in the actual system. We implemented acknowledgement messages corresponding to each control message in the mechanism to prevent decreasing IoT system availability because, when the system is installed on a remote environment, some connection errors occur due to bad radio wave conditions depending on the location. The sender can determine that the connection was lost and try reconnecting to the receiver if an acknowledgement message is not received within a given time. In this paper, we set the time limit as 20 s.

4   Evaluation and Discussion

In this section, we evaluate the applicability including performance of the priority control mechanism in an actual system that uses different mobile networks to those used in [5]'s evaluation. In this evaluation, the priority control mechanism uploaded data from IoT devices to an application server in accordance with the scenario. Table 1 shows the scenario. This scenario was made by using requirements from the target system. We used two evaluation indicators: the sending ratio of each priority (the ratio of data that could be transmitted within the evaluation times) and the average transfer complete time for each priority (the required time from the generation of data in the IoT devices to complete transition). If all the sending ratios with a higher priority are higher than those with a lower priority and all the average transfer complete times with a higher priority are shorter than those with a lower priority, we can say the proposed mechanism applicable in actual System.

Table 1. Scenario of this evaluation

Data type	Data amount	Data generation interval	Data interval	Priority
Camera (small)	About 220 KB	1 min	5 min	2
			1 min	3
Camera (large)	About 2 MB		10 min	4
			1 min	5

Figure 3 shows the architecture of the greenhouse data-collection system that was used for the evaluation in this paper. The greenhouse data-collection system has 12 camera devices. The priority control mechanism uploads data generated by these camera devices to a cloud server. We installed Raspbian 8 onto Raspberry Pi 2 and used them as IoT devices. Similarly, we used Ubuntu 14.04 LTS as the application and broker servers. The installation site is an agricultural faculty field in Shizuoka University. We used WiMAX2 for the system's mobile network. The average mobile network throughput was 2.30 Mbps (measured by iPerf) at the installation site. The evaluating time was from 3:20 PM July 18 to 10:00 AM July 20 (43 h).

Figure 4 shows the results of the sending ratio and average transfer complete time for each priority. The sending ratios with a higher priority were higher than those with lower priority. In addition, all the average transfer complete times with a higher priority were shorter than those with lower priority. Therefore, proposed mechanism could ensure bandwidth immediately for data that has high priority because it determines which data to send using the application's requirement. These results show that the priority control mechanism could satisfy minimum requirements of the actual IoT system.

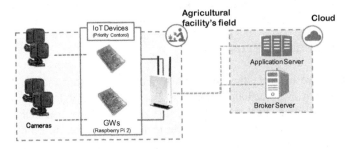

Fig. 3. Architecture of greenhouse data-collection system

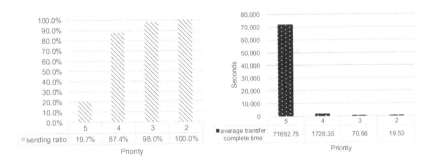

Fig. 4. Sending ratio and average transfer complete time for each priority

However, the average transfer complete time for the highest priority was too long (19.53 s) because the calculated transfer time was 0.75 s if the bitrate was 2.30 Mbps and the data size was 220 kBs. Therefore, the average transfer complete time was too long regarding network throughput. Figure 5 shows the amount of received bitrates that were calculated per 20 s. As shown in Fig. 5, there was dispersion over the course of time in the received bitrates, especially during the daytime. We consider that it was caused by a long round-trip time in this environment. When mobile networks that have long round-trip times are used, the priority control mechanism spends time sending and receiving control messages between each element. Furthermore, the average round-trip time of the mobile network was 702 ms (measured by ping) at the installation site. Therefore, the performance of the current priority control mechanism is affected by the round-trip time. We should solve the problems of the long average transfer complete time and uneven bitrate through a mobile network that has a long round-trip time.

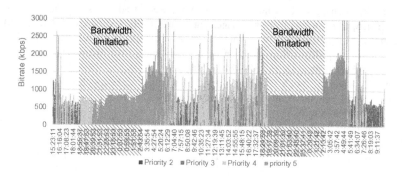

Fig. 5. Received bitrates calculated every 20 s

5   Conclusion

In this paper, we evaluated the applicability of a priority control mechanism in an actual remote monitoring IoT system. We improved the mechanism in accordance with the system operations. We evaluated proposed mechanism in an actual remote monitoring IoT system, a greenhouse data-collection system as actual remote monitoring IoT system. We showed that the priority control mechanism satisfied the minimum requirements of the actual IoT system. On the other hand, the proposed mechanism's performance deteriorated when it was used over high round-trip time networks. In future work, we will overcome this performance problem in high delay network. Furthermore, we will evaluate our mechanism in various network environments.

Acknowledgements. This work was partially supported by the JSPS (KAKENHI JP26280028) and the Cooperative Research Project Program of the RIEC, Tohoku University.

References

1. Smith, T.F.: Towards a definition of the Internet of Things (IoT). IEEE (2016). http://iot.ieee.org/images/files/pdf/IEEE_IoT_Towards_Definition_Internet_of_Things_Revision1_27MAY15.pdf
2. Atzori, L., Iera, A., Morabito, G.: The Internet of Things: a survey. Comput. Netw. **54**(15), 2787–2805 (2010)
3. Gubbi, J., Buyya, R., Marusic, S., Palaniswami, M.: Internet of Things (IoT): a vision, architectural elements, and future directions. Future Gener. Comput. Syst. **29**(7), 1645–1660 (2013)
4. Cisco Visual Networking Index: Global mobile data traffic forecast update, 2014–2019. Technical report, Cisco (2015)
5. Tachibana, T., Furuichi, T., Mineno, T.: Implementing and evaluating priority control mechanism for heterogeneous remote monitoring IoT system. In: Adjunct Proceedings of the 13th International Conference on Mobile and Ubiquitous Systems: Computing Networking and Services, pp. 239–244. ACM (2016)

6. Sheng, Z., Mahapatra, C., Zhu, C., Leung, V.C.: Recent advances in industrial wireless sensor networks toward efficient management in IoT. IEEE Access **3**, 622–637 (2015)
7. Palattella, M.R., Accettura, N., Vilajosana, X., Watteyne, T., Grieco, L.A., Boggia, G., Dohler, M.: Standardized protocol stack for the internet of (important) things. IEEE Commun. Surv. Tutor. **15**(3), 1389–1406 (2013)
8. Sheng, Z., Yang, S., Yu, Y., Vasilakos, A.V., McCann, J.A., Leung, K.K.: A survey on the IETF protocol suite for the Internet of Things: standards, challenges, and opportunities. IEEE Wirel. Commun. **20**(6), 91–98 (2013)
9. MQ Telemetry Transport. http://mqtt.org/
10. Sharma, R., Kumar, N., Gowda, N.B., Srinivas, T.: Probabilistic prediction based scheduling for delay sensitive traffic in Internet of Things. Procedia Comput. Sci. **52**, 90–97 (2015)

Lecturus: Collaborative Mobile Phone Lecture Recording

Amnon Dekel$^{(\boxtimes)}$ (ID), Yonit Rusho, Ofir Aghai, Vidran Abdovich,
Avishay Hajbi, Max Zemsky, and Rami Cohen

Shenkar College of Engineering, Design, Art, Ann Frank 12, Ramat-Gan, Israel
{amnoid,yonit,ophirg,vidrana,avishayh,
maxz,ramic}@se.shenkar.ac.il

Abstract. We present the Lecturus Mobile Phone based lecture recording system. Lecturus allows a group of students, connected via social networks, to collaboratively record, photograph and annotate a lecture in real time. A key motivation was to minimize attention to the recording process itself and maximize attention to the lecturer. This was achieved by A. breaking a complicated task of recording and annotating a lecture into simpler sub-tasks (recording audio, taking photos, adding textual annotations) and distributing those tasks among the participants. B. simplifying the tasks to minimize their cognitive load. C. Uploading and allowing participants to later view, manage, edit and share their recording via RESTful web services.

Keywords: Digital media · Cognitive load · Human computer interaction
Mobile computing · Web services

1   Introduction

For thousands of years students have been looking for ways to best remember a lecture that they attended. Initially they used poetry and song as a memory enhancement mechanism [1, 6]. Later, with the development of tools for writing and drawing (charcoal, ink, pens, papyrus, parchment, paper), they took notes and drew illustrations as ways of retaining access to information over time and space [1, 6]. These tools were the main methods of personally recording information for over 3000 years [6]. The late 19th century and the 20th century saw the development of new media capture and recording technologies (Still Image Photography, Audio Recording and Moving Image Cinematography). As these technologies matured, they became more capable (i.e. movies synchronized with sound, higher quality recordings) as well physically smaller and less expensive. This enabled the use of these tools in more personal settings, as well as in the lecture hall [7]. The last few decades have seen such devices falling in price to become available for most middle-class students if they wanted them. The second decade of the 21st century has continued this trend, with mobile phones taking over as the main media recording device for billions of people, replacing the stand-alone camera, the portable video camera and the tape recorder. The mobile phone has become the new universal recording device, enabling the creation of more than 3 billion photos and 400,000 of *hours* of video per *day* [2, 3].

© ICST Institute for Computer Sciences, Social Informatics and Telecommunications Engineering 2018
K. Murao et al. (Eds.): MobiCASE 2018, LNICST 240, pp. 265–270, 2018.
https://doi.org/10.1007/978-3-319-90740-6_21

Lecturus is a project developed at the Shenkar College of Engineering, Design, Art that explores how to merge lecture recording with today's ubiquitous social networks, enabling a group of connected students to record a lecture in a distributed and cooperative fashion and then later view, manage, edit, search and share their peer co-created recordings via RESTful web services.

1.1   Issues with Lecture Recording with Mobile Phones

Has the ubiquity, capability and low cost enabled the smart phone to become a viable tool in recording lectures by students? In some cases it has, but because such recordings must be performed by a single user, not many users are willing to invest the time and effort of recording a lecture on their own. A typical scenario would see a student asking permission from the lecturer to record the lecture. If they opt to record just audio, then they could place the phone near the lecturer (on a table or on the lecture podium). If they wanted to record video, they would keep the phone with them and need to hold it up to keep the lecturer or the board and screen in the field of view being recorded. If they opted to take still images of the board or screen then they would launch the phone camera application and raise the phone to take a picture each time they wanted to capture a photo. Each of the cases described above have different attention demands (picking the phone up, launching the camera or audio recording application, taking a picture, etc.). Lastly, having captured the media from a lecture, they must edit it: organize the files, decide which photos to use and then manually connect between the photos and any text annotations they might have created. With time-based media such as audio or video, the process is much more demanding: the student must search though the captured media material in a linear fashion to connect between any point of interest (photos, annotations) and the time of their occurrence within the recording itself. All this makes the task too time consuming or difficult for most people in most cases.

2   The Lecturus Peer Lecture Recording System

The Lecturus project was designed to enable students to make use of the mobile phone as a peer lecture recording device, while minimizing the difficulties described above. We defined the following top level goals for the project:

1. Ensure that the process of recording a lecture does not get in the way and grab too much *attention* from the lecture itself.
2. Allow students to easily *capture* rich media recordings of lectures within an academic context.
3. *Store* the recordings and their associated materials online and enable users to view, edit and share their recordings.

2.1   Minimizing Attention Issues

Our first priority in designing the system was to ensure that the students who use the system suffer the least amount of multitasking attention deficits. We did not want that the use of the system will steal attention away from the lecturer and thus needed to find a user flow that would minimize, as much as possible, the user interactions with the system during the lecture. Our solution focuses on two factors: a. *Spreading the task* across more than one student and b. *minimizing interface focus* during use.

Spreading the Task: If a task demands too much attention to be performed, then one possible solution is to divide the task between several different actors. As can be seen below, after a new recording is set up by one of the students (defined as the Owner), they then proceed to invite a set of friends to participate in the actual recording process. Most of the rest of the functions are available to all participants in parallel, thus *minimizing the amount of **actions** each participant needs to perform.* We divided the task into the following sub-tasks:

1. Setup:

    a. Creating a new Recording: Connecting the recording to a specific course and a specific class and giving it a name. [Owner]
    b. Setting the Text Tags to be used in the recording. [Owner]
    c. Inviting friends to participate in the recording. [Owner]
    d. Receiving a notification to participate in the recording. [Invitees]
    e. Agreeing to participate in the recording. [Invitees]

2. Recording:

    a. Recording a continuous audio track of the recording. [Owner]
    b. Taking photos and saving their creation time-stamps to synchronize them with the audio recording. [All Participants]
    c. Adding text annotations and saving their creation time-stamps to synchronize them with the audio recording. [All Participants]
    d. Ending a Recording. [Owner]

3. Post Recording:

    a. Listen to the recording while seeing each photo and text annotation at the correct time during playback. [All Participants]
    b. Edit the location of photos and text annotations within a recording, including the option to delete them. [All Participants]
    c. Change the privacy setting of each recording (Public or Private). [Owner]
    d. Sharing a recording. [Owner]

Minimizing Interface Focus: Since we want the users of our system to keep their attention focused on the lecturer, we looked for a way to minimize the actions they would need to perform to take photos and add textual annotations. Since all other functions are not needed during the recording phase, they were removed from the interface during the recording. This left us with taking photos and adding annotations:

1. **Taking a Photo:** Since taking a photo forces the user to raise their phone to aim the lens to the target area in the visual field, we opted to use the physical motion of raising the phone from the table and moving it into a vertical orientation as the trigger that launches the camera. By doing this we minimize the attention needed to find and place the finger on the phone buttons needed to launch the camera or the

need to unlock the phone and then launch the camera. *By sensing that the phone has been moved into a photo taking "position" the system helps minimize attention demands.*

2. **Adding Text Annotations:** It was obvious to us that we did not want students to manually type text annotations on their phone because this will steal attention away from the lecturer and will thus be counter-productive [4]. Thus, we decided to offer a group of 4 pre-set annotations (that can be edited *before* the recording begins) that are presented as 4 buttons on the screen. During the recording students need only tap the buttons to add that annotation and save it's time-stamp. *Although this task demands attention, it is a small amount of attention for a lot of cognitive reward.* See Fig. 1d, e.

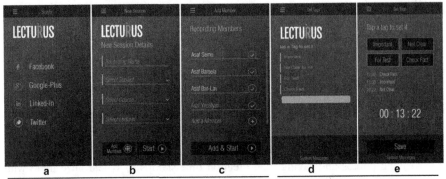

1. Using Social Networks to Invite Participants   2. Setting & UsingText Tags

Fig. 1. 1: Social Network Screens: a. Select the Social Network. b. Enter Recording details then Add participants. c. Select participants from the selected social network. 2. Setting Text Tags Screens: d. The Edit Tag screen that is available *only before starting* a recording. e. Tag Button Screen: Note the four Large Text Tag buttons available during the recording

2.2 Adding Participants Using a Social Network

Since a recording using the lecturus system is handled by a group of peers, the recording owner must first invite his or her friends to participate in the recording. When a user joins the Lecturus system they are asked to log in using one of the existing Social networks (Facebook, Google Plus, LinkedIn, Twitter). The service then allows them to invite participants to a recording from their social network contacts. See Fig. 1a–c. Each invitee receives a notification to participate in the recording. If they accept, they are added to the active participant list. Once the owner starts the recording, all participants are notified and can add photos and annotations as they see fit.

2.3 Online Access to Recorded Content

To minimize data loss in case of a network disruption, all media is continuously uploaded in chunks during a recording. Once a Recording is finished, all its online materials are transcoded and made available for personal viewing, editing and Sharing. See Fig. 2.

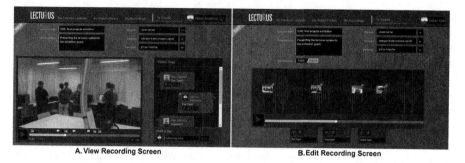

A. View Recording Screen   B. Edit Recording Screen

Fig. 2. A. View recording screen. Includes audio playback, synched photos, and synched text annotations. B. Edit recording screen. Move photos and annotations. Edit annotations.

2.4   System Overview

The Lecturus system was built using Web technologies. The Mobile Client was developed as a Hybrid Application using HTML/CSS/JS based web pages inside an Apache Cordova wrapper that enabled access to phone functionality via the Android Native Platform API for recording audio and sensing phone motion. A NodeJS server was developed to gather recording blocks, merge them into single files and transcode them to a web friendly format, save the media files (audio and images) on a Cloudinary service and the text annotations and media time-stamps into a MongoDB database service. This data is accessed via a Web Client that allows users (recording owners and participants) to view, edit, search and share the recordings on their large screen web browsers. See Fig. 3.

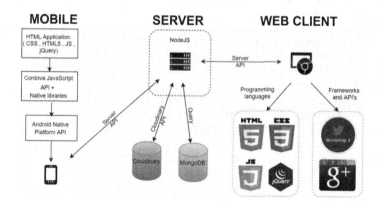

Fig. 3. Lecturus system structure and data flows

3   Results and Future Work

The Lecturus project was designed to enable students to merge the capabilities of the Smartphone with a peer based service to collaboratively record lecture recordings while minimizing attention deficits to participants. A prototype of the service was developed and tested within the Software Engineering department at Shenkar. To facilitate the process, the service was linked to the institutional course database making it easy for users to add a new recording within the context of a course name, lecture date and lecture room.

Testing was done with a group of 7 students, over a period of two weeks, during which they were asked to use the system to record several lectures. Participants were randomly selected to be recording "owners" who had to set up a new recording, invite participants and then end the recording. All participants also tested the online web interface to view, edit and share recordings. Tests showed the utility and usability of the system, with multiple 90 min recordings successfully recorded, uploaded, transcoded, viewed, edited and shared. All in all, the participants had no problem in understanding the service, editing the text annotations, inviting recording participants and creating recordings. They did comment that it was not always clear to them if the recording was being successfully uploaded and saved during the recording process. We are planning to improve system feedback to make this clearer. The one major missing piece that most users requested was the option to record video. We are now planning to develop a video recording module for future testing.

References

1. Brady, W., Elkner, J.: Introduction information and communication technology (Chapter 1). In: History of Information Technology (2017). http://openbookproject.net/courses/intro2ict/history/history.html
2. Cakebread, C.: People will take 1.2 trillion digital photos this year — thanks to smartphones (2017). http://www.businessinsider.com/12-trillion-photos-to-be-taken-in-2017-thanks-to-smartphones-chart-2017-8
3. Donchev, D.: 36 Mind Blowing YouTube Facts, Figures and Statistics – 2017 (2017). https://fortunelords.com/youtube-statistics/
4. Dynarski, S.: Laptops Are Great. But Not During a Lecture or a Meeting. New-York Times (2017). https://www.nytimes.com/2017/11/22/business/laptops-not-during-lecture-or-meeting.html
5. Global smartphone sales to end users since (2007). Statistica.com https://www.statista.com/statistics/263437/global-smartphone-sales-to-end-users-since-2007/
6. Hardy, L.: The Ordinary Man's Guide to the History of Information Technology. CreateSpace Publishing Platform (2010)
7. Lecture Recording. https://en.wikipedia.org/wiki/Lecture_recording

On-Body Smartphone Position Detection with Position Transition Correction Based on the Hand State

Anja Exler[(✉)], Christoph Michel, and Michael Beigl

Karlsruhe Institute of Technology (KIT), TECO, 76131 Karlsruhe, Germany
exler@teco.edu

Abstract. Smartphone users tend to store their devices at manifold on-body positions: in their trouser pocket, in their backpack, on the table, or simply in their hands. Depending on the position, it might be required to adapt the ringtone and notification type to enhance their perception. To do so, the smartphone needs to be able to automatically detect the device's position.

In this paper, we present an approach to detect the on-body position of the smartphone based on the smartphone features such as accelerometer data. In addition, we propose a position transition correction (PTC) algorithm to improve the position detection. The PTC assumes that each position transition involves the position "hand" as the user has to hold the phone into their hands to take them out of one position and place them another.

We gathered data from 20 participants and ran different classification methods. The KStar classifier achieved an accuracy of 81.97%. By applying the PTC we were able to correct about 50% of the errors on a simulated transition sequence, leading to an accuracy of almost 90%.

1 Introduction

By now, smartphones became an essential part of our everyday lives. They support us, but they can also be a burden by exposing us to an information overflow and to persistent availability. Different works already mention the importance of the smartphone position, e.g. for choosing an appropriate notification modality [3,4]. However, automatically inferring the on-body smartphone position is not an easy task. Different researchers already addressed this issue, e.g., [1,4–9]. Using common classifiers, we show that predicting the on-body position is possible with acceptable accuracy of up to 81.97%. To improve the accuracy, we introduce a position transition correction (PTC). We assume that each position transition has to involve the "hand" state: to take the smartphone out of the trouser pocket and into the backpack, it is necessary to pick up the phone, hold it in the hand and move it by hand from one position to the next one. Hence, we further assume that an apparent transition that did not include a hand state

© ICST Institute for Computer Sciences, Social Informatics and Telecommunications Engineering 2018
K. Murao et al. (Eds.): MobiCASE 2018, LNICST 240, pp. 271–276, 2018.
https://doi.org/10.1007/978-3-319-90740-6_22

might be an error and not an actual position transition. Our correction mechanism builds up upon these assumptions and corrects the prediction results – leading to an increase of the accuracy and a decrease in errors.

2   Related Work

Smartphone position detection was investigated in different ways before. Some researchers started by recognizing the user's activity. Kunze et al. [6] first identified a walking activity before identifying the device position. They claimed that, while walking, certain movement patterns manifest themselves which help to classify the positions head, breast, and wrist. They applied a majority voting on the walking sequence and achieved a recognition accuracy of up to 100%. Vahdatpour et al. [8] also relied on a two step approach. First, they identified walking sequences using unsupervised activity discovery. Next, they used support vector machines (SVM) to classify the on-body regions lower arm, upper arm, and head. Using a model trained on 500 randomly drawn samples from a dataset with 2500 entries, they achieved an accuracy of 89%.

Alanezi and Mishra [1] go one step further. They also start by running an activity recognition. However, they do not limit themselves to the walking activity, but follow different classification strategies based on the recognized activity. They present a design for a recognition system and a first prototype.

There is also related work that does not rely on a former activity recognition but directly classifies the position. Kunze and Lukowicz [5] classified positions during different everyday activities. Using a hidden markov model (HMM) and a window size of 6 min, they achieved an accuracy of 82%. After merging front and back trouser pocket into one class, the accuracy rose up to 92%. Shi et al. [7] combine measurements from accelerometer and gyroscope to estimate the rotation radius. Afterwards, they calculate features based on the rotation radius and the angular velocity. They considered the positions chest pocket, trouser pocket, belt bag, and hand. A five-fold cross-validation using a SVM achieved an accuracy of 91.69%. Wiese et al. [9] relied on accelerometer data to detect smartphone positions and investigated the usefulness of other sensors. The accelerometer data alone yieled an accuracy of 79%. By including further sensors such as proximity sensor and ambient light sensor they pushed the accuracy up to 85%. Fujinami [4] investigated smartphone position detection based on the accelerometer only and yielded an accuracy of up to 80.1% for nine different position classes (around the neck (hanging), chest pocket, jacket pocket (side), front pocket of trousers, back pocket of trousers, backpack, handbag, messenger bag, and shoulder bag) and 85.9% for five different position classes (merging the four types of bags into one class and the two trouser pockets into one class).

It seems promising to rely on smartphone features, especially accelerometer data. Some researchers already considered the hand position. Antos et al. even mentioned the meaningfulness of a hand state as transition between different positions [2]. We will combine these ideas and present a smartphone features-based position recognition and a position transition correction based on the hand state.

3   Common Smartphone Positions

To assess where users store their smartphone commonly and which positions we should consider in our specific investigations, we ran a short online survey. Overall, 76 persons participated, aged between 17 and 36. We asked them with which frequency they store their phone in a specific position: trouser pocket, backpack, jacket pocket, purse, shirt pocket, wristband, belt bag, back pocket, on the table, or in the hand. The results are depicted in Table 1. Based on these results, we decided to consider the following positions: trouser pocket, hand, backpack, purse, and on the table.

Table 1. Results of the online survey to assess most common smartphone positions over all activities (sit, stand, walk, jog, ride a bicycle) in %.

Position	Frequency
Trouser pocket	53.22
Hand	37.40
Backpack	31.62
Jacket pocket	24.44
Purse	23.11
Table	21.71
Shirt pocket	5.26
Wrist	2.11
Belt bag	0.64
Back pocket	0.26

4   Predicting the Smartphone Position

4.1   Data Assessment and Feature Selection

We wrote an Android application to assess smartphone data. We considered features derived from data gathered using the accelerometer, gyroscope, proximity sensor, light sensor, and screen activity. Data was downsampled to 30 Hz and partly transformed using Fast Fourier Transformation (FTT). We investigated different windowing schemes and chose a step size of 120 and an overlap of 60 as it yielded the best results.

We considered the following features: average per frame, average of the FFT bin, FFT max bin index, DDT sum of the first/second/third/fourth quarter, highest/lowest/last value of the frame, first/third quantile, root mean square, standard deviation, sum of all values, squared sum, variance, and number of zero crossings. This leads to a total number of 198 features (11 sensor measurements * 18 features). To reduce the number of features for the final classification, we ran different feature evaluation mechanisms, namely: SymmetricalUncertAttributeEval, ReliefFAttributeEval, OneRAttributeEval, CorrelationAttributeEval, InfoGainAttributeEval and GainRatioAttributeEval. In each case, the features derived from the accelerometer measurements yielded the best results.

4.2 Study Design and Sample Description

We collected data from 20 subjects (6 female, 14 male) in-field. We asked the participants to perform at least the activities sit, stand, and walk, and optionally to jog or ride a bicycle. During each activity, the phone was stored at each considered smartphone position – excluding the combination hand and bicycle due to security concerns. For each combination of subject, activity, and position we collected one minute of data.

4.3 Classification

As mentioned above, we preprocessed the data and ran a feature selection to identify the best features. Using these features, we trained different classifiers provided by WEKA[1], namely a support vector machine (LibSVM), two tree-based methods (RandomForest and RandomTree) and two instance-based approaches (KStar and IBk). We decided to use leave-one-person-out cross-validation. The accuracies per classifier are shown in Table 2. The highest accuracy of 81.97% was achieved by the KStar classifier.

Table 2. Accuracy for recognizing smartphone positions per classifier in %.

Classifier	LibSVM	RandomForest	RandomTree	KStar	IBk
Accuracy	81.29	81.01	77.24	81.97	81.73

5 Position Transition Correction (PTC)

5.1 PTC Theory

Antos et al. [2] already labeled the state during a position transition as *hand*: their subjects used their hands to change the device's position. We assume that every significant position transition is realized using the hand. This assumption can be illustrated by the following example: a user takes the smartphone out of their trouser pocket (p_0) using their hand (h) and places it in their shirt pocket (p_1):

$$TrouserPocket\ (p_0) \rightarrow Hand(h) \rightarrow ShirtPocket(p_1)$$

Consider the following, exemplary classification result:

$$TrouserPocket\ (p_0) \rightarrow ShirtPocket\ (p_1) \rightarrow TrouserPocket\ (p_0)$$

If we assume that a hand position has to appear in between any other two positions then this example must be a recognition error. Either, the hand state was missed, it was misinterpreted as a shirt pocket, or the device stayed in the

---

[1] https://www.cs.waikato.ac.nz/ml/weka/.

trouser pocket the whole time and was wrongly recognized as being in the shirt pocket.

Our TCP mechanism would inspect every window of data within the sequence. First, we look for each hand transition in the sequence. Next, we perform a majority voting on the transitions in between to decide in which position the smartphone is during that subsequence. An example for a successful correction is visualized in Fig. 1.

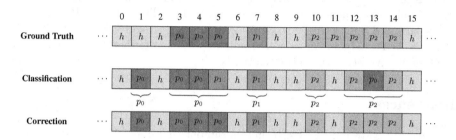

Fig. 1. A sequence correction that successfully reduced the number of errors.

5.2 PTC Evaluation

As input we use a simulated sequence. The sequence was created from ground truth data and transformed by using probabilities taken from the confusion matrix of the classifier results we gained from the leave-one-person-out cross-validation.

To rate the PTC, we compare the ground truth information with the PTC-corrected version of the simulated sequence. Thanks to the PTC almost 50% of all errors could be reduced and the accuracy was increased to about 90%. However, we have to note that a good detection of the hand position is essential for the correct functioning of the PTC.

6   Conclusion

This paper focused on predicting the smartphone position based on smartphone features while the phone is stored at different positions during different everyday activities.

First, we ran an only survey to assess common smartphone positions for common activities such as sit, stand, walk, jog, and ride a bicycle. We identified hand, trouser pocket, backpack, purse, and on the table as positions.

We collected data from 20 participants while they underwent different everyday activities and stored the smartphone at different positions. Concerning sensors, we considered accelerometer, gyroscope, proximity sensor, ambient light sensor, and screen activity. After running different feature selection algorithms provided by WEKA, we decided to focus on accelerometer data only. We only relied on the sensor measurements and did not run an activity recognition first. Using common classifiers, again provided by WEKA, we achieved recognition accuracies of up to 81.97%. The results have to be treated with care as we only had a limited amount of data. However, we required a confusion matrix to simulate a position transition sequence. For this use case, the amount of data was sufficient.

We also proposed a position transition correction (PTC). The PTC mechanism assumes that each position change has to include a hand transition. Applied to a simulated sequence of position changes, the PTC reduced the errors by about 50% and improved the recognition accuracy to about 90%. We propose to enhance the PTC by introducing a minimum duration for hand transitions or to combine it with other correction methods.

References

1. Alanezi, K., Mishra, S.: Design, implementation and evaluation of a smartphone position discovery service for accurate context sensing. Comput. Electr. Eng. **44**, 307–323 (2015)
2. Antos, S.A., Albert, M.V., Kording, K.P.: Hand, belt, pocket or bag: Practical activity tracking with mobile phones. J. Neurosci. Methods **231**, 22–30 (2014). Motion Capture in Animal Models and Humans
3. Exler, A., Dinse, C., Günes, Z., Hammoud, N., Mattes, S., Beigl, M.: Investigating the perceptibility different notification types on smartphones depending on the smartphone position. In: Proceedings of the 2017 ACM International Joint Conference on Pervasive and Ubiquitous Computing and Proceedings of the 2017 ACM International Symposium on Wearable Computers, pp. 970–976. ACM (2017)
4. Fujinami, K.: On-body smartphone localization with an accelerometer. Information **7**(2), 21 (2016)
5. Kunze, K., Lukowicz, P.: Using acceleration signatures from everyday activities for on-body device location. In: 2007 11th IEEE International Symposium on Wearable Computers, pp. 115–116, October 2007
6. Kunze, K., Lukowicz, P., Junker, H., Tröster, G.: Where am i: Recognizing On-body positions of wearable sensors. In: Strang, T., Linnhoff-Popien, C. (eds.) LoCA 2005. LNCS, vol. 3479, pp. 264–275. Springer, Heidelberg (2005). https://doi.org/10.1007/11426646_25
7. Shi, Y., Shi, Y., Liu, J.: A rotation based method for detecting on-body positions of mobile devices. In: Proceedings of the 13th International Conference on Ubiquitous Computing, UbiComp 2011, pp. 559–560. ACM, New York (2011)
8. Vahdatpour, A., Amini, N., Sarrafzadeh, M.: On-body device localization for health and medical monitoring applications. In: 2011 IEEE International Conference on Pervasive Computing and Communications (PerCom), pp. 37–44, March 2011
9. Wiese, J., Saponas, T.S., Brush, A.B.: Phonepriception: enabling mobile phones to infer where they are kept. In: Proceedings of the SIGCHI Conference on Human Factors in Computing Systems, CHI 2013, pp. 2157–2166. ACM, New York (2013)

Taxi Dash: Serendipitous Discovery of Taxi Carpool Riders

Briane Paul V. Samson[(✉)] [iD] and Yasuyuki Sumi

Future University Hakodate,
Hakodate, Hokkaido, Japan
b-samson@sumilab.org, sumi@acm.org

Abstract. During winter, scheduled bus services can experience delays in locations where extreme and persistent snowfall affect road conditions. Commuters rushing to school or work often choose more flexible modes like taxis. However, taxi fares are more expensive for a single passenger, most especially students. In this paper, we present the design and implementation of a carpool application for taxi services in Hakodate, Japan. Considering the high level of shyness among Japanese university students, the application intends to facilitate serendipitous discovery and group formation among Japanese students expressing intent to take taxi services.

Keywords: Group formation · Carpooling · Web applications
Human-centered computing

1 Introduction

The main motivation of this application is the scenario of students waiting patiently for a delayed bus to arrive, specially in the morning while going to school. Instead of walking to school under harsh weather conditions, they usually take the taxi alone, but doing so on a regular basis would not be economical. Thus, a taxi carpool solution is suggested to alleviate the expensive fare.

Forming groups for taxi carpools can easily be accomplished off-line, even without the help of digital solutions, since students are already waiting in proximity around bus stops. However, the high level of shyness among Japanese students [1,2] creates a barrier for on-the-fly group formation to happen.

Existing solutions like Uber[1], Grab[2] and Wunder[3], offer rider-sharing but they mostly operate with private car owners. Grab offers taxi hailing in its application but it has yet to open its services in Japan.

Our solution allows users to easily join taxi carpool groups being formed within their vicinity. We simplify the user experience by focusing on the scenario

---

[1] https://www.uber.com/en-JP/.
[2] https://www.grab.com/sg/.
[3] https://www.wunder.org/.

© ICST Institute for Computer Sciences, Social Informatics and Telecommunications Engineering 2018
K. Murao et al. (Eds.): MobiCASE 2018, LNICST 240, pp. 277–281, 2018.
https://doi.org/10.1007/978-3-319-90740-6_23

Fig. 1. Taxi Dash lowers the barrier and simplifies the experience of group formation through a context-aware application.

of people waiting for the morning bus going only to the university (Fig. 1). It is assumed that they are already waiting around bus stops. This paper describes the design and implementation of the current application, as well as the architecture of the solution.

2 Design and Implementation

This section provides the detail of the overall architecture of the solution and the current implementation of the Taxi Dash application.

2.1 Overall Solution

The Taxi Dash solution implements a Model-View-Controller architecture. The user-facing application is implemented as a web application instead of a native mobile application for cross-compatibility and scalability. This design decision ensures that the application can have responsive rendering regardless of mobile device resolution and form factor.

The solution is designed to be context-aware. The meetup points shown to users are collected from Google Maps. When a user tries to join or organize a trip, we filter them using a distance radius of 500 m to ensure that they can quickly move to a meetup point. Initially, we only provided bus stops as meetup points but based on user feedback, these can be hard to find for taxi drivers. Thus, we decided to replace them with points-of-interest (POIs), convenience stores, and other known establishments with enough parking space for waiting. While we have removed bus stops from the list of meetup locations, we still made sure that the new locations are located near bus stops going to the university.

The current limitation of this implementation is that getting the location of the user takes a relatively longer time. On our most recent tests, it takes around 2–4 s for the browser to get the location.

2.2   Application Design

For the application, we followed Material Design to ensure simplicity and good usability. It is a visual language that leverages on classic good design principles. With a sizable adoption rate among regularly used applications like Asana and Airbnb, along with Google products, we can assure its familiarity. Lastly, we wanted to keep the look and feel of the web application as close as possible to a mobile application.

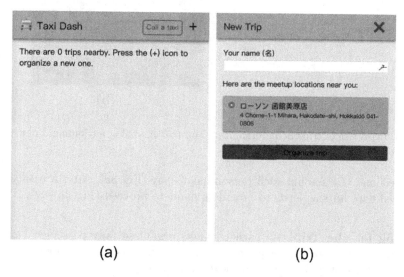

Fig. 2. (a) The home page showing no organized trips, and (b) a list of meetup points nearby for organizing a new trip.

Organizing a Trip. After the location of the user is detected, a list of trips being organized nearby are shown. If there no trips nearby (Fig. 2a), s/he can organize by tapping the (+) icon. First, the user must enter his/her name or nickname (Fig. 2b). Then, a meetup location must be selected from a curated list shown to the user. It only shows locations within a 500 m range, ordered from nearest to farthest. The nearest option is selected by default.

To simplify the experience, users can only select from the curated meetup locations provided, unlike other location-based applications. Each trip assumes that everyone is going to the same location, which in this case is the university.

Lastly, each trip is assigned a unique trip name (i.e. *Trip Yuki* in Fig. 3a). This can be used to easily identify passengers at the meetup location, if in the case of multiple trips organizing there.

Joining a Trip. If there are trips already organized near the user, they will be shown, with the closest meetup location as the first option. Aside from the name of the trip and meetup location, the user is also shown the number of available

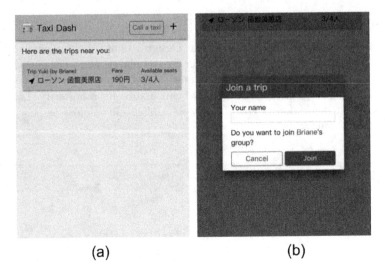

Fig. 3. (a) A list of trips being organized, and (b) the dialog for joining a new trip.

seats left and the amount each person has to pay (Fig. 3a). After a user selects a desired trip, he/she needs to provide a name to proceed (Fig. 3b).

Waiting for the Trip. As each trip gets organized, any passenger can call the taxi company or hail a passing taxi. They can copy a number from the pre-defined list of taxi companies shown in Fig. 4a.

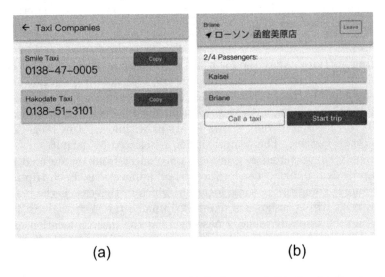

Fig. 4. (a) The list of taxi companies in Hakodate, and (b) the details of a trip the user just joined.

Leaving a Trip. Passengers, even the organizer, can leave the trip any time as long as the trip hasn't started yet (Fig. 4b). If everyone leaves, the trip will be canceled and will not appear in the list of available trips.

3   Usability Evaluation

In its early stage, a preliminary usability evaluation was conducted using the System Usability Scale [3]. It is short but a reliable assessment of the usability of any system. It is an industry standard and valid even with small sample sizes.

With an initial sample of 5 respondents, the application yielded a fair average score of 59.9. For those who gave low scores, they noted the low robustness and compatibility issues with other desktop browsers (i.e. MS Edge).

4   Conclusion and Future Work

We have developed a web application that lowers the barrier of group formation among Japanese students for taxi carpooling purposes. In its current implementation, we were able to cover the critical use case scenarios but has only received a fair average score in the preliminary usability evaluation.

For future work, we want to further improve the responsiveness to other form factors and resolutions, implement notifications for newly organized trips, and a dashboard for taxi drivers to highlight areas with increasing taxi demand. We are also considering the option of organizing a carpool and picking up passengers along the way. Additionally, we want to evaluate its effectiveness in promoting carpooling with more respondents. Our ultimate goal is to experiment on further simplifying this experience like in the case of the Amazon Dash button[4] where a user can push the button whenever s/he wants to join a taxi carpool group and s/he can leave without anything done if s/he can't wait.

References

1. Sakuragi, T.: Association of culture with shyness among Japanese and American university students. Percept. Mot. Skills **98**(3), 803–813 (2004). 6
2. Pryor, B., Butler, J., Boehringer, K.: Communication apprehension and cultural context: a comparison of communication apprehension in Japanese and American students. North Am. J. Psychol. **7**(2), 247–252 (2005)
3. Brooke, J.: SUS-A quick and dirty usability scale usability and context. Usability Eval. Ind. **189**(194), 4–7 (1996)

---

[4] https://www.amazon.com/ddb/learn-more.

User Attribute Classification Method Based on Trajectory Patterns with Active Scanning Devices

Kenji Takayanagi[1]([✉]), Kazuya Murao[1], Masahiro Mochizuki[2],
and Nobuhiko Nishio[1]

[1] College of Information Science and Engineering, Ritsumeikan University,
1-1-1 Nojihigashi, Kusatsu, Shiga 525-8577, Japan
`gibson@ubi.cs.ritsumei.ac.jp`, {`murao,nishio`}`@cs.ritsumei.ac.jp`
[2] Research Organization of Science and Technology, Ritsumeikan University,
1-1-1 Nojihigashi, Kusatsu, Shiga 525-8577, Japan
`moma@ubi.cs.ritsumei.ac.jp`

Abstract. Technologies for grasping the distribution and flow of people are required for urban planning, traffic planning, evacuation, rescue activities in case of disaster, and marketing. In order to grasp what kind of attribute the distribution and flow of people are formed, this paper proposes a method that estimates the attributes of users. As a method of estimating user attributes, we utilize probe request frame of Wi-Fi that smartphones are emitting. Probe request frame includes MAC address, enabling us to acquire the movement trajectory of a user by tracking the MAC address. By using the feature values obtained from the movement trajectory of the user, users are roughly classified into several types. In this paper, we focus on the user attribute estimation in underground city comprising of stations, shops, restaurants and so on. Through the practical experiment at Osaka underground city, we confirmed that the proposed method can classify the users into commuter or not by using the intervals between probe request frames.

Keywords: People flow analysis · Attribute estimation
Spatiotemporal data · Probe request frame

1 Introduction

There is a demand for technology to grasp the distribution and flow of people for urban planning, traffic planning, evacuation, rescue activities in case of disaster, and marketing. As a related service, there is a store congestion status notification service provided by Google[1]. This is based on the anonymous data aggregated from the users who enabled the location history of Google to determine crowded time and staying time. When deploying such services, information on time and

---

[1] https://blog.google/products/search/know-you-go-google/.

© ICST Institute for Computer Sciences, Social Informatics and Telecommunications Engineering 2018
K. Murao et al. (Eds.): MobiCASE 2018, LNICST 240, pp. 282–288, 2018.
https://doi.org/10.1007/978-3-319-90740-6_24

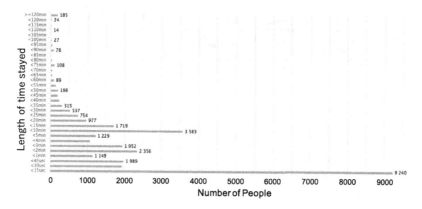

Fig. 1. Distribution of the length of time users stayed near a lunchbox store in the station.

place is required for fine granularity even in an indoor space such as a commercial facility. We focused on devices with Wi-Fi and have proposed a system that can inexpensively grasp the distribution and flow of people [1] thus far. With this system, it is possible to grasp the flow of people and the number people who are not moving. However, there is a problem that it is not easy to grasp what kind of attribute influences the distribution of the number of stayers. Actually, we investigated the distribution of time the users stayed from probe request frame obtained from sensors installed near a lunchbox store in a station as shown in Fig. 1. Figure 1 shows that the peaks appear at 15 s, 2 min, and 10 min. It can be inferred that the peak at 15 s probably passed through the lunch box store. On the other hand, the peak at 2 min and the peak at 10 min probably are those who dropped in near the lunch box store comprising of regular customers buying the boxed lunch quickly and first-visit customers taking long time to decide what to buy. In other words, our interest is shifting to grasp what attributes of people affect the distribution of the number of stayers. Therefore, in this paper, our goal is to find actions such as walkthroughs, commuters, shoppers, and facilities stakeholders.

2 Method

This section explains how to collect probe request frames, how to deal with MAC-randomized device, how to generate a moving path and how to cluster moving paths in order to find user attributes such as walkthrough, commuters, shoppers, and facility workers.

2.1 How to Collect Probe Request Frames

The overall system configuration diagram is shown in Fig. 2. A device such as a smartphone accompanied by a Wi-Fi function periodically transmits a probe

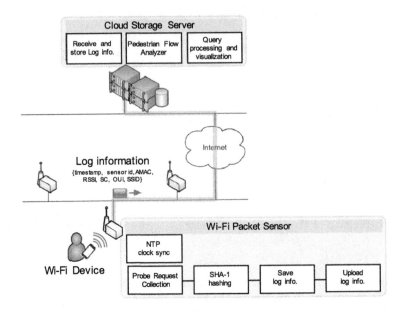

Fig. 2. System overview.

request frame to connect to a Wi-Fi access point. Distributively arrange sensors that can collect probe request frames in the environment where the station and the commercial facility are close. The MAC address of the collected information is anonymized by SHA-1 algorithm for the consideration of privacy. This anonymized MAC address is called an AMAC address.

Our method uploads these pieces of information to the cloud storage server and utilize those accumulated information to estimate attributes.

2.2 How to Deal with MAC-Randomized Device

This section describes the influence of the MAC-randomized device. MAC-randomized device indicates a device that has a dummy MAC address randomly changed. The reason why such a dummy MAC address is transmitted from the device is to protect the privacy.

A device with a dummy MAC address can be specified by checking the second least significant bit of the first octet of the first 24-bit product vendor code which is called OUI (Organizationally Unique Identifier) as shown in Fig. 3 [2].

The ratio of the probe request frame including randomized MAC address and the ratio of the MAC-randomized device among the probe request frames observed from February 18, 2017 to March 18, 2017 are shown in Fig. 4. From the Fig. 4, the average randomization rate (blue line) of all probe request frames observed on a day is about 13 % on average. It is considered that this is because the number of probe request frames transmitted from MAC-non-randomized devices is frequent. The average randomization rate (orange line) of all devices

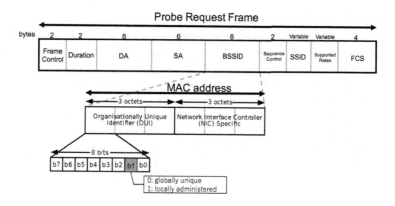

Fig. 3. Randomize bit of MAC address.

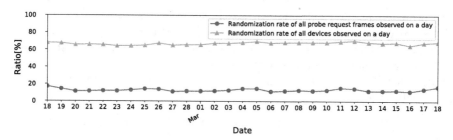

Fig. 4. Ratios of probe request frames and devices with randomized MAC address. (Color figure online)

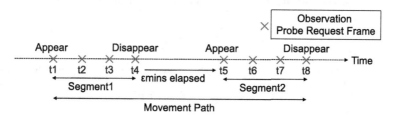

Fig. 5. Example of movement path generation.

observed on a day is about 67% on average. More specifically, it is difficult to identify two different frames emitted from a same device, therefore devices with randomized MAC have to be eliminated in the user attribute estimation.

2.3 Movement Path Generation

When there are observed probe request frames arranged in chronological order as shown in Fig. 5, probe request frames whose intervals are within ϵ seconds are grouped as a segment, and one or more segment groups are called movement paths. This movement path is generated on a daily basis. In addition, a probe request frame observed after ϵ-second interval is regarded as appearance, and the last probe request frame in the segment is regarded as disappearance. It can be said that the segment composed of appearance and disappearance is within the observation area.

Then, a method of deciding the threshold ϵ when creating a segment, but since the probe request frame transmission interval differs for each model of the device, a histogram of probe request frame transmission intervals is investigated for each vender that can be known from the MAC address. The third quartile of the histogram created by each vendor is set to ϵ. The reason why we set the third quartile to ϵ is that the segment breaks more than necessary and effective feature values cannot be obtained if the mode is set to ϵ.

2.4   Movement Path Clustering

The proposed method extracts feature values from each segment. Four kinds of feature values are employed: average path length, average speed, variance of speed, and time stayed. Using these features, we estimate user attributes: walkthroughs, shoppers, and facility workers each segment. In addition, focusing on segments, there are intervals in which user device is not found. Definition of these features are as follows:

– Average Path Length: Calculating the length at each sensor hop in the segment.

$$\bar{l} = \frac{\sum_{k=1}^{n} l_k}{n}$$

– Average Speed: Calculating the speed at each sensor hop in the segment.

$$\bar{v} = \frac{\sum_{k=1}^{n} v_k}{n}$$

– Variance of Speed: Calculating the speed at each sensor hop in the segment.

$$\sigma^2 = \frac{\sum_{k=1}^{n} (v_k - \bar{v})^2}{n}$$

– Time Stayed: Calculating the time difference between the appearance time and the disappearance time in the segment.
– Idle Time: Calculating idle time difference between the disappearance time of a segment and the appearance time of the next segment.

In this section, we describe a method for estimating the attributes of commuters by using the feature value of idle time between segments. This feature value is obtained from a movement path composed of two or more segments. As a result of investigating the number of segments per movement path on a weekday, 77% of a movement path consist of one path and 23% of movement paths consist of two or more paths. Figure 6 shows the clustering result of idle time using K-means++ clustering method (K = 2) between segments. Two clusters colored in blue and orange shows the first peak and second peak, respectively. Figure 7 shows a histogram of devices that appeared first time on a day at each hour. Colors in the bars show two clusters obtained in Fig. 6. From the Fig. 7, high peak appears at 8 a.m., which is the morning commuting time zone. Another peak appears at 6 p.m., which shows workers going back home. On the other hand, there can be seen people who spent 2 to 3 h around this area evenly in the evening. From these results, we have confirmed that commuter attribute.

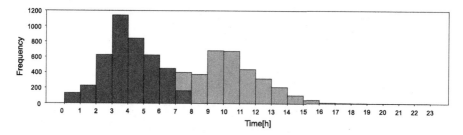

Fig. 6. Clustering result of idle time between segments (K = 2). (Color figure online)

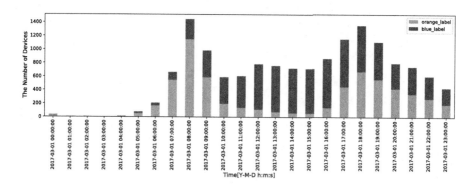

Fig. 7. Time distribution of idle time between segments of the day. (Color figure online)

3   Conclusion

In this paper, we estimated the user attribute by using the feature amount obtained from the movement trajectory generated by using probe request frame. In fact, we estimated the commuter attribute from the idle time between segments, which is the feature values of clustering, using the data on the first day of the weekday. As a result, a characteristic mountain was seen when commuting in the morning and returning home in the evening.

References

1. Fukuzaki, Y., Mochizuki, M., Murao, K., Nishio, N.: Statistical analysis of actual number of pedestrians for Wi-Fi packet-based pedestrian flow sensing. In: Proceedings of the 1st International Workshop on Smart Cities, pp. 1519–1526 (2015)
2. Robyns, P., Bonné, B., Quax, P., Lamotte, W.: Non-cooperative 802.11 MAC layer fingerprinting and tracking of mobile devices. Secur. Commun. Netw. **2017**, 1–26 (2017)

Author Index

Printed in the United States
By Bookmasters